MUDDLING T
MADAG

Dervla Murphy was born in 1931, of Dublin
parents, in County Waterford, which is her
home base. From childhood she wished to
write and to travel. At the age of fourteen
she had to leave school to look after her
invalid mother, but she continued her
education by reading widely and cycling in
Europe. After her mother's death in 1962
she cycled to India and worked with
Tibetan refugees before returning home to
write her first two books. Her next journeys
were to Nepal and to Ethiopia; then in
December 1968 the birth of her daughter
put a temporary stop to adventuring. In
November 1973 she and Rachel set off on
their first long journey through the
Karakoram with an ex-polo-pony and in
1978 walked 1300 miles through the
Peruvian Andes with a pack mule.

Dervla Murphy is the author of many
travel books, including *Full Tilt, Eight Feet
in the Andes, Where the Indus is Young, On a
Shoestring to Coorg, The Waiting Land* and,
most recently *Cameroon with Egbert*.

CENTURY TRAVELLERS

MUDDLING THROUGH IN MADAGASCAR

Dervla Murphy

ARROW BOOKS

Century Travellers

Published by Arrow Books Limited
20 Vauxhall Bridge Road, London SW1V 2SA

An imprint of Random Century Group

London Melbourne Sydney Auckland Johannesburg
and agencies throughout the world

First published in 1985 by John Murray Ltd
Century Travellers trade paperback edition 1986
Arrow edition 1990
3 5 7 9 10 8 6 4

Front cover illustration: The Hutchinson Library

Printed and bound in Great Britain by
The Guernsey Press Co Ltd
Guernsey, C.I.

ISBN 0 09 972880 X

Definitions

Muddling Through: 'to attain one's ends in spite of blunder after blunder'

Muddling On: 'to get along in a haphazard way through makeshifts'

Oxford English Dictionary

Contents

ACKNOWLEDGEMENTS

My gratitude goes to:

Rachel Murphy, whose faith in this book, when various vicissitudes had reduced the will-to-write, became my main inspiration, and whose editorial help at the end was invaluable.

Toni Madden and Hilary Bradt, who generously shared their links with and knowledge of Madagascar, and whose comments on the draft typescript provided much needed guidance and encouragement.

The Rajaoana family, whose kindness was beyond measure.

Diana Murray, whose heroic editorial work came at a time when the author couldn't see the wood for the trees.

Hallam Murray, who devoted much time and thought to the choosing of illustrations.

Barbara Wace, Jane Wilson, Jamie Brown, Adrian Lewis, Hilary Bradt and Rachel Murphy, who provided illustrations from which to choose.

And finally – special thanks to Lucia, who will never understand how much she helped.

To all our Malagasy friends —

Those whose names we can remember,
Those whose names we have forgotten,
And those whose names we never knew.

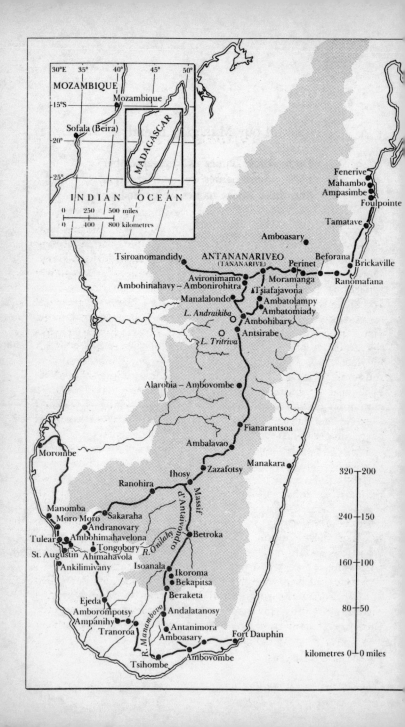

Introduction
A Bit of History

Once upon a time – about eighty million years ago – the break-up of Gondwanaland left an isolated island (some 1,000 miles long and 300 miles across) lying 250 miles off East Africa's coast. During this 'continental drift' era, when Madagascar was slowly separating from Africa, Australasia, South America and the Indian Deccan, the highest forms of life were primitive placental and marsupial mammals. From these, on Madagascar, no large, vigorous, predatory creatures developed. Instead Evolution wandered down a peaceful byway, not being very inventive, which is why zoologists and botanists now describe the island as 'a living museum'. Most of its plant and animal life is unique, though its geological structure and geographical features have much in common with Southern Africa. Fittingly, the coelacanth was first found in Madagascar's deep surrounding waters, having survived there almost unchanged for many millions of years.

Despite countless man-hours of academic toil, no one is sure – or ever likely to be – exactly when Madagascar's first settlers arrived. But it is certain that few fertile areas of the world remained so long uninhabited; the earliest archaeological evidence of human occupation dates from about AD 900. It is also certain that Malagasy* culture has Malayo-Polynesian roots. The language belongs to the Malayo-Polynesian group though about twenty per cent of its modern vocabulary is Bantu, with a sprinkling of Sanskrit, English, French and Arabic.

At one time it was assumed that the proto-Malagasy had sailed straight across the southern Indian Ocean to Madagascar, a distance of almost 4,000 miles. Now the most widely accepted theory is that migrant traders, in large twin-hulled outrigger

* pronounced 'Malagash'

canoes, made the journey by comparatively easy stages: from Sumatra to the Andaman Islands, to Ceylon, South India, the Maldives, the Laccadives and so across the Arabian Sea to Socotra and finally (during the first century AD?) to Azania, now known as Kenya and Tanzania. There they found empty spaces, a good climate, varied trading opportunities and a sparse, undeveloped population on whom it was easy to impose their own culture.

During the next few centuries – according to this theory – more and more Polynesians settled on the African coast, then gradually moved inland, introducing new food plants wherever they went: taro, yams, bananas, coconuts, breadfruit. This novel notion of growing food, instead of merely hunting and gathering it, contributed to a Bantu population explosion, one of the causes of the eventual settlement of Madagascar. Another cause was Arab domination, by the tenth century, of Indian Ocean trade.

The island's sporadic settlement extended over centuries, beginning perhaps as much as 1500 years ago with small groups establishing themselves on the north-west and west coasts. Larger groups came later and, having had more contact with the rapidly expanding Bantu, were less obviously Polynesian. These new arrivals settled on the south and east coasts, as well as among the original migrants. Madagascar's mountainous and densely forested interior remained for long unexplored; it could be approached only through the valleys of the Onilahy, Tsiribihina and Betsiboka rivers, which run into the Mozambique Channel. Probably the first people to venture up those valleys and discover the high central plateau were the Vazimba, a tall, strong, dark-skinned tribe with curly though not frizzy hair. The second, main migration apparently pushed these early settlers inland. Then, much later, they were pushed west again when the Merina arrived on the plateau. They ended up in the Bemaraha Mountains as troglodytes who food-gathered in the forest; now the majority live in primitive hamlets on remote heights. The Merina tradition that the Vazimba are indigenous to Madagascar has been rejected by anthropologists.

The exact origin of the Merina, the largest and most enterprising of Madagascar's eighteen main tribes, remains a mystery. Scholars offer contradictory explanations for their light brown skin, straight black hair and impeccable Polynesian features. Some argue that they are descended from Malayan or Javanese migrants who landed on the east coast of Madagascar no more than seven or eight centuries ago and were never in the African melting-pot. Others maintain that their ancestors were among the earliest groups to settle in Africa, when there were few Bantu around, and that they married only within the tribe – making it taboo to do otherwise – during all those centuries when later settlers were being slightly miscegenatious. There are several other theories with which I won't detain us. The 'late arrival' theory, favoured by the Merina themselves, seems to me the most plausible. But whenever and from wherever they arrived, the pioneer Merina evidently found it necessary, on reaching the plateau, to combine intermarriage with military conquest – a popular formula, throughout Malagasy history, for settling territorial disputes. The minority of Merina who do not look pure Polynesian tend to be tallish and rather dark with slightly wavy hair.

The Polynesian/African genetic experiment had happy results, unlike many inter-racial mixes. When the proto-Malagasy settled on the Great Red Island they had already become, despite marked variations in physique, colouring and features, a homogeneous people united by their language, their animist religion and a distinctive, stable culture. On the practical level they had retained three important characteristics of their Polynesian heritage: highly developed fishing skills, rectangular wooden huts built on stilts in rainy regions and the ecologically disastrous technique of slash-and-burn rice cultivation. In Africa they had learned about animal husbandry and they brought to Madagascar the ancestors of those huge herds of magnificently horned hump-backed zebu which still dominate the social and religious rituals of millions. These animals have become a symbol of Malagasy culture; they appear on the coinage, the stamps and many printed cotton skirts and *lambas*. (The *lamba* is sometimes worn as a shawl and sometimes, by both men and women, as a sarong.)

Madagascar was not 'discovered' by Europeans until 10 August 1500 when an off-course Portuguese ship sighted an unexpected mass of land. Gradually the sailors realised that it was an unknown island and named it 'St Lawrence's Island', after the saint of the day. Portuguese geographers then decided that this must be the Arabs' 'Isle of the Moon' and the 'Madagascar' of which Marco Polo had heard rumours as he crossed Arabia.

No sooner discovered than attacked. In 1506 and 1507 the

scattered Arab trading settlements along Madagascar's north-west coast were destroyed by the Portuguese, during a relentless campaign against their main rivals in the spice trade. Subsequently a few half-hearted efforts were made to explore the Malagasy coasts. But it quickly became obvious that the island was without precious metals, precious stones or rare spices, that the coastal fevers were exceptionally virulent and that the natives' reactions to *vazaha* (foreigners) were unpredictable. So Portuguese attentions were returned to the African mainland.

Between 1613 and 1619 a Portuguese Jesuit, Fr Luis Mariano, zealously investigated many coastal villages with soul-saving in mind. He preached doggedly, often risking his life, but found it impossible to persuade the Malagasy that Hell awaits the wicked. He therefore decided they could never be converted to Christianity and went home. Two hundred years later he was proved wrong when Christianity – though not his version of it – came to play an extraordinarily important part in the formation of modern Madagascar.

Towards the end of the eighteenth century the Merina rulers moved out from their plateau homeland to take control of most of Madagascar, though the formidable southern semi-desert, and a large area of the west coast, south of Majunga, remained unconquered. In 1810 the accession of King Radama II to the recently established Merina throne coincided with Britain's seizure of Mauritius from the French. The eighteen-year-old king, eager to bring the whole island under Merina authority – a difficult task, given the nature of the terrain and the turbulence of certain tribes – welcomed the practical and moral support of the first British Governor of Mauritius. Robert Farquhar had offered this support as part of his strategy to stop the export of slaves from Madagascar and undermine France's claims to have gained sovereignty over the entire island in the seventeenth century; Britain did not covet Madagascar but was anxious to keep it French-free.

To strengthen Anglo-Malagasy ties, Farquhar urged the radical Nonconformist London Missionary Society – already interested in Madagascar – to send missionaries and artisans to Imerina where the young king was impatient to introduce European education and craftsmanship to his people. In February 1818 the LMS duly despatched two young Welshmen, David Jones and Thomas Bevan, with their brides, to settle in a region where no one had ever seen a white woman. By February 1819 Mr and Mrs

Bevan and their new-born daughter, and Mrs Jones and her new-born daughter, had all died within six weeks at the port town of Tamatave. For centuries the notorious 'Malagasy fever' (cerebral malaria) had been one of Madagascar's main defences against the outside world and during the nineteenth century 'General Tazo' (fever) and 'General Hazo' (forest) made their names as the most efficient officers in the Malagasy army.

When the bereft David Jones at last reached Imerina, on the central plateau, he reported home: 'King Radama is exceedingly kind and affable. He is a great advocate for education and esteems the instruction of his people in the arts of civilisation more than gold and silver.'

Having commented that in general the Merina of all classes were more civilised than many of the inhabitants of Wales, Mr Jones had to add (one can almost see his pen trembling with horror): 'The greatest sins of all they are guilty of, are adultery and fornication which reach to the highest pitch among the people universally so that there are few husbands and wives who are not guilty of adultery and not one young person above ten years of age I believe free from fornication.' The spread of Christianity did little to alter this happy-go-fucky situation. Fifty years later, the education of Malagasy girls was often interrupted by pregnancy from the age of twelve on, and at twelve or thirteen many left their mission schools to marry.

When King Radama dictated a letter to the LMS, requesting as many missionaries as were available, he insisted that they must include builders, carpenters, tanners, weavers and blacksmiths. Being suspicious of French designs on his country he also communicated with Paris, turning down an offer of Catholic missionaries. It could do his people no good, he pointed out, to be disputed over by mutually antagonistic Christian sects. His own attitude to religion was cynical. While rejecting the taboo-ridden animism of his ancestors he remained unimpressed by Christianity as an alternative and saw the missionary presence as a means to material and social, rather than spiritual and moral, advance. He could have found no better people for his purpose than the men and women of the LMS. Between them they possessed all the qualities needed to meet the Malagasy challenge. They were tough, kind, democratic, resourceful, energetic, versatile and adaptable. At times their adaptability led them to compromise quietly when orthodox Anglicans or Roman Catholics would have raised the theological roof. As a result of this flexibility Malagasy Christianity has a flavour all its own and the high percentage of Malagasy who regularly attend church is almost a world record for the 1980s.

David Jones was soon joined in Antananarivo by another young Welshman, David Griffiths, and together these two, personally assisted by a keenly interested and intelligent Radama, provided the Malagasy with a written language based on the Roman alphabet. They then translated and printed texts for the rudimentary schools already founded, in which it was soon possible to use the senior pupils to teach the juniors, so quick-minded and avid for learning were the Merina young. Next, and most important of all for the Welshmen, came the translation of the Bible, a daunting task to which their more advanced students contributed as the years passed. By 1826 the New Testament had been completed and the Old was coming along nicely. To us this seems an astonishing achievement on the part of two men from humble homes in the Welsh mountains who first had to learn Malagasy themselves, and then devise a script, while simultaneously establishing an academic educational system and supervising the training of artisans. How many 'experts', laden with what electronic equipment, would now be despatched to a Third World country to implement such a programme?

After King Radama's death in 1828 reactionaries took over and during their régime many Malagasy Christians were martyred in unspeakable ways – which drew more of their compatriots to Christianity, instead of frightening them off. Yet despite the fervour of the ordinary Merina no monarch was converted until 1869. Then Queen Ranavalona II and her Prime Minister-cum-lover were baptised together and soon after married in church.

Prime Minister Rainilaiarivony – industrious, astute, diplomatic – was the real ruler of Madagascar from 1864 to 1896, during which time he had to marry three Queens for reasons of state. Queen Ranavalona's conversion seems to have been genuine but the Prime Minister's was a matter of political expediency and required him to put his country's good before his personal affections. Before marrying the Queen in church he had to divorce his wife, Rasoanalina, to whom he was devoted and by whom he had had sixteen much-loved children. (To make matters worse, Ranavalona II was some fifteen years his senior and not too well preserved.) The couple were baptised by a Malagasy pastor and, significantly, there were no Europeans present at this historic ceremony. By 1869 Nonconformist Protestantism had been accepted as a Malagasy religion; having no colonial government support helped. Catholic missionaries in Madagascar have always been handicapped by their French connection.

In 1890 the LMS could – and did – boast of 1,224 churches, 59,617 members and 248,108 adherents, the majority in Imerina. (I have been unable to discover how the precise figure for 'adherents' – a suspiciously ambiguous term – was arrived at.) By then Christianity had transformed important aspects of Malagasy life, without undermining the traditional culture. On the plateau Quakers worked in harmony, as is their wont, with the LMS. Elsewhere the Jesuits (chiefly on the east coast) and the Norwegian Lutherans (chiefly in the south) had established their own missions. But the alliance between the LMS and the ruling Merina meant that Nonconformism enjoyed a special position throughout Madagascar, which it retains to this day.

In 1862 Dr Andrew Davidson of the LMS founded Madagascar's first medical service but in the 1880s the Quakers took on the main burden of medical work. Both the French Jesuits and Norwegian Lutherans included doctors among their pioneer missionaries, the Catholics specialising in the care of lepers. A government medical service was set up in 1875 and its personnel, unlike most Merina government servants, received salaries. By 1880 there were several fully qualified Malagasy doctors. A few took degrees in Edinburgh, including Dr Ralarosy who organised a village dispensary scheme as trained Malagasy nurses became available.

Before the French took over in 1896 primary education, especially in the villages, was left almost entirely to the churches. The Malagasy preacher was usually the teacher, too, and used the local chapel as his schoolroom. In 1880 the Prime Minister made elementary education compulsory for all children over seven, only a decade after it had been introduced in England and two years before it was introduced in France. Already some 40,000 pupils were regularly attending Protestant schools and by 1894 the number had risen to 137,000. To cater for this educated public the missionary printing presses, largely LMS-run and Merina-operated, produced a steady flow of textbooks, dictionaries, religious works, hymn-books, newspapers, monthly and quarterly journals and a scholarly *Antananarivo Annual* dealing with various aspects of Malagasy life. When the French took over, the vast majority of the plateau population, of both sexes, was literate and numerate, a fact which distinguished Madagascar from any other colony of the time.

The French conquest tempted Jesuit missionaries to tell the more credulous villagers – especially the Betsileo – that they must become Roman Catholics to avoid being considered disloyal to France. Some Jesuits also commandeered Protestant churches, accusing their Pastors of treachery, and had many of their clerical rivals arrested and several executed. When these activities were reported to the first French Governor-General, Galliéni, he ordered the Jesuits out of the stolen churches, assuring the Malagasy that they were at liberty to worship how they chose – or not at all. Although himself a fervent atheist, Galliéni eventually acknowledged the achievements of the LMS and co-operated with them.

Galliéni ruled for nine years and 'pacified' those regions never subdued by the Merina. The new unified state cost many Malagasy lives, though not as many as were lost during the unsuccessful campaigns of King Radama I and Queen Ranavalona I.

Unfortunately the second Governor-General, Augagneur, was a rabid anti-cleric who at once announced his determination to separate Church and State. He banned teaching in churches, thus closing ninety per cent of the rural schools because few villages could afford a separate building. But no one could de-educate Antananarivo's intellectuals, some of whom formed an anti-colonial movement long before such enterprising behaviour had been dreamed of elsewhere. During its early years this group lacked strength, cohesion and consistency, yet it contained the seed of today's Malagasy nation.

As a colonial possession Madagascar was utterly unlike any of the European colonies in Africa, though in one way comparable to British India. There too the people of various states had long been accustomed to bureaucratic and/or hierarchical institutions of their own, however ramshackle these may have become by the time the British arrived.

Alfred Ramangasoavina, a former Malagasy Minister of Justice, liked to remind *vazaha* that one cannot talk of Madagascar's accession to independence in 1960. Before the French conquest the Merina Kingdom had been internationally recognised as an independent sovereign state, therefore in legal terms the country recovered its independence in 1960. It was not, like so many African ex-colonies, a new-born state with artificial borders – arbitrarily drawn, in defiance of ethnic realities, as a result of European meddling and haggling. Yet there were several crucial differences between the old and new Madagascars. Throughout most of the nineteenth century the island was ruled by a Merina oligarchy not fully in control of all regions; the 1960 Republic was a union of Madagascar's eighteen tribes, enjoying (at least in theory) equal rights.

To understand present-day Franco–Malagasy relations, it is necessary to think back to August 1896 when a law was passed in the French Parliament declaring Madagascar a French colony. At once General Joseph Simon Galliéni took over the island, with full civil and military powers and explicit instructions from the Prime Minister, André Lebon – 'The system which consisted merely in exercising the protectorate* over the dominant race is now set aside. The authority of the sovereign power must now be applied by the authority of the chiefs of each separate tribe.' The intention was immediately to downgrade the 'dominant race' since the Merina were the greatest threat to French control over the new colony; during the brief French Protectorate, Merina officials had been secretly organising widespread rebellion from Antananarivo.

However, General Galliéni soon realised that he needed the assistance of those people described by the Reverend William Ellis as 'more numerous, industrious, ingenious and wealthy than those of any other part of the country' – people who already had considerable experience of governing two-thirds of the island. The last Prime Minister, Rainilaiarivony, had set up an administrative hierarchy, with regional governors and deputy-governors, which was accepted by the majority of the population. So Galliéni ignored his own Prime Minister's directive (colonial governors could get away with that sort of thing before the days of instant communication) and retained the existing structure, using as subordinates to the French district commissioners those Malagasy officials (usually Merina) who had been serving the

* The Protectorate was established in 1890 by the Convention of Zanzibar, a Franco–British treaty allowing Britain to retain Zanzibar in return for relinquishing all interest in Madagascar as a colony.

monarchy. To expedite this bureaucratic dovetailing, he encouraged all French officials to learn the language and until the 1940s most senior administrators spoke fluent Malagasy.

Yet the Merina were gradually and inexorably downgraded, though not at once deprived of all senior positions. In the regional training schools set up to supply the junior staff for the administration, and overseers and accountants for the settlers' plantations and commercial firms, no Malagasy were trained to take on senior posts. Also, admission to Antananarivo's lycées was strictly controlled; given the high average intelligence of the Merina, it would have been dangerous to educate them *en masse* beyond primary level. Of the limited number of lycée students, only a few of the Merina élite – hand-picked for political reliability, though the hand-picking did not always work – were allowed to study at French universities. This restriction did much to inflame Malagasy nationalism, as did the dual judicial system: French laws for the colonists and a brutally unjust code, known as the *indigènat*, for the Malagasy. Under the *indigènat* district commissioners could sentence any Malagasy – without trial – to fifteen days imprisonment for not cultivating enough rice (enough, that is, in the estimation of the French authorities), or for not paying taxes, or for refusing to provide unpaid labour.

The Merina upper classes were most sensitive to educational and promotional restrictions. But the operation of the *indigènat*, the imposition of taxes and the much-abused forced-labour system were resented by every section of the population. Under the monarchy, Imerina's large feudal estates had been cultivated by serfs and slaves and each area's *fokon'olona* (rural commune) had obliged freemen to contribute annually to public works, either by giving a sum of money or a certain number of days labour, known as *fanampoana*. Colonial apologists used the Merinas' possession of slaves as justification for the French system of forced labour, which was a particularly dirty trick. Malagasy domestic slavery was not criticised even by the Reverend Ellis, a commentator ever eager to condemn the effects of 'the barbarous laws of Madagascar . . . partaking of the inconsistency, superstition and cruelty which characterize the public and domestic regulations of most heathen nations'. And the Reverend T.T. Matthews – another LMS apostle who laboured in the Malagasy vineyard during the last thirty years of the nineteenth century – admitted that 'Domestic slavery in Madagascar was the mildest form of slavery, and in most cases the slaves were regarded as almost members of the family and treated as such'. His only complaint was that 'even the mildest form of domestic slavery was utter ruination to all family morality. For, even in the days when polygamy was rampant, a man's female slaves were all at his mercy, and were practically his concubines, or those of his sons, or both.' However, since 'family morality', as defined by the LMS, never got a look in anywhere on the Malagasy scene, this objection carries little weight.

All over the world, in rural societies with a limited – or no – cash economy, corvée systems operated, and still operate. Someone has to construct communal irrigation channels, mend bridges, maintain tracks, clear canals and so on. It is however one thing to contribute labour for the good of one's own community and quite another to be forced to work, far from home, for the benefit of foreign settlers. When Galliéni made a law, one month after his arrival, requiring every healthy male between the ages of sixteen and sixty to work for the French on fifty days out of each year, for nine hours a day, on minimum wages, he created France's most intractable problem in Madagascar. Yet as the ruler of the new colony he had no alternative. A man of flawless personal integrity, he was far from being the worst type of colonial administrator; indeed, by nineteenth-century standards he seems almost benign. But the French Parliament was impatiently demanding tangible rewards to justify the colossal expenses, both financial and human, of the military conquest; and without forced labour there could be no rewards. The formal abolition of slavery a few years earlier – ironically, a result of the pre-conquest French Protectorate – had left the highlands without any dependable labour force; and the east coast had never had one.

In these two main areas of French settlement and exploitation, entirely different types of property rights had been traditionally recognised. On the central highlands, in Imerina and the territory of the Betsileo immediately to the south, most of the fertile land formed large feudal estates – whose cultivators, on the abolition of slavery, had automatically become the *de facto* owners of as much land as was necessary for the survival of their families. Along the steep, wet, densely forested east coast, the Antasaka, Antaimoro and Betsimisaraka tribes had for centuries practised slash-and-burn mountain-rice cultivation and obtained all the food, clothing and building materials they needed from the surrounding forests. So neither the highland peasants nor the coastal tribesmen (who had always been freemen) felt any urge to work for the French. They didn't need cash – it was as simple as that. Therefore, like many another colonial ruler, Galliéni pronounced that 'Taxation is an indispensable stimulant to the energy of the native'. Put more crudely, if you impose a tax, and operate a legal system that allows men to be jailed for not paying it, people will have to earn money, either by working for wages or by producing surplus food, though they may have no need or wish to enter a cash economy.

Throughout the colonial era, the provision of adequate labour for the settlers' purposes remained the administration's biggest problem. Marcel Olivier, Governor-General from 1924 to 1930, wrote: 'Without the effective support – let us be frank, without the pressure – of the administration, nine-tenths of the European enterprises would disappear for lack of manpower. The freedom of the worker to choose his job should only become part of the laws of a country when the obligation to work has become a customary practice.'

This is a classic example of the imperialist mind in action, transposing European standards to a non-European context, purely for the colonists' benefit, and assuming that the 'natives' ' failure to view things from the European angle was a moral defect instead of a preferred way of life which did no harm to anyone. We Westerners tend to congratulate ourselves, nowadays, on the disappearance of such attitudes; but our congratulations are premature. The activities of most multinational companies throughout the Third World also demonstrate a total disregard for local needs and traditions, though their motives and methods are more cleverly disguised. Some people prefer the old-style colonial bluntness. At least the exploited 'natives', or their political leaders, knew exactly what they were up against.

However, 'exploitation' was not the name of the whole game. Colonialism brought genuine benefits as well as appalling hardships to the Malagasy, as to many other peoples. Throughout the vast areas unsuited to European settlement, most of the locals, by then accustomed to the hierarchical structure of Merina rule, effortlessly transferred their loyalty to French district officers. And many of these, when not influenced by powerful settlers, showed much paternalistic benevolence, being prepared to work hard, and uncomplainingly endure the most spartan of living conditions, for 'their' people.

Galliéni saw health-care as one of his main duties. Soon after his arrival he expressed appreciation of 'the perseverance of the missionaries in these praiseworthy efforts, which the Hova (Merina) Government had tried to emulate; a hospital having been built by its orders, and an attempt having been made to create a school of medicine, which resulted in the training of a few doctors and midwives'. The missionary medical services, restricted by lack of funds, were quickly and efficiently extended by ordering the well-equipped Medical Corps of the Army of Occupation to give free treatment, and build dispensaries, wherever it went (which was most places). The new hospitals, orphanages and dispensaries were 'to be kept up' – Galliéni ordered – 'by means of contributions by the villages, but, where necessary, subsidized by the local budget'. He also founded a new School of Medicine in Antananarivo, opened maternity homes and established training centres for midwives. Antananarivo's main dispensary provided free advice and medicines, and thousands of booklets on hygiene were distributed – with remarkable results, because of the high literacy rate. Some hospitals had to be enlarged to accommodate women VD patients. Among the Malagasy no shame attached to those diseases and the victims, having read their booklets, were soon blocking hospital entrances. The population of Madagascar was three million – or so – when the French took over. It is now nine million – or so.

After Galliéni's departure in 1905 the forced-labour laws were increasingly abused, separating many men from their families for two or even three years. The influential forest-concession and plantation owners knew how to tame their local French district commissioner, who was supposed to look after the workers' interests. Official labour statistics for 1943 record 3,810,000 compulsory 'man/days'. It is not astonishing that the 1947 Rebellion was at its most frenzied in such areas as Manakara and Ambatondrazaka, where the plantation owners were especially notorious for their cruelty.

Galliéni's successor, Victor Augagneur, made promotion for Malagasy officials, in the Departments of Education and Health, conditional on their becoming Freemasons. This proved a useful 'divide and rule' implement since most educated Merina were devout Christians whose consciences forbade them to join an anti-clerical Freemasonry.

Augagneur also decreed, in 1909, that certain Malagasy, after fulfilling numerous stringent conditions, could become French citizens with full civil rights, thus escaping the indignities of the *indigènat*. This was his way of implementing Galliéni's policy that the leading families should be allowed to regain some power once Madagascar had fully accepted French rule. Not many were able or willing to take advantage of the decree; there were scarcely ten thousand Malagasy-French citizens in 1960, out of a population of six million. But this group's influence was disproportionately great and most of its Francophile members were absorbed into Colonial Society.

Whether or not he became a French citizen, the educated Malagasy who was good at his job was accepted as an equal by his French colleagues and regularly invited to their homes – a situation almost unimaginable in British India and quite unimaginable in British Africa. Senior French administrators were rarely prejudiced in the crude, colour-conscious British way; intellectual parity was their main criterion for the establishment of social relations. And because the Merinas' intellectual development had been conditioned by generations of contact with European educationalists, and by some experience of European universities and much experience of European literature and thought, the colonists found them easier to get on with than France's Asian 'subjects', whose more sophisticated cultures were inaccessible to all but a few exceptional European minds. The average administrator had little in common with most of his settler compatriots; 'chancers' were numerous in Madagascar, where limited scope for profit meant less competition and fewer bureaucratic controls than in the more prosperous and better-organised colonies. Similarly, many Merina found that they had a greater intellectual affinity with the French than with the majority of their fellow-Malagasy. Thus lasting Franco–Malagasy friendships flourished and intermarriage was acceptable; one of the last Governor-Generals had a Malagasy wife. The children of mixed marriages usually rose high in the government service and Franco–Malagasy matings, in or out of wedlock, produced no equivalent to the pathetic Anglo-Indians.

However, only a minority chose this degree of co-operation and integration with the colonists. Meanwhile many middle-class Merina, with allies from their own élite and from other tribes, were supporting that nationalist movement which was more or less active – though not often united – throughout the whole period of French domination.

Merina pride had been deeply wounded by the degradation of their kingdom to colony status and the abrupt loss of power, prestige and possessions. Yet many soon recognised that the European development of Madagascar might benefit the island in general and their own tribe in particular, if the *indigènat* and educational restrictions could be abolished or at least modified. This realisation, combined with the natural mildness of the Malagasy temperament, meant that Malagasy nationalism never became a movement of extremists. Indeed the term 'nationalism', though generally used, is imprecise in this context; most of Madagascar's so-called nationalist leaders, before the Second World War, were not seeking to overthrow the administration but simply to ameliorate the harshness of colonial rule.

One of the pioneer leaders was Ravelajaona, a Protestant clergyman and a scholar whose encyclopaedia – *Treasury of the Language and Things of Madagascar* – is still used. His party of moderate intellectuals, 'The Christian Young People's Union', included several relatives of the Royal family and was banned by Augagneur. In 1913 Ravelajaona published a series of articles on Japan, in a Malagasy-language journal, explaining how an Asiatic people could profit by a study of Western science and technology. This series had a lasting effect on many young Merina who had been humiliated and frustrated by the French refusal to allow them academic freedom and the jobs for which their talents fitted them.

Three years later, in the middle of the First World War, a group of Malagasy nationalists tried to organise an armed uprising. (Probably these were The Christian Young People's Union who, following their banning, had become a secret society not unlike the Irish Republican Brotherhood of the same period.) When the conspiracy was discovered some five hundred 'intellectuals' were arrested and forty-one were accused of incitement to revolt. The jumpy settlers spread rumours of a German plot involving the discovery of barrels of poison and enough gunpowder to kill every French citizen on Madagascar. This was pure fantasy, but to soothe the colonists each defendant was given a viciously heavy sentence on the flimsiest of evidence. However, no Malagasy was executed; the French were less politically myopic than the British in Ireland during that same year. Most of the prisoners were freed in 1918, the rest in 1921 under a general amnesty. As in Ireland in 1916, the majority of the population were uninterested in (if not actually disapproving of) the activities of the conspirators. And, again as in Ireland, at the time of the attempted uprising many Malagasy were fighting with their colonial masters against the Germans.

During the First World War 46,000 Malagasy were recruited and 2,368 killed in action. The return home of these troops, bearing hard-won battle honours, changed the nature of the nationalist movement. No longer was it dominated by thwarted Merina academics. Having served France on terms of equality in Europe, the ex-soldiers were disinclined to revert meekly to the status of second-class citizens in their own land. They were mainly responsible for the rapid spread of political agitation during the 1920s. And as the numbers of educated Malagasy grew, all over the island, so did the demands for equal civil rights, though as yet only a tiny radical minority was seeking complete independence.

The French dedication to free speech was severely tested at this time – and proved genuine. The career of Jean Ralaimongo, a Betsileo schoolteacher who had volunteered to fight in Europe, well illustrated French tolerance of 'constitutional' opposition to the colonial régime. In Paris, immediately after the war, Ralaimongo shared a room with Ho Chi Minh and returned to Madagascar in 1921 already known as a potential 'trouble-maker'. Yet he was received by the Governor-General, Hubert Garbit, who warned – 'I don't want anyone coming to upset my Malagasy under the pretext that they are unhappy when they are not unhappy.' (Such self-deceptions enabled many colonial officials all over the world to exploit their fellow-men with a clear conscience.) Despite the fact that Ralaimongo was obviously hell-bent on 'upsetting' as many Malagasy as possible, Garbit then allowed him to travel freely throughout Madagascar, collecting evidence for a critical report on the administration which he published on his return to Paris. Moreover, in spite of the controversy aroused by this report, he was permitted, a few years later, to settle in Diego Suarez – the French naval and military base at the northern tip of Madagascar – from where he organised a long campaign on behalf of the peasantry which provoked many settlers to hysterical rage.

As France's Socialist and Communist parties gained strength during the 1930s, Madagascar's nationalists received increased support in the French Parliament. After the 1936 election of Leon Blum's Popular Front, the Malagasy were granted the right to form Trades Unions, though only of workers who could speak and write French. Also, press censorship was lifted, forced labour – apart from a maximum of ten days a year for public works – was abolished in theory (in practice it continued until 1946) and all political offenders were granted an amnesty. From then on nationalist demands were supported by the many Leon Blum followers among the colonists and by influential non-Communist political parties within France. As a result, there was a spontaneous upsurge of pro-France emotion at the beginning of the Second World War and the nationalists voluntarily ceased their propaganda campaigns.

During the war Madagascar was occupied from May 1942 by Allied (mainly British) troops, after an ill-organised invasion through Diego Suarez; the British army did not distinguish itself on that occasion but the navy saved the day.

With the establishment of the French Union in 1946 all France's colonial subjects acquired French citizenship and equal rights – again, in theory. In practice, Madagascar's post-war difficulties meant that forced labour actually increased after the system had been legally abolished. This continuing dependence on 'conscripted workers' is believed to have been one of the main causes of the 1947 Rebellion. Another was the extreme hardship inflicted on the Malagasy by rampant black-marketeering and the corruption of the official Rice Marketing Board, to which all farmers were compelled to sell surpluses at artificially low prices. A third factor was what we would now call a 'fundamentalist revival' among the *ombiasa* and their followers – especially in the south. These 'heathen sorcerers', as the Reverends Ellis and Matthews called them, had never ceased to resent the intrusion of European ideas and Christian practices, to which they rightly attributed their declining power.

At that time of transition – a year after the creation of the French Union – confusion prevailed throughout Madagascar. The peasants' loyalty to their French district commissioners had been irreparably damaged by the Allied occupation; the political parties were far from united; the *indigènat* and various other restraints on political activity were gone; many settlers were resisting proposals to lessen their privileges by introducing some degree of 'power-sharing' in the new National Representative Assembly (NRA). Many colonial administrators were also protesting against being made accountable to local Malagasy politicians – the time could not have been riper for anyone interested in promoting rebellion.

The Rebellion broke out on the evening of 29 March 1947, the day before the first meeting of the newly elected NRA. Strangely, the organisers have never been clearly identified, perhaps because most were soon killed and nothing had been put on paper. Many Malagasy cherish private convictions about exactly who was responsible where: but nothing can be proved. Certainly the Rebellion was carefully planned. It broke out simultaneously in such widely separated places as Moramanga, Diego Suarez and Manakara – and anyone with experience of Madagascar's communications problems will appreciate the significance of that. For some unknown reason the capital's rebels cancelled their plans at the last moment, but elsewhere their comrades soon had about one-sixth of the island under control, mainly in those areas where land and labour disputes had been endemic for half a century.

Guerrilla warfare continued for about a year, with little evidence of any centralised command. Scattered groups of peasants, meagrely supplied, opposed the French troops with spears, axes, slash-hooks, shotguns; they had only a few modern weapons stolen from military bases. In October 1947 several units of the Foreign Legion and thousands more Senegalese troops arrived as reinforcements. This extra Senegalese 'input' was, to say the least, unfortunate. During that historic night of 29 March, when Moramanga's army camp was attacked by some two thousand men armed with slash-hooks and spears, scores of Senegalese soldiers were surprised and killed before they could reach their guns. The survivors massacred a never-established number of the local non-combatant population, which surprised no one. The Senegalese – a permanent part of the French garrison – had long since gained a reputation for unprovoked deeds of random savagery. It was only to be expected that when provoked the slaughter would be hideous. To have loosed these troops on the entire island, for eighteen months, with a mandate to 'repress rebellion', was the most dreadful crime committed by the French in Madagascar.

In December 1948, when 558,000 surrenders had been registered, the Rebellion was declared officially over. A subsequent Commission of Enquiry was told by General Garbay and the French High Commissioner (who under the new French Union régime replaced a Governor-General) that the Rebellion's Malagasy victims numbered between sixty and eighty thousand. Most of those were villagers who had fled to the forest to escape military reprisals and died of disease or starvation. Along the east coast almost every family lost some of its members. The French lost about a thousand troops and thirty settlers, the majority Creoles.

To the Malagasy, the massacres of the Senegalese troops have become the epitome of barbarity and injustice. Most Malagasy are gentle, peaceable people – brave enough when necessary, but with no warrior-cult, no tradition of glorifying war. Their happy state of geographical isolation means that, apart from their own ritualistic slave-hunting tribal wars (which by definition involved few deaths), they have enjoyed a comparatively unbloody history. Never before had they experienced anything like the horrors of the twenty-one-month repression of the Rebellion. The eighteenth-century Merina 'unification' campaigns, and Galliéni's 1896–1904 'pacification' campaign, seem mild in comparison. It would therefore be understandable if the acid of unforgiving hate had ever since been corroding Franco–Malagasy relations. But though we did hear the Senegalese atrocities being mentioned with shudders of retrospective terror, we also got the impression that the French authorities of the day are not held directly responsible for all that happened. Many Malagasy seem to have chosen to regard the Rebellion and its repression as so atypical of Franco–Malagasy relations that both 'incidents' are best not mentioned when the colonial history of the island is being discussed. In 1967 the first government commemoration of the Rebellion's victims was organised; but President Tsiranana prepared for this occasion by repeatedly urging the Malagasy not to dishonour their dead by vengefully brooding on past wrongs. (We could use a Tsiranana in Ireland today.) In 1970 Nigel Heseltine wrote: 'Twenty years after this conflict it could be said that the psychological wounds had healed ... The settlement of the consequences of the Rebellion are greatly to the credit of both Malagasy and French. It cannot have been easy to forget, and in fact the events have not been forgotten. But they are remembered with an objective dignity, and any return to the extreme forms of xenophobic nationalism, as appears occasionally in fringe newspapers of small opposition groups, has been resolutely rejected by the mass of the population as well as its leaders.'

The Malagasy word *Fihavanana* has – perhaps not surprisingly – no exact English equivalent. It was translated for us by a Merina friend as 'benevolence and friendship towards all one's fellow-

men' and it describes one of the most obvious Malagasy characteristics. As our friend said, 'The basis of our Malagasy philoso-
phy is this: it is better to lose money than affection.'

Fihavanana goes a long way to explain why the transition to
independence was so painless in Madagascar. And it was helped
in its operations by the personalities of André Soucadaux,
France's last High Commissioner, and Philibert Tsiranana,
Madagascar's first President.

Tsiranana was a Tsimihety from the Ankaizina region in the
north-west, a schoolteacher from a poor peasant family, like so
many of Madagascar's political leaders. A man of high intelligence and by nature a reconciler, he had always believed that
Madagascar should move gradually towards independence in
friendly co-operation with the French. In 1954 he founded a new
political party; at first based in his native province, it soon spread
to include all the coastal peoples and some Merina moderates. In
January 1956 he was elected to the French National Assembly as
representative of the Malagasy people of West Madagascar. A
year later he was leading a coalition of coastal parties, which had
reduced the Merina parties to a minority in the Malagasy National Assembly. This proof that the workings of democracy could
protect the majority from any reassertion of Merina dominance
was a necessary condition for the granting of full independence.
Tsiranana was a close friend of André Soucadaux, a Socialist with
a real affection for the Malagasy, who was eager to do all he could
to assist in the establishment of a stable republic.

On 15 October 1958 Soucadaux appeared before the Malagasy
National Assembly and declared – 'The Government of the
French Republic solemnly recognises the establishment of the
state of Madagascar, and the abrogation of the Law of Annexation
of August 6, 1896.'

During the next twenty-one months, Soucadaux and Tsiranana
continued to work as a team to bring about an efficient transfer of
power. Their task was made easier by the fact that independence
had been patiently negotiated with France, not wrested from a
reluctant government by force. The Malagasy leaders had not just
emerged from jail, or from guerrilla hide-outs in the bush, to take
control. The Ministry of the Interior was the first to be staffed
entirely by Malagasy, with only a few French advisers, and by
Independence Day the armed gendarmerie, the civil police and
the security services had been under Malagasy control for eight-

een months. By that date too almost all French senior civil servants had been withdrawn and the 'Accords Franco–Malagaches', dealing – among other things – with the status of French residents in Madagascar, had been signed on 2 April 1960. Most of Tsiranana's ministers were ex-civil servants, with years of experience in the senior ranks of the administration, and in 1960 he invited three famous nationalist leaders, who had been unjustly exiled to France after the 1947 Rebellion, to return home and accept ministerial portfolios. This was a moving gesture because in the past he and they had been implacable political opponents. All three came home and two – Ravoahangy and Rabemanana-jara – became ministers. Only the seventy-four-year-old Raseta declined the invitation.

On 26 June 1960 the Tsimihety peasant's son watched the red, white and green flag of the new republic being raised over the Queen's Palace in Antananarivo, sixty-four years after the last Merina monarch, Queen Ranavalona III, had watched the red and white Merina standard being hauled down as she was carried to exile on a litter – with an escort of Senegalese troops.

It had all been very civilised. No French residents felt it necessary to leave Madagascar abruptly; however they may have deplored their loss of top-dog status, they knew they had nothing to fear from the new régime. There were no disconcerting changes in the commercial life or administrative structures of the country and more than twenty years after Independence Madagascar still has several thousand French residents, most of whom have become Malagasy .citizens. By now there have of course been many changes – not only disconcerting but, according to the French 'old guard', catastrophic. Their children and grandchildren do not see Madagascar as a country with a future; very few of them remain on the Great Red Island.

1

The Slow Red Road
to the Great Red Island

Everything about Madagascar is surprising: its terrain, flora, fauna, people, language, history, religion, politics – and the fact that it doesn't have an embassy in London. For British and Irish travellers the nearest source of visas is Paris, where Rachel and I went visa-hunting in April 1983. We were not leaving for Madagascar until June but a prolonged and strenuous hunt seemed likely. In general, the more obscure a country the more convoluted its bureaucracy.

We stayed with Toni, an old friend who lives in an eighteenth-century attic in the Latin Quarter, and over the years has done us more good turns than you could reckon on a lama's prayer-beads. On our way home from Baltistan, for instance, she nursed me through an almost lethal attack of food-poisoning picked up between Karachi and Moscow. Rachel was then aged six and a half and had much enjoyed her three-month mid-winter ride through the Karakoram on a retired polo pony, though we lived mainly on dried apricots and the night temperatures often dropped to minus twenty degrees. Three years later she and I trekked some twelve hundred miles with a mule through the Peruvian Andes: also quite a rough journey. Now Rachel was fourteen and a half – suddenly as tall as her mother – no longer a juvenile appendage. On our way to Paris I wondered, slightly apprehensively, how the mother–daughter relationship would withstand Malagasy hardships. The days of being a stoical foal-at-foot were certainly over for Rachel, and I reckoned that travels with a fourteen-year-old would be *different*. Which they were.

Toni had spent the previous month gently persuading the Embassy of the Democratic Republic of Madagascar that our summer plans could help the Malagasy tourist trade, which may partly explain why it took us only eighteen minutes to get our visas. But it must also be said that the Malagasy Embassy in Paris is singularly unbureaucratic. As you appear, before you've said a word of self-identification, swarms of small pale-brown happy-looking people, with soft welcoming voices, smile delightedly; and no one is interested in trivia like passport numbers and health certificates. True, our visas cost £22 each and were valid for only one month. But if tourists come at the rate of two a week, or thereabouts, you've obviously got to make the most of them.

Samuel Rajaona, a Malagasy colleague of Toni's, invited us to a corner of Madagascar in a Parisian apartment block to meet his wife and son. French is Madagascar's first European language but the Rajaonas also speak fluent English and gave us much practical advice, supplemented by a marked map of Madagascar, a list of possibly useful addresses, a street plan drawn by Samuel to help us to find his niece in Antsirabe – to whom he promised to write, preparing her for our arrival – and a chit in Malagasy requesting village headmen to tolerate and, if necessary, assist us. This last document was more important than I realised at the time. Madagascar's pervasive *fady* (taboos) still operate powerfully in rural areas, *pace* the LMS. We were moved by the Rajaonas' imaginative kindness. The warmth of this 'welcome-in-advance' seemed like a blessing on our journey.

Samuel presented to us his only copy of an irreplaceable volume published in 1975 for Air Madagascar. This soon became our favourite of many eccentric guidebooks. It radiates an endearing guilelessness as it explains how many roads have fallen into disrepair and become impassable, how many taxi-services no longer exist, how many beaches have sharp-edged mussel-shells making it dangerous to go 'bear-footed' (*sic*). We felt that tourist-evasion was not going to be one of our problems as we read this description of the area around Vohimasina:

'where are the ruins of a Corsair Fort, with wells disposed at an isoceles triangle. There are five unimportant hotels, except maybe the Bamboula Hotel where are two bungalows with three beds. To South at Ambilalamaitso are many private villas but the hotel is not opened regularly. There is only one restaurant keeper, Mr Marcelle, who prepares nice meals but only for a limited number. Swimming in the sea is prohibited because of sharks. And the swimming-pool in the lagoon has to be re-built. Camping sites there are. Hunting

and fishing give excellent results there. And with an out-
board one can make nice trips beholding delightful landscapes on the Pangalaues canal. With a good boat driver
knowing this water way one can reach Akanin'ny Nofy (the
Nest of Dreams). Akinin'ny Nofy is pretty dormant for the
now being, in spite of the presence of the motel with attached
buildings of a really good standing but more or less closed. It
is a region of salted lakes and there are many waterfalls. Let
us also mention lemurs, reptiles (inoffensive), nice flora,
medicinal plants. For hunting there are winged games.'

At once 'pretty dormant for the now being' became embedded in
Murphy-speak.

At Heathrow, on 28 June, Rachel guarded our 'hand-luggage'
(her rucksack, weighing thirty-five pounds) while I took my
rucksack (forty-five pounds) to the BA desk. Ahead of me a stocky
young Nigerian stood beside five gigantic leather suitcases on
wheels. When he was charged £647.50 for excess baggage I
shuddered in sympathy. But he nonchalantly produced a wad of
sterling, peeled off thirteen £50 notes – which scarcely diminished
the wad – and had to be reminded to pick up his change. How the
other half spends . . .

The weedy Englishman behind the desk – exhausted by all
those suitcases – scowled at our 'Aeroflot to Antananarivo' tickets.
'Blimey! Somewhere else no one ever heard of!' He disappeared to
find out the code letters and the restive queue behind me wondered why Aeroflot can't check in its own passengers. I smirked
inwardly. Travel snobs enjoy this sort of thing when everyone
around them is labelled for dog-eared destinations like New York,
Hong Kong, Karachi, Lagos.

Aeroflot is commendably austere: no wasteful bumph in the
seat-pockets, no duty-free luxuries for sale, no professional (or
other) smiles from the cabin-staff. But our lunch was good, apart
from a macabre white wine which only the Russians could
swallow. These were in the majority: well-groomed middle-aged
men with pale faces, fat briefcases and, it seemed, many worries.
They brooded silently over pages of figures, graphs and diagrams.
They were, perhaps, a trade delegation.

We landed at Moscow in brilliant sunshine. Beside the runway,
peasant women wearing headscarves were languidly raking hay in

golden meadows; if there is a production target for haycocks it was not bothering them. Ninety minutes and several long queues later we were in the nearby Airport Hotel, a gaunt glass and concrete block which for transit passengers like us, staying overnight without visas, is literally a prison. All its doors are guarded twenty-four hours a day by armed men, impassive but alert in smart green uniforms. Others of that ilk supervise one's fifty-yard walk from the bus to the hotel entrance, and back again when departure time comes. Any passenger who steps out of line provokes a yell and a scowl from the nearest guard. The general effect is of a neurotic mistrust holding the Soviet psyche by the throat.

While waiting for a lift to the eighth floor we enjoyed the English version of a multilingual notice: 'Each room is smoothly supplied with water, heat, light, ventilation and other communal services . . . Hotel personnell cleans without violating passengers' tranquillity.' We glanced around us. 'Tranquillity' seemed not the *mot juste*. Overbooking on the Aeroflot scale can only be described as an unnatural vice and we were surrounded by passengers at various stages of bewilderment/rage/despair/hysteria – people who had thought they were about to leave for London, Lima or Ulan Bator but found that instead they were condemned to two, three, even four days in the Airport Hotel *without* their luggage and *without* access to their country's diplomatic representative in Moscow.

Our room was not supplied, smoothly or otherwise, with soap, towels or lavatory paper. The sheets were clean but torn and damp, the electric light was too dim to read by, the ventilation was nil and the wall-long window locked. We got the key from our obese, expressionless floor-lady (why was it not left in the window?) and recklessly took out binoculars to study the landscape. Our view was limited to a tall forest of birch and pine beyond the narrow road leading to the airport. Only by standing on the table-shelf beneath the window could we see Moscow – a grey smudge along a cloudless horizon. In the cool of the midsummer evening a few smartly dressed off-duty hotel staff were sauntering, smoking, chatting and joking far below us. One young couple met outside the door of the kitchen-annex, which also had its armed guard, and hurried away into the forest. The bird life consisted of two fractious crows, two wheeling kestrels and three hopping sparrows; Marxism had not got to them and they were behaving just like Irish crows, kestrels and sparrows. We put away our binoculars and went downstairs to observe the resident fauna.

Our fellow-internees, like ourselves, had all been attracted by Aeroflot's sensationally low fares and were travelling alone, or in pairs or family groups; Intourist looks after packaged tourists elsewhere. During the next twenty-four hours we talked with three Ethiopian students, a young Japanese woman journalist, two Swedish archaeologists, a Hong Kong Chinese family complete with granny, an elderly Kenyan couple flying for the first time and terrified, two Swiss ornithologists going to Tashkent, two portly Sudanese gentlemen with surprisingly strong views about Northern Ireland, a young Danish couple going home after three years hitch-hiking through Africa, an even younger Sinhalese couple with a minuscule new-born daughter in a carry-cot – and Belgians going to Libya, Pakistanis going to Britain, Spaniards going to India and young Arabs going all over the place. There were also many Malagasy on the way home (circuitously) from France or Italy. On our return to the airport we were joined by many more – Moscow University students on Soviet scholarships – and one of these told us that ninety-five per cent of the passengers carried on Aeroflot's weekly flights to Antananarivo are Malagasy.

Despite our prison's mixum-gatherum, the Malagasy were readily identifiable. They looked conspicuously cheerful and relaxed; their numerous small children were neither spoiled nor cowed and behaved admirably under stress; their dignified self-confidence – distinctive though hard to describe – contrasted strongly with the brash arrogance of some of our younger Asian and African fellow-internees.

Malagasy charm is founded on natural good manners and spontaneous amiability, yet behind this one senses a reserve that makes one feel honoured to be accepted by a Malagasy as a friend. In Paris we had met only Merina; here we were seeing a tribal cross-section and physical differences were marked, sometimes even within the same family group. Few Malagasy could be mistaken for true Africans, yet negro genes are often as obvious as Polynesian.

We left Moscow at 10.15 p.m. on 29 June. As we gained height the sun became visible – a vast red balloon balancing on the earth's sharp rim beneath an eerie violet sky. Four other *vazaha* (foreigners) were on board: two taciturn young German women planning to trek in the eastern rain-forest and two elderly excited

Norwegian women going to visit Lutheran medical missionary friends in Antsirabe. They had never before left Europe and spoke no word of French or English. On my right Rachel had a window-seat; on my left sat an endearing seven-year-old, son of an Italian father and Malagasy mother. Pappa was a small gentle ageing man, touchingly devoted to his three children; he spoke fluent Malagasy and seemed no longer a *vazaha*. Mamma was a generation younger, fat, kind and jolly with a broad brown face and a gurgling laugh. The two tall, slender, dark-skinned men in front of us had finely cut features and wore tweed suits (it was mid-winter in Madagascar) and bottle-green Homburg hats. All night they talked and laughed, their gestures gracefully express-ive, their white teeth flashing.

During the seventeen-hour flight five meals were served, be-tween four long refuelling stops; these combined quantity with quality and what we couldn't eat I squirrelled away for future reference.

At Simferopol in the Crimea the midnight air was balmy but the dreary cramped transit lounge had only one 'Ladies' and one 'Gents', which caused a few catastrophes among abruptly awakened junior passengers.

At Cairo we had to stay put because the Soviet and Egyptian governments have fallen out; armed uniformed men strolled casually to and fro on the tarmac while our plane was receiving attention.

At Aden the 6 a.m. heat savaged us even as we descended the steps; within moments sweat was visibly streaming off everyone. In the squalid transit lounge, stinking of stale piss, the ceiling-fans were not working and much of the nasty plastic seating had disintegrated to expose dangerously inflammable guts. The fly-blown cafeteria, the enormous duty-free department and the Soviet-stocked bookshop were closed. Women in yashmaks queued patiently at an unattended bank counter, the ragged airport staff went mad with lust when they saw Rachel, and the Norwegians' camera was confiscated because they tried to photo-graph each other under a notice in Arabic. Seeing them verging on tears I intervened and successfully bullied the bullies.

At Nairobi the temperature was perfect, the sky grey, the breeze cool, the airport buildings First World-ish. An abundance of duty-free goods and folk-art souvenirs was tastefully displayed on both sides of a high-ceilinged circular arcade, freshly painted and spotlessly clean. Here the Norwegians were tricked into paying $US7.50 for a tiny bottle of nail-polish. Touchingly, they sought me out; and in my novel role as guardian angel I talked grimly to the Kikuyu merchant – six foot four and surly in proportion – about police and trading licences. Reluctantly he returned the precious dollars, but only after a senior Kenyan army officer had coincidentally appeared nearby. Meanwhile Mrs Nilsen had lost her boarding-pass, at which we all panicked. (I had lost mine at Moscow Airport but Rachel found it just in time, under a restaurant table.) She was however allowed on without it; the hard shell of Soviet bureaucracy hides many a tender heart, as our own Moscow adventures have more than once reminded us.

Next came the excitement of Kilimanjaro, rising alone and snowy out of a softness of cloud – scarcely ten miles away across the cinnamon Nyiri Desert. Then we were staring down at the Indian Ocean's smooth blue width, through a scattering of motionless cloudlets far below. These created the illusion that the sky was underneath as well as above; from that height, in the equatorial noonlight, the two blues were identical.

Since leaving Moscow our Malagasy fellow-passengers had remained exuberant: even Aden failed to depress them. Somehow they generated a celebratory feeling which we, heading for an unfamiliar and unimaginable country, were very much in the mood to share. Over the Mozambique Channel this feeling intensified and their joy was palpable. Eagerly they took it in turns to peer through the windows and at last their beloved coast appeared – flat, red-brown, indented, surf-fringed. Up and down the plane we saw them smiling at each other, for once not saying much, their big brown eyes lustrous with happiness.

This was our first glimpse of the Malagasy's profound patriotism – as distinct from nationalism, of which the majority are innocent. They love their Great Red Island with a religious fervour linked to those peculiar forms of animism and ancestor-dependence which underlie their culture and have not been weakened – only modified – by the influence of Christianity. In 1837 the Rev. William Ellis of the LMS noted: 'Often, when setting out on a journey, they take with them a small portion of their native earth, on which they often gaze when absent, and invoke their god that they may be permitted to return to restore it to the place from which it was taken.' Nowadays a popular proverb, frequently printed along the hems of *lambas*, expresses this same spirit – 'The zebu will lick bare stone, and die in the earth of the place he loves.'

Even from 35,000 feet, we could see an alarming amount of bare stone between the coast and Antananarivo. The most quoted description of Madagascar is not flattering – 'an island with the form, colour, consistency and sterility of a brick'. This seems not much of an exaggeration as one gazes down on a barren landscape where centuries ago the fires of slash-and-burn cultivators became out-of-control infernos, still vivid in the folk-memories of several tribes. The central plateau (average height 4,000–5,000 feet) is a muddle of low mountains on which erosion has left cruel wounds, looking from the air like giant red fans. Occasionally symmetrical volcanic cones and massive misshapen granite peaks rise above wide valleys holding narrow red-brown rivers which fill their beds only during the summer rains. The crust of hard red clay that covers most of the island seems particularly obvious in winter, when the coarse grass which somehow sustains millions of zebu is sparse and brown.

As we lost height thread-like paths could be seen crossing the hills, linking tiny hamlets, and red tracks wound through the more populated valleys; we were soon to discover that these are motor-roads, catering for very few motors. Then we were over the Imerina heartland where stubble-brown paddy-fields separated the many villages, each with at least two churches. In the near distance rose the mighty rock of Analamanga, the ancient Vazimba fortress on which Andrianjaka, founder of the Merina kingdom, built a royal enclosure (the *rova*) from which grew Antananarivo. As we touched down the Malagasy cheered and clapped and burst into song; so infectious was their delight that at last Soviet smiles appeared.

2

Antananarivo:
'Tana, City of Beauty'

One of Toni's Parisian contacts was awaiting us at the entrance to the 'Arrivals' area. Small, slim and beautiful, Oly imperturbably guided us through a dense and dangerous bureaucratic jungle. We had been warned that the capital's airport officials represent all that is worst in modern Madagascar; and when we looked at them crouching behind their desks, poised to spring on defence-less *vazaha*, we could believe it. But Oly, an Air Mad hostess, warded off all predators, however grand their uniforms, with a subtly menacing insouciance that recalled the tougher Merina Queens.

Soon we each had an armful of forms, including an engaging leaflet which said:

> 'MALAGASY DEMOKRATIC REPUBLIC: MINISTRY OF HEALTH – *Sanitary Control at Frontiers* – IMPORTANT ADVICE: – Keep this ticket during one month. If you are ill or you does not feel weel durîng this time, you should show this ticket to the doctor to help him for taking care of you.'

Cerebral malaria remains such a hazard that the government has undertaken to provide all *vazaha* victims with free medical treatment on presentation of this leaflet. Whether or not these official good intentions could be implemented outside – or even inside – Antananarivo is a question we luckily cannot answer.

When all formalities had been completed (or not, as the case might be) Oly guided us to the bank. But then duty called and she had to leave us to discover for ourselves the whimsicality of Malagasy logic.

It was 4.05 p.m. and an international flight had just arrived. It is illegal both to import FMG (Malagasy francs) and to change money outside a bank. Yet the airport bank had closed at 3 p.m.

and the nearest alternative was fifteen miles away. For the Malagasy passengers, all met by jubilant relatives, this did not matter, and it would be uneconomic to keep a bank open to serve six *vazaha*; so this contretemps was part of the price to be paid – willingly, in our case – for an almost tourist-free country.

It's an ill-wind . . . Several taxi-drivers, grinning all over their faces, converged on the two German girls and ourselves as we stood irresolute by the shuttered bank. They amicably competed to take us (COD) to the Hilton Hotel where the Tourist Bank would certainly be open. We did a not too unreasonable deal (£3.35 each), but that drive to Tana – the capital's universally used nickname – was marred by our companions' contempt for the illogical inefficiency of the Malagasy. We felt they should have stayed at home if logic and efficiency were so essential to their peace of mind.

Our ebullient taxi-man displayed another sort of Malagasy illogic. He believed that if you drive fast enough, on either side of a narrow road, everything else in sight – rickshaws, poultry, pedestrians, buses, cars, pigs, handcarts – will have to get out of your way just in time. Because of this unsoothing delusion, we merely glimpsed tall, winter-bare roadside trees and gushes of colour as flowering shrubs spilled over high walls around French colonial villas and crowded suburb-villages of brick or wood or tin shacks and loads being carried on heads and butchers, fruit-sellers and ironmongers occupying cubby-hole stalls and long-legged panic-stricken cocks squawking and scattering as we sped past. Twice we swerved violently on corners to avoid oncoming overloaded buses. Only when we had skidded to a halt did I realise that my fists were tightly clenched and fear-sweaty.

Tana's Hilton looks like a Hilton and is by far the tallest building in Madagascar. But that afternoon its vast foyer was empty and its reception-desk unmanned. Wandering down long silent corridors of standardised affluence, we saw no other *vazaha*. At intervals gorgeously uniformed servants emerged smiling from alcoves and niches; clearly we were not Hilton material, yet their welcoming handshakes were as genuine as the surrounding glamour was phoney.

The young woman behind the bank-desk had high cheek-bones, a milk-chocolate skin and long orange finger-nails. She wore a coral necklace and expensive scent and was our first grumpy Malagasy; perhaps she has too much time for introspection. Dismissing my traveller's cheque she said brusquely, 'Tomorrow, please! Come back tomorrow – this is now five-ten and the business has stopped at five.'

The wall-clock over the door said 4.45, as did all our watches – including Miss Grumpy's. When I pointed this out she sighed theatrically, then opened the safe. We were baffled; it took us a few days to learn that the Malagasy treat time as something pliable. They do not argue about day and night – the sun's movements are incontrovertible – but otherwise time is there for man's convenience and may be manipulated according to individual needs or moods. This is one reason why Madagascar has never got its industrial act together; the fundamental characteristics of the Malagasy cancel out Western priorities. There is supporting evidence for this statement around every corner in Tana.

Outside the Hilton we consulted our guidebook which said – 'There are many touristic folders on Antananarivo so we need not describe the town.' It did however list hotels and we wondered about the Auberge du Soleil Levant – 'twenty-four bungalows handicapped by the absence of running water'. Finally we settled on the Hotel Lido – 'in the midst of the Zoma, very nice panarama from the solarium'. The Friday Zoma is Tana's famous market and by chance we had arrived on a Thursday. Traditionally each town's market was known by the day on which it was held and 'Zoma' means 'Friday'. (In fact Tana's market now operates daily – only more so on Fridays.)

Malagasy exiles call their capital 'Vohitsara' (City of Beauty) and truly Tana is a wondrous place. It has grown on the sides of a Y-shaped rock-mountain as vegetation grows on an embankment, the houses finding spaces where they could – balancing on ledges, clinging to precipices, tucked between boulders and trees, peering down onto each other's red-tiled roofs. Around the base of this granite rock lie flat paddy-fields, now slightly encroached on by a new district, Ampefiloha, where the alien Hilton towers over jerry-built government ministries that have aped its incongruous functionalism.

Happily Ampefiloha is a small district and unlikely to expand in the near future. Soon we had left it and were rustling through autumn leaves by the tree-fringed shore of Lake Anosy, created when the ancient marshes were drained. The still water reflected a simple First World War Franco-Malagasy memorial obelisk, standing on an islet smothered in fabulous ferns, jacaranda trees and bougainvillaea vines.

We followed a tarred road, lavishly pot-holed, never suspecting that its name (Route Nationale No. 7) would be engraved on our hearts within a month. Then we asked the way of two graceful girls escorted by a shy smiling youth. They silently beckoned us to follow them and we panted up a long zig-zagging flight of broken stone steps, very narrow and steep between ramshackle flower-bedecked dwellings. The stench of stale urine was asphyxiating and here we first heard the rhythmic thud of rice being pounded in stone mortars – Madagascar's signature tune. The gradient eased as we passed the bullet-riddled ruins of a modern government building wrecked during the 1972 'protests'. Moments later we were on a wide colonial shopping street near a small, tree-shaded park – the Place Colbert. Before we could adequately thank them our guides had disappeared down another precipitous alleyway.

As we crossed the park – on the spine of one mountain ridge – the western sky suddenly flared to an unreal flamboyance of orange, crimson, purple and copper. Jet-lag breeds subjective reactions and I took this conflagration personally, as a welcoming gesture from the local spirits. Tana is famed for its sunsets but we never again saw anything quite so spectacular.

Suddenly we were overlooking the Zoma on low ground far below, where the arms of Tana's Y-mountain diverge. Hundreds of off-white cotton umbrellas were shading small stalls crowding around a dozen substantial buildings – the lock-up shops of prosperous merchants. Each building had a tiled red-brown roof, high-peaked, then curving prettily towards the eaves; the façades were broken by vaguely Moorish arches giving access to shadowy arcades.

There is no twilight in Madagascar and as we descended a wide flight of steps, lined with traders' stalls, darkness came. Half-way down was the Hotel Lido, where a lame youth with tightly curled hair and a mild stutter showed us to our room on the top floor. He was profusely apologetic, but ineffectual, when the door refused to lock. The window latch was also broken, the ceiling was coming undone and the 'hot' tap gave forth only a grudging trickle of cold water containing interesting fauna. For £7 (sterling) this seemed poorish value – until we opened the shutters to see the Zoma being dismantled by candle-light, and a myriad windows glowing dimly gold on the amphitheatre of mountain opposite our own cliff.

Forgetting jet-lag, we hastened out.

Most of the stalls had already been cleared and their umbrellas folded; each umbrella has bamboo ribs and a stout six-foot branch as handle. The only illumination came from guttering candles, or oil-wicks in minute tins flickering below brown faces amidst the few remaining piles of fruits and vegetables. We stumbled more than once into open drains, or over mounds of noisome refuse and chunks of broken paving. Small sleeping children were curled up inside raffia mats by the parental stalls and the traders were now catering for each other, bartering an over-ripe hand of bananas for a lump of sizzling hot pork-fat, or an orange for a bunch of onions, or a mug of coffee for a limp lettuce, or a handful of tiny dried fish for three squashed tomatoes, or a snifter of crude home-made rum (the 'ardent spirits' so unsuccessfully opposed by the LMS) for a skinny roast chicken. Cheerfully loquacious men and women, wrapped tightly in their *lambas* against the winter night (for us just pleasantly cool), squatted around toadstool-shaped tin charcoal stoves grilling meaty or fishy titbits, or brewing bitter herbal (veronia) tea in battered rusty tins retrieved long ago from some affluent dump-heap. Mothers were simultaneously suckling babies and stuffing rice into the mouths of toddlers while fathers counted takings or packed unsold goods into round floppy raffia baskets. Three aged down-and-outs shuffled between the empty stalls, pausing often to grope hopefully through piles of invisible refuse. They begged from us, timidly, asking if we were French as they peered up at our candlelit faces. They had never heard of Ireland. Before returning to the hotel we bought bananas at a stall where the price was clearly chalked on a piece of wood. When I offered the correct number of coins the merchant laughed and shook his head and handed me back 50 FMG. Bananas go cheap after dark.

Clanging metal bars and rattling corrugated iron woke us at sunrise; big stalls were being prepared for Friday's Zoma. Most umbrellas were still folded, looking like those slim mushrooms that grow in cowpats, but as we watched from our window, while eating a breakfast of Aeroflot leftovers, they suddenly blossomed everywhere – even up the steep flight of steps opposite our own. The sky was overcast and the air autumnal chilly; herbal-tea-sellers were doing a brisk trade. Just below us whole families were unloading ancient motor-vans, the five- and six-year-olds skipping through the throngs jauntily balancing baskets of vegetables on diminutive heads. Other traders used hand-carts or wheelbarrows, or bicycles or bus-roofs. But most goods arrived on a human head, which in Madagascar can bear loads of formidable weight and preposterous bulk. The younger women also carried babies on their backs and were followed by a straggle of unwashed offspring; Madagascar is said to have one of the world's highest birth rates. The adolescent girls moved with marvellous grace but too many wore European-style clothing, garish and ill-cut. How much lovelier they would look wearing traditional skirts and shawls! Through binoculars we watched deft brown hands building fruits and vegetables into pyramids or towers or rotundas or rectangular walls; this task obviously encourages the stall-holders to express their creativity in friendly competition. Being midwinter, the range of nuts and fruits was restricted: peanuts, oranges, lemons, bananas, expensive strawberries. The vegetables were almost all of boring European extraction: carrots, onions, cauliflowers, potatoes. We remarked on the gaiety of the noises that filled the grey chilly morning; it suggested a public holiday rather than the start of a long day's work.

By eight o'clock it was difficult to squeeze between the stalls and, being taller than the average Malagasy, our eyes were perilously within range of protruding umbrella ribs. Few shoppers were buying in bulk and Rachel noted that those few had the air and apparel of servants from rich households. The Friday Zoma is, it seems, as much a social occasion as a shopping expedition. And for the *vazaha* it is total immersion in Tana life. Every sense is engaged – by a swirl of unfamiliar smells; by the bold colours of exotic merchandise and tribal fashions; by the musical surging of the Malagasy language as buyers and sellers haggle, discuss, advise, tease, condemn, laugh, protest; by the textures of homespun silk *lambas*, scaley tree-barks, dried shreds of animal skins and feathery bunches of freshly picked herbs; by the weird flavours of spicey titbits hot off charcoal and containing God-knows-what.

Suddenly my mind leaped to a typical Western supermarket: neon-lit, sterile, odourless, computerised, TV-guarded, its chemically sprayed fruits and steam-scoured vegetables bred to standardised shapes, sizes and shades, its shelves shiny and bright with slick deceptive packaging, its wan and bored check-out staff scarcely acknowledging the customer's humanity. Surely the

Zoma way is better than our way? Is there not a value beyond calculating in the links between producer and consumer, seller and buyer, Nature and Man?

On a long flight of wide, shallow steps, leading to the Upper Town, we realised that we were in the Recycling Department, as Rachel put it. Those steps were thronged – they serve as one of the capital's main streets – and trade was brisk. The merchants were selling grubby well-worn clothes, piles of plastic footwear, Nestlé milk tins containing home-made floor-wax, antibiotic injection phials refilled with traditional remedies, mountains of multico-loured, multishaped buttons, rows of empty bottles, tins, jars and boxes scavenged from embassy garbage-sacks, historically valu-able collections of old locks, bolts, keys, hinges and spare parts gleaned from deceased motor-vehicles, bicycles and sewing machines – and stacks of disintegrating French romantic novels and French magazines, few dated later than 1971, accompanied by the latest issues of bargain-price French-edition Soviet news-papers. We noticed that these last were less popular with browsers than the ancient magazines.

Most goods were displayed on wooden trestles, though some had been spread over a chalked-out area of step. Apart from the second- (or fifth-)hand garments, which were being continuously rummaged through, everything was neatly – even tastefully – arranged: this was no jumble sale. The young men attending the hardware-cum-machinery stalls were doing a steady trade and looked proud of their merchandise – as well they might, in a country where business life often grinds (literally) to a halt for lack of some minor spare part. The collectors of ex-embassy containers (usually elderly women or young girls) had washed and polished their finds, and graded them according to size, shape and mate-rial. As we stood admiring one such display Rachel said, 'You should hire a freight plane and set up business here!' – an allusion to my psychopathic and space-consuming inability to throw away any re-usable object. There was an air of achievement about this Recycling Department, which depends on individual enterprise, ingenuity and persistence. Anyone can pick up a telephone and order a consignment of new bedside lamps or bicycles from a wholesaler; not everyone can find a suitable replacement for broken switches or pedals.

Friday's Zoma also overflows onto the Avenue de l'Indépend-ance, Tana's main thoroughfare. This dual carriageway leads to a memorable railway station, the sort of thing that might happen if a Moghul mosque mated with a Venetian palace. Here up-market stall-holders sell fresh orchids, cheap jewellery, bed-linen and blankets, shoddy new furniture, crudely made toys, lengths of printed cotton, raffia work, semi-precious stones, wood-carvings mainly for the vestigial tourist-market, kitchen ware – and mass-produced landscape scenes so horrendously ugly that one doubts afterwards if one has *really* seen them.

Within deep arcades are dozens of spacious colonial shops, unkempt and almost empty. On their shelves faded French advertisement placards replace the goods advertised; and behind long plate-glass windows dust accumulates around their meagre remaining stock. No one will buy these goods, we were told, because they are defective, being displayed only to take the bare look off emporia where once it was possible to purchase anything, however rare or luxurious, that was available in Paris.

In 1845 Queen Ranavalona I became suspicious of the activities of *vazaha* traders on the east coast and banned all foreign goods. But fifty years later, at the end of the 'Anglo–Malagasy friendship era', Tana's shops were offering Cheddar and Cheshire cheeses, Keating's Insect Powder, Suffolk kippers, Bartlett pears and tinned Oxford sausages. Now all foreign goods have again been banned, by President Didier Ratsiraka, as part – his supporters say – of a harsh but wise campaign to force the Malagasy to become self-sufficient in manufactured goods. Others blame the ban on Madagascar's economic collapse after Ratsiraka's régime cut the link with the French franc and spent \$US300 million on Soviet arms – a sum which Western economists reckon is only \$US20 million less than Madagascar's export earnings for 1982.

The Malagasy do not take kindly to industrialisation, as Jean Laborde, the French architect and entrepreneur, discovered in the 1830s when he established several large factories near Tana. Then the Malagasy abhorred such work, and they still do. Under Queen Ranavalona I the problem was easily solved; Laborde used forced labour, providing food and lodging but no pay, and imposing ruthless military discipline. At the first opportunity – in 1857 – these wretched slaves destroyed all his machinery, work-shops and factories and for a century thereafter the Malagasy were free of any large-scale industry. But over the same century they developed a taste for imported manufactured goods, which the country can no longer afford, and President Ratsiraka's industrial pioneering has not so far been a great success. Billions of francs have been squandered on a fertilising plant that cannot produce fertilisers suited to Malagasy soil, on a tannery for which no hides are available and on a battery plant now idle for lack of money to buy raw materials.

Half-way down the Avenue de l'Indépendance we were shocked by the Hotel de Ville, war-battered and scorch-marked. This ugly relic of civil strife gives Tana's main street an uneasy look, yet it must have been quite a handsome building before 13 May 1972. On that date it was attacked, as a symbol of the pro-French 'Establishment', after police had fired indiscriminately into a student-demo-cum-strikers'-march peacefully protesting against the policies of Philibert Tsiranana, the first President of independent Madagascar. Under his rule foreign trading was restricted almost entirely to France, French advisers remained in most government departments, 3,500 French sailors used the only Malagasy naval base – at Diego Suarez – and French aid balanced the national budget.

We were told that the Hotel de Ville has been left in ruins as a reminder of the sacrifices made to turn Madagascar into a 'Marxist Christian' state – President Ratsiraka's description of his own régime. This somehow seems implausible; more likely no cash is available for its restoration. It certainly serves as a reminder of Madagascar's political instability, something not normally evident as one explores the capital's laughter-filled streets where children play exuberantly and greet the *vazaha* warmly, good manners curbing their curiosity. True, we noticed in the Zoma pairs of young unarmed soldiers, wearing camouflage battledress and red berets, and their relations with the crowd seemed slightly strained. In 1981 a riot started near the market when students stoned soldiers. The official figures later said – 'five dead, forty-four wounded'. Rumour said – 'eight dead, eighty wounded'. Those students represented both left and right, which is not as irrational as it may sound. A Christian Marxist government can scarcely avoid displeasing everyone. However, even those who most dislike President Ratsiraka's ramshackle ideology concede that he is an able man with enough maturity to admit in public to some of his own mistakes. Despite his ill-judged industrial ventures he may do more good than harm if he survives.

The President's survival is a matter about which he himself seems pessimistic. He lives in the Ambohitsorahitra Palace

(French Colonial Renaissance) and when we blithely approached it, as gawping tourists approach Buckingham Palace or the White House, we were turned back by heavily armed soldiers while still some fifty yards from the railings – behind which anti-aircraft guns lurk among tall trees. One theory explains these weapons by referring to the President's conviction that Pretoria is keen to eliminate him. Another theory maintains that he is afraid of no one but invented a South African threat to justify his irresponsible purchase of Soviet guns, tanks, MIG-21s and MIG-17s. (Madagascar's MIGs are rumoured to be no longer airworthy and those we saw at the airport did look under-exercised; grass had grown quite high around them.) A third theory suggests that the President lives in terror of his political rivals; his predecessor, Colonel Richard Ratsimandrava, was assassinated in 1975 after six days in office. In Tana political controversies generate as many theories, few capable of proof, as there are interested Malagasy. But elsewhere we learned that the armed forces, if not the President himself, are indeed jittery about South Africa's attitude to Malagasy socialism.

In 1975 President Ratsiraka wrote his *Boky Mena* (*Red Book*) in which he adapted Marxist principles to Malagasy needs. At once the Western media, which only occasionally glances at Madagascar, yelped – 'Communist!' And then they turned away again, since the island's domestic politics are not circulation-boosters. Yet within days of arriving in Tana one's antennae have registered that the President is not running a Soviet-type régime, whatever else. Madagascar's politics, like its wildlife, are unique to the island – and are now evolving rapidly, unpredictably and so far not as attractively as the flora and fauna.

Tana's population of half a million (it was about ten thousand in 1820) is predominantly Merina though representatives of every tribe are to be found in the capital. Happily it is still free of the Third World's worst urban problem – swarms of starving peasants squatting in shanty-towns. But the national population graph is ominous; from four and a half million in 1945 to nearly ten million in 1983, with about a third of the population under ten.

The Government Information Minister, Mr Bruno Rakotomavo, admits that Tana is 'the town that has suffered most during the present economic crisis'. Yet despite its outward appearance of a once well-maintained colonial city now grievously neglected, it does not have a Third World aura. By our standards it is poor, but not desperately so. Compact and idiosyncratic, it is an intimate, personal place – a big village with the panache of a capital. Thus it is a complex place, as the Malagasy are a complex people, and it would be futile to try to describe it by likening it to anywhere better known. It is – and one hopes it will long remain – superbly *itself*.

Large churches of various denominations rise above the crowded dwellings, recalling the importance of one-up-manship to nineteenth-century Christians. No less conspicuous is the colonial legacy of schools, colleges, institutes, hospitals, banks – the majority handsome buildings, also dominating their surrounding areas. Yet by now all these landmarks have somehow lost their 'European-ness' and merged into the general enchanting craziness that is Tana. Neither the nineteenth-century missionaries nor the twentieth-century colonists damaged the integrity of this place. They came, they preached, they exploited – but they didn't conquer.

Until the mid-nineteenth-century the use of stone or concrete was considered sacreligious in the Merina sacred city. The oldest houses are therefore of wood and the finest of these may be found in the Upper Town around the royal *rova*, now known as 'the Queen's Palace'. This is a district of charming oddities where many dwellings have long, flower-filled, delicately carved wooden balconies, looking from a distance like aprons brimming with scarlet blossoms. One house has a wing resembling a bell-tower – painted blood-red, with mock-Romanesque windows set high under a steeply sloping roof. Another sports a pale pink tower wearing a comical square tin roof like a Christmas cracker hat. Often such happy extravagances are attached to otherwise conventional two-storey stone dwellings; no doubt they were added as families grew in number or prosperity. Some stand on wooden stilts, some on brick pillars; all are cunningly contrived to fit a quart of humanity into a pint pot of mountainside.

One brick cottage with a steep tiled roof and neat dormer windows would not startle in an English village. Close beside it an even smaller cottage has a pale blue tin roof with a crimson-shuttered dormer; only in Tana could corrugated iron actually add to the beauty of a townscape. Overlooking these is an elegant three-storey villa of rosy brick, its russet roof broken by an extraordinary variety of dormers in unexpected places, its windowless gables showing how effectively brick can be used to pattern a façade. Higher still, a gazebo of stone-pillared balconies, enclosed by lacy wood-carving, has wide orange-shuttered windows: its three sharply peaked tin roofs are surmounted by copper orbs and sceptres. Beside this outburst of eccentricity rises a tall, slim, white-washed house, split into three levels: one dormer window is also a side-door and from the fanciful fretwork roof a catwalk leads to a cliff-face. Everywhere laundry flaps on balcony clothes lines, half-hiding exuberant pot-plants and vines; and between the dwellings – where one has to walk in single file – small shrubs somehow find space to grow at odd angles. I do not recall seeing two identical buildings in the whole of Tana. Each home is the product of its owners' inventiveness.

In Ambohidahy, the colonial commercial district, one realises the true meaning of the word 'recession'. After a long search we came upon what seemed to be Tana's last packet of envelopes. Rachel could find no picture (or other) postcards to send her schoolmates. No street-plan was available, nor could we find any of those 'touristic folders' mentioned by our guidebook; where there is almost no tourist-trade it is not worth reprinting such 'literature'. The absence of other *vazaha*, apart from a remnant enclave of French residents, adds immeasurably to Tana's charm. In most non-European capitals the presence of hundreds or thousands of fellow-Westerners creates an inescapable 'them-and-us' atmosphere in which youngsters like Pierre and Joseph would never have approached Rachel and me, volunteering to guide us to the *rova*.

Both were seventeen-year-old schoolboys, taller than the average Merina. Joseph wanted to practise his French, Pierre – most unusually – his English. (Few Malagasy now speak English: and outside of the main towns not many speak French.) Our response to Tana astonished these lads; from their elders they had acquired the notion that it has become a shamefully scruffy city 'not fit for tourists'. Already we had observed among the older generation of middle-class Merina a tendency to apologise for the fact that 'Tana is not what it was'. Their apologies were of course oblique; the Malagasy are never obvious and anyway are too proud to criticise their country openly. But it is sad that some youngsters are being led to compare Tana unfavourably with what they can see of other capitals on the blurred and jerky black-and-white screens of Malagasy television. (Mercifully all the few television aerials are indoor.)

As we climbed steeply towards the *rova*, Rachel took several photographs of the Lower Town and the surrounding valley. Then, as we were approaching an army post high above the road, our friends insisted that she conceal her camera. No one had warned us of any local restrictions on photography but the boys' fear was so palpable that we did not argue.

Soon we passed the (accidentally) burnt-out ruin of Andafianaratra Palace, a startling pink and white edifice of colossal proportions, completed in 1872 for the Prime Minister. Four massive corner towers, each supporting a bloated mushroom of masonry, are still connected by three tiers of balconies once enhanced – our friends said – by some of the finest wood-carving in Madagascar. Before the 1976 fire it had a glass dome which must have made it look even curiouser.

Nearer the *rova* we received another architectural shock, this one uncompromisingly Greek: Queen Ranavalona II's wall-less Judgement Hall, which has sixteen stone columns twenty-five feet high with clumsily carved capitals. It dates from 1881 and stands on the edge of a cliff overlooking the tranquil village-dotted countryside far below – an appropriate position, as hurling people over cliffs was the favoured Merina method of public execution.

Alas! the Queen's Palace was being repaired so the *rova* – strewn with building materials – had been closed to visitors. Frustrated, we peered through the open main gate in a monumental stone archway surmounted by a bronze eagle with outstretched wings. According to Pierre, this bird represents Radama I's crack troops – known as 'eagles' because they stood sentry, day and night, on this *rova* hilltop.

The open gate, and a walk around the periphery, allowed us to see most of the *rova*'s bizarre conglomeration of constructions; these prompted Rachel to murmur that we were probably missing nothing, aesthetically, by being excluded from the museum. The original palace (Manjakamiadana) was a simple wooden building on which the French architect, Jean Laborde (the same who used slave labour) elaborated in the 1840s. Then, between 1868 and 1873, an astonishing Scotsman named James Cameron devised, by Royal Command, a stone 'shell' for the palace. He was so carried away by this commission that he added four Italianate towers, a Loire Château roof and a façade of ten late mediaeval cloister arches – five up and five down – beneath a Haussmann balustrade. The result seemed to me entirely pleasing as a decoration on Tana's highest point, though if one met it in Europe one might be tempted to smile.

Also within the *rova* are what seem at first glance to be a pair of twee seaside chalets. In fact these are The Kings' Tomb and The Queens' Tomb, which since 1897 have held the bodies of rulers formerly buried at Ambohimanga, the ancient royal 'city'. Amongst those present is Andrianampoinimerina, who began the political unification of Madagascar in the late eighteenth century and rested for eighty-seven years at Ambohimanga before being taken to the capital in a silver boat casket. The last ruler of Madagascar – Queen Ranavalona III, who died in exile in Algeria in 1917 – returned to Tana in 1938 and was reburied with ceremonial flourishes that are still remembered. Joseph told us that behind those tombs – invisible from the gate – are seven small tiled houses holding the bodies of those who ruled before Andrianampoinimerina. (In those days the Merina 'kings' were really tribal chiefs, later upgraded.) Only three Merina rulers are excluded from the royal burial place, two because they were dethroned and one because he died of leprosy. The reverence with which the boys spoke of all these burials and reburials suggested that the traditional beliefs of the Malagasy are not weakening among the younger generation.

In bemusing contrast to the royal mausoleums is a smallish church, the Royal Chapel, that might have been designed by Wren. Queen Ranavalona II laid the foundation stone soon after her baptism and the architect was William Pool, an English LMS builder. He must have been a man of many moods because he was also responsible for the singularly un-Wren-like Andafianaratra Palace. Pierre and Joseph did not share our enthusiasm for this golden-stoned gem. Pierre remarked that Queen Ranavalona I (she who ordered Madagascar's early Christians to be flung off a 600-foot precipice) was a 'strong leader' who recognised Christian missionaries as the thin end of the colonial wedge and sought to preserve 'the religion of our ancestors'. In 1895 – he added – many peasants blamed the French conquest on the monarch's desertion to Christianity, which meant forfeiting the protection of the ancestors. We knew both boys to be Christian, yet he sounded as though he approved of the peasants' attitude. I longed to discuss with him the role of Christianity in present-day Madagascar. But then I looked at his serious young face – bronze and smooth-skinned, with wavy hair falling over a high forehead into slightly slanting eyes – and I sensed that any probing on such matters would be considered unmannerly. The Malagasy character contains more than a soupçon of oriental inscrutability.

As we left the *rova* an invisible two-man army band began to play Schubert's *Marche Militaire* with tremendous verve; in winter this sundown concert is a daily event. The boys lived nearby so we returned to Analakely on our own, by a new route down the grassy slope below the Grecian columns.

The equatorial sun was slipping perceptibly towards the horizon, its gentle brilliance pouring across the plain far below us – glinting gold on water channels between green market gardens and grey-brown paddy-stubble, emphasising long gashes of dark red earth, laying grape-purple shadows on the distant encircling hills. Then all colours merged into the grey-blue of a brief dusk and, from above, the National Anthem signalled the lowering of the Malagasy flag on the Palace roof. I am always disquieted by the zeal with which ex-colonies cultivate such nationalistic trimmings, often while excoriating every aspect of the culture in which they are rooted. National anthems and flags symbolise something peculiarly European; they are derived from ancient – and long since perverted – ideals which are utterly alien to the spiritual or emotional inheritance of a country like Madagascar.

We were soon lost; even in daylight Tana's geography baffles *vazaha*. But it was fun being enmeshed in a network of ladder-like paths connecting scores of hillside dwellings to each other – though not, so far as we could determine, to anything else. Occasionally those paths became tree-trunk bridges across narrow chasms. Often they wandered through back (or front) yards, past open living-room doors revealing families eating mounds of rice by candlelight. The two *vazaha*, tripping over jerry-cans, hen-coops and rice-baskets, caused much amusement. Several kind people gave us detailed directions in Malagasy, which they took it for granted we would understand. (The French were good at learning it.) When at last we stumbled – literally – onto one of Tana's few tarred roads, it was by accident.

These roads have no corners, only curves; thus we went around in circles for another half-hour, noting landmarks like church spires, then ten minutes later seeing them below us when they should have been above. In desperation we tried one of the wide flights of concrete steps that link Tana's various 'shelves' in the city centre. Many steps once had reinforcing metal bands along their edges and these have now come unstuck in enough cases to present a fearsome night-time hazard.

Equally hazardous are the unlit footpaths beside the tarred roads. The Malagasy have a penchant for removing huge slabs of pavement to expose deep holes containing esoteric interweavings of sewage-pipes, water-pipes, thick cables and thin wires. All over the world urban authorities enjoy exposing their subterranean technological wonders, but usually the exposure is temporary and it is the custom to provide warning lights and protective barriers. Not so however in Tana, where these death-traps are permanent features of the city scene. Rachel was convinced they'd been opened the day before the French left and were unlikely to be closed until the Russians came. We never saw anyone working near them and, in most cases, no chunks of pavement were awaiting replacement; these have apparently been removed to serve a more useful purpose elsewhere. Within such chasms the liquid mud is always malodorous and, if the percentage of straying sewage is high and the dead cats are very dead, it exhales near-lethal fumes.

Eventually Rachel decided that we should go through a mountain, as the road ahead of us did. Her usually reliable sense of direction had been atrophied by Tana but at this point – perhaps reactivated by hunger – it told her, correctly, that Analakely District lay beyond that tunnel. Plunging into its pitch-blackness, we felt grateful for the absence of human hazards in Tana.

Several Malagasy had warned us that their capital is now a suppurating mass of pick-pockets, muggers and cut-throats. We doubted this; the Zoma has its share of professional pick-pockets but there is no nastiness in the city's atmosphere by day or by night – no undercurrents of vicious violence or anti-*vazaha* resentment, no vulgar whistling or winking or jostling in reaction to an attractive young girl. The innate Malagasy dignity makes Tana seem truly civilised, whatever may be the state of the drains.

Only one car passed us in the tunnel. This capital goes early to bed and even the Avenue de l'Indépendance, where the nightlife would be if there were any, is virtually deserted by 8 p.m.

The Malagasy language is a joy to listen to but a torment to pronounce. Luckily however the most important words are manageable: *aza fady* and *misaotra* (please and thank you). Also, it helps that many Malagasy, especially among the Merina, have

European first names which may be used if one is desperate –
though at some risk of giving umbrage, the Malagasy sense of
decorum being strong. Oddly enough, a compatriot of ours is
partly to blame for the intractability of Malagasy As She Is
Written.

James Hastie was born in 1786, to a prosperous Quaker milling
family in Co. Cork, but he rejected pacifism and ran away from
home to fight in the Mahratta War. At the age of thirty-six, as
Sergeant Hastie, he landed at Tamatave, having been chosen by
Governor Farquhar of Mauritius to tutor two young Merina
princes. He was accompanied by the first horses to set hoof on
Madagascar but few of these English thoroughbreds survived the
gruelling climb to Imerina.

This courageous, shrewd and kindly Irishman contributed
more to the Anglo–Merina alliance than any other individual.
Among his contributions was some assistance to the LMS
pioneers as they struggled to wed Malayo-Polynesian sounds to
an incompatible Latin alphabet. The missionaries were also being
helped by one Sergeant Robin, a deserter from the French army
who arrived in Madagascar a year after Hastie, taught King
Radama I to read and write in French, became his secretary and
was mainly responsible for France's continuing influence in Imerina throughout the British era. Unfortunately for posterity, the
two sergeants disagreed about the pronunciation of vowels and
consonants. Whereupon, according to one story, the King poured
oil by decreeing that consonants be given an English pronunciation and vowels a French pronunciation. This must have seemed
to him an ideal solution, bound to mollify both his friends, but the
result was catastrophic.

Rachel's flare for languages (not inherited from her mother)
prompted me optimistically to buy off a Zoma book-stall *An
Elementary English–Malagasy Dictionary* published in Tana in 1969
by the Lutheran Press. But even Rachel quailed on finding the
following:

'accommodation – ny zavatra ao an-trano ilain' ny vahiny
  na mandry izy na misakafo
bar – hazo atsivalana amin' ny lalana
beach – moron-dranomasina torapasika
buffet – fanaka fitoeran-dovia sy hanina
come on – mihaona na mifankahita kisendrasendra

daytime – ny fotoana anelanelan ny fiposahan'ny masoan-
dro sy ny filentahany'

and so on down the alphabet to:

'Zoo – saha misy bibidia hojeren' ny mpitsangantsangana'.

Perhaps Madagascar should scrap the LMS system and start
again?

The road from Analakely to Tana's *saha misy bibidia hojeren 'ny
mpitsangantsangana* is, by local standards, quite straightforward.
But we found all the gates padlocked and there were no helpful
notices about opening hours. This alarmed us; we were leaving
Tana next morning and had been told we could get our lemur-
reserve permits only at the zoo.

We were searching for some break-in point when a car
approached, passed us – then abruptly stopped and backed. It
was old and well groomed, like most Tana vehicles, and its
youngish driver – dark-skinned, with Arabic features – was also
well groomed. 'You have a problem?' he asked. Then he volunteered to drive us back to the main gate, where he would endeavour to solve our problem. In Tana we benefited from many
such spontaneous acts of kindness.

Louis spoke basic English and his opening remarks recalled our
Air Mad guidebook. 'Now this zoo is no good. You will not enjoy
it. Ten years ago it was very good. Now there is nothing to see.
Most of the animals have died. They had nothing to eat and
nobody cares any more.' As we searched for someone with a key he
elaborated on his country's woes, concluding: 'So here we have
every trouble – no money for roads, no books for schools, no
medicines for hospitals, no tyres for cars, no food in the shops, too
much black market, nothing except for smugglers who bribe. It
makes me sad in the heart! What was good before is now bad –
bad, bad, bad!'

This blunt talk was novel to us; usually such complaints are
merely hinted at through those stylised circumlocutions cultivated by most Malagasy. In an odd way Louis seemed to need the
sadness in his heart, rather as a masochist needs flagellation. An
Irishman also condemns his government with relish, but generally there is a self-righteous implication that if *he* were running the
show all would be well. Louis however was almost taking a share
of the blame, criticising himself as part of the Malagasy 'thing'

that had gone wrong. It is unlikely that this was a conscious attitude, that he ever thought in terms of the individual citizen's responsibility; yet as we talked a feeling of diffuse guilt came through strongly. Perhaps this is an extension of the Malagasy sense of close physical identification with their country, which itself is tied to their intimacy with their ancestors. Of which more anon.

Tana's botanic garden-cum-zoo, skilfully laid out on a hillside, may once have been a delight but now rows of empty cages give it a stricken appearance – though we rejoiced that such cramped cages *were* empty. As Louis had predicted, we did not enjoy it. (In even the best of zoos my rapture is modified.) Most of the few surviving lemurs (ring-tailed) live on an isle in a lakelet. Before permit-hunting, we sat on winter-brown grass watching them playing in a dead tree, and being fed over-ripe bananas and stale bread by a keeper who paddled across six yards of deep water in a canoe.

The Directorate of Scientific Research was founded by the French for the study of demography, geography, agricultural genetics and medicinal herbs. Only one room was occupied, by a giggling gaggle of adolescent girls dissecting frogs. Here we learned that lemur-reserve permits are in fact issued by the Bureau d'Eaux et Forêts, which has its offices several miles away, near our hotel. When we sought admission to the Natural History Museum an amiable rotund gentleman, wearing gold-rimmed spectacles and a halo of spiky silver hair, was desolate. 'The key – no!' he exclaimed. 'My colleague I think have in his pocket for an accident – I am sorry! I am full of apology – tomorrow you come back and I have key – yes?'

'Perhaps,' we murmured, not wishing to seem unforgiving. Then we said, '*Misaotra*', shook hands and departed. Shaking hands is important in Madagascar – something more than a formality. To omit this little ceremony can be construed as a deliberate insult.

I thought later about the sadness in Louis's heart and the missing key and reflected that most of Madagascar's inefficiencies and apparent stupidities involve the breakdown or misapplication of imported technologies or ideas. A semi-Western life-style, such as the French imposed on Malagasy towns, cannot be maintained without a modicum of organised work on the part of the adminis-trators and their staffs. But the Malagasy are amenable only to those outside influences which they deem benign – and which include neither the 'Work Ethic' nor the 'Save and Prosper' ideal, not to mention their decadent child the 'Rat Race'. Many Malagasy seem indifferent to comfort, convenience, cleanliness and efficiency, yet this does not mean that Madagascar is hopelessly corrupt or unable to run itself. The Malagasy have their own set of priorities, among which kindness, good manners, tact, generosity, fortitude of spirit and family loyalty rank high. By our standards their country is at present falling to bits, literally as well as metaphorically. Yet if they can avoid being blackmailed, bullied or otherwise lured into an alliance with either bloc, the Great Red Island may still be in harmony with its ancestral spirits as it enters the twenty-first century. And to the Malagasy this harmony is what matters most of all.

The Bureau d'Eaux et Forêts (Department of Waterways and Forests) occupies three small rooms, crammed with filing cabinets and desks, on the fourth floor of a modern government building in what seems to be Tana's diplomatic quarter. Six-foot snake skins, giant mounted butterflies and the skeletons of extinct mammals decorate the walls. Dead beetles the size of dogs (chihuahuas) protrude from open drawers. The courteous staff of three generate no sense of urgency about the protection of waterways, forests or wildlife.

A not-so-young woman with a streaming cold peered at us through a veil of wavy raven hair. Between sneezes she indistinctly asked us to leave our passports in the next room and return for our permits at 4 p.m. – it was then 11 a.m. This seemed too speedy to be true: had we misheard her? 'There must be a snag,' muttered Rachel, who grew up in the hard school of Asian and South American bureaucracy. But there wasn't.

At 3.58 p.m. we were graciously received by the Chef de Bureau, sitting plump and beaming behind a desk disconcertingly paper-free. He shook hands, presented us with our permits, advised us how best to avoid spear-carrying brigands in the lawless south and remarked, with chilling cheerfulness, that soon all lemurs will be extinct because they are so tasty.

Conservation is low on the list of official Malagasy concerns. Repeatedly we got the impression that it is seen as another form of Western exploitation, a left-over from colonialism which brings well-paid *vazaha* experts into the country to lecture the natives on how they should use their meagre resources. If drought or floods have reduced an area's food supplies, why not catch as many lemur as possible for the pot? If I were the mother of hungry children , would I not urge my husband to hunt anything edible? It is easy to be a committed conservationist on a full belly.

In Madagascar only rich tourists, who are content to fly from A to B seeing almost nothing, can hope to follow a set plan: and even they have their problems. In most regions the sort of self-propulsion we favour is out; neither the arid southern deserts nor the humid eastern rain-forests encourage cycling or long-distance trekking. So our Malagasy journey was, as they say, unstructured, though three widely scattered objectives provided a provisional framework. These were: a mountain trek in Imerina (to gratify my deepest longing), snorkling around the coral reefs off the west and south-east coasts (to gratify Rachel's deepest longing) and looking for lemurs in the Isalo Massif and the rain-forests (to gratify a common longing).

We had considered going to Nosy-bé, Nosy Komba and Nosy Tanikely, three islands off the north-west coast which offer the best snorkling and lemur-watching in Madagascar. But then we were warned that there are four *real* tourist hotels on Nosy-bé; and these include a 'Holiday Inn' of surpassing ugliness – for 'high-quality tourism' – built in 1977 on the most beautiful of the island's beaches. It was also rumoured that live tourists may occasionally be observed in that area, wearing bikinis, listening to transistor radios and applying sun-tan lotion. Our flesh crawled and we scrubbed the north-west.

In Tana we discovered that no reliable information is ever obtainable about public (or indeed private) transport throughout the rest of Madagascar. It therefore seemed that we must leave the attainment of lemurs and coral reefs in the laps of the ancestors, who we hoped were regarding us favourably. But at least the mountains were easily reached. They surround the capital and at seven o'clock one cool grey morning we shouldered our rucksacks and set out to trek to Antsirabe through the Ankarata – a distance of some 130 miles as the Murphys walk.

3
Ambling through the Ankaratra

'Bustling' is not a word that could ever be applied to the Malagasy; like the Irish, they believe in 'not killing themselves'. But, as we left Tana, Route Nationale No. 1 was thronged and quietly animated. A mile-long market was being set up and, with a guesstimated eighty per cent of Malagasy still engaged in agriculture (mainly subsistence), markets are where the action is.

Almost every head in sight was wearing a burden of saleable goods, from the grey-wispy head of a limping granny under a sack of cabbages to the frizzy black head of a tiny girl in a flounced pink frock under a tower of newly woven raffia baskets. Tongas were being drawn by pairs of briskly trotting, fine-boned, glossy ponies, the majority well-fed and groomed. Madagascar's equine population is restricted to the flat plain around Tana; the fate of the first horses to arrive, with James Hastie, made future importers cautious. But some race-horses are bred in Imerina, and Tana has its clique of keen race-goers. Each ramshackle tonga was packed with produce and people, so inextricably mixed that only unrelated arms, legs and heads – the last usually decorated with happy grins – were visible between bundles of firewood, live hens, sacks of rice and rolls of raffia bedmats. From within these cargoes came squeals of laughter, snatches of song and greetings shouted to passing friends. A few myopic men sit in Tana offices dreaming and planning (fortunately mostly dreaming) about a 'strong industrial base' for Madagascar. But how much laughter and song would there be among a crowd of Malagasy workers commuting to a factory?

This was a 'down-market' market; none of the traders had motor-vans and the bulkier goods – second-hand furniture, bales of hay and the like – were piled high on speedy two-man-power rickshaws. These are pulled by one runner and pushed by another who on level ground uses only his forehead, keeping his hands clasped behind his back. The Malagasy call these vehicles *pousses-pousses* because when ascending steep hills the puller repeatedly urges his mate to 'Pousses-pousses!' (push-push!).

Soon we were surrounded by paddy-fields, some being prepared for the spring sowing by pairs of zebu drawing ploughs not much less primitive than those we saw in the Andes. Several men followed each plough, breaking huge clods with short spades. The women play their part later, during sowing, re-planting and harvesting.

We planned to turn off Route Nationale No. 1 fifteen miles west of Tana, at Arivonimamo, where a dirt road leads into the Ankaratra range. This brief Route Nationale (it ends abruptly at Tsiroanomandidy) has an astonishing velvet-smooth tarmac surface; we were to see nothing else like it in Madagascar. Of the country's 22,800 miles of so-called 'motor' roads only ten per cent are tarred and only twenty-eight per cent permanently usable; the rest are washed away annually during the rains. And even the tarred stretches tend to be of uncertain temper: on a good day it takes five hours to drive the 105 miles from Tana to Antsirabe.

Suddenly we heard what sounded like rifle-shots. Then round the next bend came fourteen magnificent zebu – sleek chestnut backs shading to black underparts – being driven at a fast trot by two men continuously cracking long leather thongs. These drovers were lean, dark-skinned and bare-footed, with broad features and masses of curly hair looking like red-powdered wigs. They wore only ragged shorts and *lambas* and had the aura of folk who do not belong anywhere near a city. Such drovers often maintain this steady speed for up to twenty miles. Prudently we stood on the ditch; this mettlesome herd filled the road and their wide-curving horns were long and sharp. A head tossed casually in our direction – meaning no harm – could do damage. The men ignored us as they passed.

We were gazing after the zebu – marvelling at the rhythm of their and the men's movements, which seemed part of one action – when a van-driver offered us a lift. He was a blond Italian priest, wearing slacks and an open-necked shirt and going to the next town some five miles on. We appreciated his offer; it is no fun walking fifteen miles on a hot tarred road.

Paulo had been seven years in Madagascar and took an anxious interest in local politics. He commended the President's austerity campaign. 'Madagascar doesn't have rich natural resources, so it's the only way. And of course Ratsiraka isn't a Communist! How could anyone, even if they wanted to, turn the Malagasy into

Communists? They can't be brainwashed – not by Marxists or Christians or the CIA. Yes, you will see and hear some surface signs of Communist influence – but don't be alarmed. These are only a protest against Tsiranana's outlook – his gross Capitalism, always geared to suit the French economy. Ratsiraka knows he must dodge both power blocs. Yes, he has made some very bad mistakes – he tried to turn the export trade into a State Monopoly and that was a disaster. But he is big enough to admit this – not in words because he's a politician but by loosening the government's grip on the export companies. Many complain – are disillusioned – say it was better under the French. But now some things are beginning to improve. And the people will rebel only if there's not enough rice. Rice is the one thing they won't do without. They eat more rice than anyone else in the world – an average of half a kilo every day for each Malagasy. They used to grow a surplus, for export. But that was another terrible mistake – the President reduced the price paid to the peasants so they went back to subsistence farming, and at the same time the urban population was growing. So last year three hundred and fifty thousand tons had to be imported and Ratsiraka had to ask the West for help. And still rice had to be rationed in the towns, which makes always a big black market and a lot of anger. But this policy too he has changed. He's learning, though at the expense of the poor. The rich can always dodge restrictions.'

We said goodbye to Paulo in a charming little town of redbrown houses with carved wooden pillars and balconies; the name of the place escapes me. Many towns and villages begin with 'Ambohi', but apart from 'Ambohipotsy' and 'Ambohijoky' – which somehow do stick in the memory – time has fused them in my mind to 'Ambowhatsit'. You might imagine that this 'Ambohi' is akin to the Irish 'Bally' or 'Knock'. Not so, however. The situation is much more complex – and I do not intend to analyse it.

Beyond Ambowhatsit lay neat smooth hills, low curving ridges, broad shallow valleys – a landscape long since subdued by man's needs and wounded by his ignorance. Some grassy slopes were strewn with grey rounded boulders; others were red-streaked, erosion-gored. All the valleys held rice-fields and on several ridges new pine-woods flourished. Hereabouts reafforestation efforts are consolingly conspicuous; we passed stands of eucalyptus and pine – and other unfamiliar deciduous trees, tall and stalwart – and dense coppices of 'tapia'. These look like olive trees but aren't;

their leaves feed the Malagasy silk-worm.

High white clouds drifted across an intensely blue sky, their shadows muting the reds, browns, greens and greys of the pattern below; a hot noon sun glinted silver on water-channels criss-crossing the valleys; a strong cool breeze stirred flowering mimosa by the roadside. Scents were pungent: of resin and herbs and strange aromatic shrubs, dark green and glossy. The few distant villages would have been invisible but for their (two) church towers, usually tin-roofed.

We picnicked beside a long lake, level with the road. Clumps of tough reeds broke its surface and several punting fishermen paused to stare at us, standing statuesque in tiny rough-hewn boats, their *lambas* fluttering brightly against the dark water. Here we saw white herons feeding and small blue butterflies flickering through the mimosa. Less agreeable were countless colonies of monstrous black and yellow spiders – thousands of them – suspended amidst intricate web-cities on telegraph wires and trees. As a victim of spider-phobia I felt no urge to study these remarkable creatures, but our friend Hilary Bradt, who has an insatiable curiosity about Malagasy flora and fauna, later wrote to us:

'Those lovely big black and yellow jobs that live in the telegraph wires weave golden webs that are so tough you can literally raise them with one hand and duck under as though they were a wire fence. Last century an imaginative textile person thought they might supersede the silk-worm and experimented for a while, using spider webs to produce fine silken goods. The idea never came to anything commercially, but Queen Victoria was given a pair of stockings made from Malagasy spider silk.'

Soon after lunch we were again picked up, by a Merina engineering student on vacation from a French university. He deplored our trekking intentions, asserting that to camp in the mountains in winter could only lead to hypothermia. Near Arivonimamo we were stunned to see an outburst of High Technology, the only one in Madagascar. Our driver explained proudly that this NASA-built 'earth station communications satellite' provides excellent telephone links with the rest of the world. Maybe so, but it does nothing whatever for the domestic telephone system.

Arivonimamo has grim associations that may be variously interpreted. On 22 November 1895, two months after a small French force had conquered Tana, the town's Christian Merina District Governor, and a British Quaker missionary family (parents and a small daughter) were slain during the first of many anti-French and anti-Christian uprisings. Their killers belonged to the Menalamba, a group dedicated to the elimination of all missionaries by way of restoring Malagasy traditions. They were convinced – as were their successors in the south during the 1947 uprising – that ancestral support and the *ombiasas'* magic charms would protect them from even the most modern *vazaha* weapons. (*Ombiasa* may be loosely translated as 'witch-doctor', though this is a simplification of his function in Malagasy society.) When avenging French troops were sent from Tana the Menalamba fought ferociously, losing 150 men before their retreat into the Ankaratra.

Christian *vazaha* now visit Arivonimamo to honour the memory of its martyrs by laying flowers on the monument that commemorates their massacre. But a Malagasy, Sennen Andriamirado, has recently written: 'The first national liberation movement, the Menalamba, declared itself symbolically by massacring a family of British missionaries in Arivonimamo ... This movement spread throughout the country and was only completely crushed ten years later after a long war of "pacification".' One man's martyr is another man's symbol.

Had we not been put down at the appropriate junction we might have had some trouble finding it; the quaint European custom of maintaining signposts has long since been abandoned. Anyway, it would – we then thought – be misleading to suggest that such a rain-ravaged track is ever vehicle-worthy. Soon however we were to learn that by Malagasy standards this track was an almost flawless motorway.

My spirits rose as we turned towards the high blue barrier of the Ankaratra. But I suspect Rachel was day-dreaming of coral reefs and lemurs; fast-growing fourteen-year-olds tend not to be energetic. We climbed gradually towards an isolated pudding-shaped hill, aridly brown, with one wind-deformed tree on its summit. All around shimmered the blue-green saplings of a eucalyptus plantation. Otherwise there was no cultivation until we approached a hamlet that seemed to have grown out of the earth.

Here a score of bare-footed boys, wearing blue cotton shorts, white cotton shirts and quasi-military peaked caps, were being drilled on a rocky slope. This 'Revolutionary Drill' consists of marching around in circles, thrusting forward clenched left fists in unison, scowling malevolently (presumably as one is visualising the Enemies of the Revolution) and generally looking foolish and incongruous on a Malagasy hillside. The sight of two laden *vazaha* marching dustily to nowhere provoked rebellion. Ignoring the commands of their young Sergeant-Major, several boys leaped onto the track – then suddenly were overcome by shyness, looked at one another, giggled and retreated. Probably they had assumed us to be males and on realising their mistake were unable to cope with the situation.

These curious drillings are now undertaken, with varying degrees of enthusiasm, throughout Madagascar. They form part of a Presidential campaign to restore the self-respect of rural communities, who now enjoy a degree of autonomy unknown since the Merina began the administrative unification of the island and the French completed it. Opinions differ as to whether or not this abrupt delegation of responsibility makes sense. However, Malagasy villagers have never given up the habit of working together at rice-cultivation and house-building; and their traditional organisational methods are practical, efficient and generally accepted by the whole community.

From the base of the pudding-mountain we were overlooking an immense sweep of broken countryside: red slopes, silver rivers, green scrubland, grey-brown valleys, red-brown villages. At intervals our track could be seen wriggling towards a knot of mountains some twenty miles away.

It was now time to look for a campsite and around the next corner we paused to fill our water-bottles at a wayside tap serving a scattered hamlet. Like most highland homes, these two-storeyed thatched dwellings had small unglazed windows and wooden pillars supporting an upper balcony. Merina villagers usually follow a simple traditional design, yet no two houses are exactly alike in size and decoration. We were puzzled then by the numerous ruins interspersed with inhabited dwellings; later we realised that these buildings are not very durable and that to construct a new house is often easier than doing repairs – most of the raw materials cost nothing except hard work.

Our use of the communal tap caused a sensation; within

moments men, women and children were emerging – cautiously – from their homes to stare and speculate. The majority wore rags and were so filthy one couldn't assess skin-colour, but their features and hair suggested more Merina blood than any other. The nearest group – all women and girls – stood some fifteen yards away, looking apprehensive. When I waved and smiled, as reassuringly as I could, they slowly came closer and began to exchange whispered jokes about the *vazaha*. Luckily language barriers never prevent the communication of essentials and they quickly accepted us as harmless. A torrent of questions followed and our total non-comprehension provoked paroxysms of laughter. Then even the men crowded around, and everyone shook hands, and children of all sizes came running or toddling to join in the fun.

The atmosphere changed suddenly on the appearance of a young man wearing a torn blue *lamba* and a worried expression. He too shook hands, before questioning us suspiciously – though his tone was not unfriendly. He was it seemed a person of some authority, yet too young to be Chief. I produced Samuel's 'Letter of Explanation' in Malagasy, given to us for just such an occasion. But the young man couldn't read, and was plainly embarrassed by this limitation. For a few moments he stood frowning at the sheet of paper, turning it this way and that while wondering what to do next. Then a buxom young woman with baby on back stepped forward and took it from him. She had a wild mop of uncombed hair and wore a tattered once-white skirt and a ravelling blue sweater. Slowly but without hesitation she read the letter aloud while the crowd pressed forward eagerly to listen. I have never discovered exactly what Samuel said, but it went down a treat. The young man looked relieved, the crowd laughed again and some of the children clapped and cheered. (That young woman's literacy – evidently exceptional in the hamlet – puzzled us; her standing in the community seemed no different to anyone else's.)

The Chief arrived next; his age-dimmed eyes were kindly in a wrinkled copper face. He wore a straw Homburg, tattered grey pants and a knee-length check shirt beneath a new white *lamba* obviously donned to honour us. Although he could recall only a few words of French, his dry humour repeatedly came through in the course of that evening. Having read our Vital Document, he beckoned us to follow him; his gesture was as much an order as an invitation and to have disobeyed it would have been to risk throwing the whole hamlet into a state of alarmed confusion. We were led by an indirect route to a newish mud shack overlooking paddy-fields: our lodging for the night. The Chief regretted its unworthiness – we expressed joyful gratitude – everyone was happy.

Being a guest in a Malagasy village puts a certain strain on the traveller. Paradoxically, these seemingly easy-going, cheerful, friendly Malagasy are so constrained by a complicated system of beliefs and prohibitions (superstitions, to us) that fear is one of their dominant emotions – even in the 1980s. One cannot easily detect the extent to which ancient traditions still affect the urban middle class. But probably few Malagasy have entirely discarded them, for their tentacles reach into every corner of life and are very much part of *being Malagasy*.

Anthropologists and ethnologists get extraordinarily steamed up about the origins of Madagascar's pervasive taboos (a Polynesian word) or *fady* (an Indonesian word). Some try to trace them back to Arabic sources because Malagasy *ombiasa* use the old Arabic calendar when determining *vintana* (destiny) – a process of truly mind-boggling intricacy. (The *vintana* concept profoundly affects every aspect of an individual's life.) Mild feuding takes place between those who claim Arabic influences and those who deny them, but the fact remains that Madagascar's present network of beliefs and consequent restrictions is unique. It has not been imported from anywhere, whatever tenuous links with other cultures may be discerned by excited academics through the mists of history. It expresses only the *Malagasy* way of thinking, feeling, imagining, interpreting, inventing.

The pioneer missionaries were heartened to find a country apparently without any organised, institutionalised religion: without temples, priests, scriptures, pilgrimages, shrines – all those tiresome trimmings that make it so difficult to 'convert' Buddhists, Hindus and Muslims. The Malagasy seemed easy prey: straightforward pagans who had only a few vague notions about being nice to their ancestors and were pretty certain to lap up whichever version of Christianity might come their way.

This illusion did not last long. Soon the Reverend Ellis was reporting, with his usual sonorous verbosity:

'The operation of an invisible agency, or of different agencies, they see demonstrated in the phenomena, the order, and the formation of the universe around them. Yet strangers to the sublime idea of a superintending Providence, and almost equally strangers to any rational and philosophical explanation of daily occurring natural phenomena, they promptly attribute everything to the influence of charms (*ody*), which their imaginations invent, possessing qualities and virtues adequate to the production of all the varied effects either witnessed or experienced . . . While a belief in the efficacy of these potent charms is, in the minds of these credulous people, intimately associated with a conviction of the infallibility of the *sikidy*, or divination, this again is as closely blended with a belief in some superior power . . . Their minds are not a blank, upon which truth may at once be inscribed in legible characters, but filled with vain imaginings, erroneous fancies, crude conceptions, superstitious fears, and a pertinacious adherence to the opinions and decisions of their ancestors.'

That was written 150 years ago, since when much has changed. Babies born on unlucky days are no longer put out to be trampled by zebu, criminals are no longer thrown over precipices, people suspected of witchcraft are no longer required to drink *tanghin* poison to prove their innocence. But despite these not insignificant modifications to the customs of the country, the Malagasy do still have 'a pertinacious adherence to the opinions and decisions of their ancestors'.

Without fluency in the language, and years of study, no outsider could hope to understand the whole *fady*, *sikidy*, *ody* conglomerate. Fortunately casual travellers only need to know that they are dealing with a society far more complex than it looks and to remember that they may be seen as potential dangers because *vazaha* are ignorant of local taboos and could possess mysterious powers to which the Malagasy have no antidotes. This is why so many *fady* surround the treatment of *vazaha* and why one's behaviour in a village should, as far as possible, be guided by the people. Especially in remote areas, it is easy unwittingly to insult, frighten, desecrate or appear to threaten. Thus when the Chief led us through his hamlet, it was advisable to follow exactly the path he took. Had we deviated to examine something of interest we might have infringed on an area forbidden to *vazaha* – a sacrificial site or Vazimba grave (not easily detected by the unknowing eye), or a sacred cairn, spring or tree. If we did give offence this would be no trivial matter. The whole terrified community would feel obliged to organise expensive and inconvenient rituals in an attempt to undo the damage.

It helps to enquire about particular local taboos. In the Ankaratra we might have caused panic by taking from our rucksacks a tin of ham or sausages, or a pack of salami – not that any of these was available in Tana. The Ankaratra ancestors send crop-destroying hail and thunderstorms in response to pork's polluting presence: a *fady* doubtless inherited from the Vazimba. Imerina's first settlers are said to have been implacable pork-haters and those who worship at their graves, as some still do, must avoid all contact with pigs. A pig-herd's first duty is to keep his charges away from such graves; this is even more important than keeping them out of the precious rice-fields. Elsewhere however pork is much relished by the Malagasy and pigs are among the commonest domestic animals; they even share their owners' homes at night should there happen to be a pig-napper in the area. (There are baffling regional *fady* associated with them, as with all animals and birds; a typical example is the taboo on stub-tails because a pig without a curling tail brings poverty on his owner.)

Throughout Madagascar the good name of a region requires strangers (not only *vazaha*) to be entertained as generously as local resources permit. Yet the offering of hospitality to passing travellers cannot be a spontaneous kindly gesture, as it so often is in remote areas. In itself, it is one of the precautions taken to ward off the possible ill-effects of a stranger's presence and the Chief decides where guests are to stay. Those who seem to merit VIP treatment are not expected to muck in with a family; they must be given a house to themselves and when the Chief has chosen the most suitable its owners have to move out 'for the now being' – it is *fady* to dispute his decision. Some towns and large villages have the equivalent of Indian dak-bungalows – guest-houses built by the French, in local style, for travelling officials.

Our one-storeyed, white-washed lodging was neither dwelling nor guest-house; the small Malagasy flag over the doorway marked it as a People's Executive Committee office – in theory if not in practice. A rectangular building, about eight feet by thirty, it was divided into two identical rooms, each with an unglazed window in the gable end. One room was empty; the other – ours – had a crudely made trestle-table down the centre with a wobbly bench on either side. This edifice had been constructed (by reluctant 'voluntary' labour?) with much less skill and care than the average family home. Its narrow ill-fitting door of rough planks had no fastening, its window shutters were jammed, its loose tin roof leaked and never have I slept on a bumpier mud floor.

As we unpacked, the elated crowd who had followed us from the road jostled around the doorway, commenting on our possessions with exclamations of wonder and curiosity. None of them entered the room, yet after a few moments we began to register, for the first time, a phenomenon that was to become very familiar – the powerful pong of a Malagasy gathering.

We were about to start our supper of inoffensive bread and chocolate (Malagasy chocolate is surprisingly good) when the Chief's brother arrived to supervise our entertainment. Of minute stature, he wore a long grey shirt over striped pyjama-trousers, and a dark blue embroidered skull-cap which made him look remarkably like a Chinaman. He signed to us to put away our own food, pointing to two girls hurrying across a field bearing a tin stove and a basket heaped with rice. We were expected to provide the necessary cooking utensil and everyone was aghast on dis-covering that our saucepan lacked a lid. While a small boy was fetching one the girls pulled fistfuls of dry brown grass, stuffed it into the stove's hollow base and lit it with my matches. Normally a cube of glowing charcoal would have been used; matches cost money and nowadays are not always easy to find. They had been among the many everyday items absent from Tana's shops; to get even one box it was necessary to know a man who knew a man . . .

Like most Malagasy, these villagers looked reasonably well-fed despite a wildly unbalanced diet of rice three times a day, with eggs (irregularly) as the main source of protein in the Ankaratra region – no fruit, no dairy produce, no vegetables. The only signs of malnutrition were minor chronic eye infections and some worm-distended bellies among the younger children. Magnificent teeth filled every mouth. As the Reverend Ellis noted: 'All the tribes have naturally fine and regular teeth, beautifully white, which is to be ascribed to their practice of washing them regularly, and cleaning or bleaching them by the use of a dye, or pigment, made from the laingio, a native plant.' This compliment still applies outside of the towns, but where the sugar-habit has been acquired Malagasy teeth go *very* bad.

While the rice was cooking we sat among our friends, full of that content which blesses the end of a trekker's day. Our shack faced west (it is *fady* for a house to do otherwise) and stood on a ledge of rough grassland above bare fields in which geese were being argumentative. That hamlet seemed to have no other livestock: no zebu, or dogs or cats, or sheep or goats. To our left half-a-dozen dwellings were semi-encircled by tall trees – eucalyptus, cypress and various unfamiliars. As the sun sank these houses glowed orange-red against their green background while the wide sky ahead became a glory of peach and grey-blue and russet clouds. During the night we felt less appreciative of those clouds when they were joined by many others and cold rain dripped lavishly onto our flea-bags.

In the fading light we ate gluey, saltless rice, mixed with two raw eggs donated earlier by a wordless smiling elderly woman. She had presented her gift with such formal graciousness that at once it was transmuted into something very precious. The courtesy of these bare-footed, unwashed, ragged villagers reminded me of their counterparts in the Ethiopian highlands, though the Malagasy are much jollier than the Amharas.

We were organising our 'study' on the trestle-table, to diary-write by torchlight, when the Chief returned with two candles and insisted on our torches being put away. He and Brother remained with us (but they would not sit down: another *fady*?) while the crowd outside dispersed, presumably to sup. Soon after seven o'clock they were back, reinforced by a group of earth-coated men who had been clod-breaking all day in the fields. It then emerged that the Chief had several worries, only two of which we could understand. 'Where were our beds?' 'How could the door be secured to protect us from robbers?' The rest of the evening was pure farce – something easily achieved when sign-language is the main means of communication, *fady* rules OK, and everyone is desperately anxious to be polite without feeling at all sure of the appropriate formulae.

Only the Chief and Brother entered our shack. The rest crowded outside, shrouded in *lambas* against the cold wind and creating quite a festive atmosphere as they disputed, laughed, speculated and sang snatches of what we would call ballads to enliven the *vazaha*'s evening. Several crises seemed to be simultaneously on the boil but as each Malagasy much enjoys his own eloquence these may have been of far less import than was suggested by the prolonged debates they inspired.

Two youths were despatched to find a length of rope to secure the door and six people had six conflicting opinions about how best a fastening might be improvised. But the rope was so rotten that it at once disintegrated (much laughter) when stretched. I then produced two yards of tough emergency cord and the youths worked with that, and a bent nail and a heavy stone, while Rachel threw torchlight on their endeavours – which were frustrated by the mud wall's natural tendency to collapse (more gales of giggles from outside) wherever they tried to hammer in the bent nail.

Meanwhile a few of the older men among the newcomers – members of the village council – were becoming uneasy about our credentials. Samuel's letter had to be produced again and was sceptically scrutinised; being handwritten on a sheet of lined foolscap, without benefit of printed heading or official seals, it failed wholly to reassure them. They were not antagonistic to us, personally, but were unmistakably concerned about our presence – for reasons they could not explain and we could not guess. It was probably a coincidence that their unease first became apparent when I unwittingly broke a taboo by asking the literate young woman to write her name and address in my notebook. It is, we later learned, *fady* for guests to ask the name of their host, or of his village. Despite mutterings of disapproval from some elders, our buxom friend had no inhibitions about giving us the name of the village. But she firmly refused either to tell us her own name or to write it down.

Suddenly someone said – '*Good-morning!*' very loudly, and from the blackness emerged a breathless charming young man wearing a multicoloured *lamba* and a short beard. He beamed, shook hands and said, 'English speak! You speak English – you, me, speak English all together! From polisy I come – polisy know you not. What work do you? What many years you live? I say polisy all I know of you!'

We were somewhat taken aback; the village of Ambohina-havony-Ambonirohitra had seemed an unlikely site for a police-post. 'You have polisy here in this place?' I asked, taking our passports from their permanent home in my bush-shirt pocket.

'Yes, we have one polisy – *every* Malagasy city has one polisy!'

Augustin (for such was his name) then peered around the shadowy shack, recognised Brother leaning against a wall and exclaimed, '*This* is our polisy!'

Brother – obviously pleased to have his light removed from under its bushel – bowed, smiled, nodded and echoed, 'Polisy!' But I found it hard to believe that it was he who had summoned the English-speaker to investigate us in depth.

The uneasy elders, craning through the doorway, now urged Augustin to get on with it. But he, poor fellow, was nonplussed by our passports. When I placed them under the candles he glanced at them, shook his head impatiently, pushed them aside and took out half an exercise-book page and two inches of pencil. 'Name?' he asked. 'Country you live? Many years? Work you do for get money?' He carefully inscribed my answers, then to our bewilderment squealed with excitement on hearing that I write for get money. '*Writer* you are! Please give me one book – *please*! English I study but books I have none so learn I cannot!' His round dark eyes gleamed covetously in the candlelight; and the genuineness of his book-lust so moved us (normally the Malagasy never cadge from *vazaha*) that he got the H.E. Bates Rachel had bought at Heathrow.

Augustin understood much more of Rachel's French than of my English but preferred not to admit this. 'No good young Malagasy speak French. English and Russian is good. French is bad.' Yet as we struggled to communicate he repeatedly fell into the trap of Rachel's questions and answered in the 'bad' language. He had been hoping to go to Moscow University on a scholarship but when the rice prices fell his family could not afford Tana school-fees. 'Maybe next year rice prices go good and I go back to school to study to be scientist for farming and learn to mend the mountains.' As we journeyed on through Madagascar's ravaged landscapes I often remembered that phrase – 'mend the mountains'. But do even Soviet agricultural experts know how?

All this chit-chat was visibly irritating the elders around the doorway, though the Chief and Brother rejoiced to have an interpreter; I was beginning to suspect disunity among Ambohinahavony-Ambonirohitra's council. In any case it now felt like time to end the party; we had been up before dawn and walked over twenty-five miles. Looking pointedly at my watch, I unrolled our flea-bags – thus causing the general worry about our bedding to erupt again. The elderly egg-donor vehemently argued that we should be provided with raffia-matting but for some reason (some *fady?*) this was not on. Augustin protested frantically that no *vazaha* could sleep in meagre flea-bags on an earthen floor throughout a winter night. The Chief's agitation made him look quite haggard and he was unsoothed when I showed him the space-blankets under our flea-bags – admittedly not the sort of equipment likely to impress Malagasy peasants. Finally I was driven to announcing that everyone in Ireland always sleeps on the floor, whatever the weather – and in a flash of inspiration I added that for us beds are *fady*. That settled the matter. Five minutes later Rachel was asleep and I was diary-writing.

Less than a page had been written when voices approached and the door was pushed open, causing that nail to fall out again. A delegation of smiling women, young and old, laid a colossal pot of steaming, coagulated rice on the table and then stood in a row against one wall, to watch me eat.

I did my best. But Malagasy rice is just that: rice unadorned. Salt would have helped, but I feared to give umbrage by using our own. Gallantly I shovelled it in – and soon many of our old friends came flitting moth-like towards the light from the open door. The party, it seemed, was not yet over. One girl was carrying a huge enamel mug of rice-water, the commonest beverage in Malagasy villages. This substitute for tea or coffee is made after each meal by boiling water in the emptied rice-pot, to which some burnt grains always adhere. It looks like weak China tea and it tastes like – well, like rice-water. However, in regions where water is scarce and likely to be contaminated it is of great value and comfort to the *vazaha*. Having been boiled for several minutes, to extract the flavour from the burnt rice, it is almost always safe to drink.

When Brother and Augustin returned the women shook hands, urged me to eat on and left. Then an odd thing happened. Noticing my open diary, Brother became unmistakably unnerved and even Augustin looked worried. Together they pored over the thick book, and as they leafed through its closely written pages their anxiety increased. When Augustin asked if all this was about their village I explained that most of it was about Tana. That eased the tension – slightly. Did they imagine me to be writing a spy's report, and if so for whom? Or did my diary seem to represent those mysterious powers which make *vazaha* feared? Brother's reaction was perhaps understandable, but it surprised me that a young man with ambitions to study abroad should be so upset by the note-taking of a self-confessed writer.

Rachel was now awake, though cravenly lying doggo lest she be required to join in the rice-eating marathon. When three youths arrived to tackle the door problem from another angle – with a tree branch – she inevitably got the giggles and strange muffled snorts at floor-level augmented the evening's improbability. The youths served as a screen behind which I hastily tipped the remains of the rice into a yellow plastic Heathrow bag, prudently retained for emergencies. When I had been shown how to barricade the door, by wedging the branch across it, the youths tied our cord to the branch, and then to a nail hammered into the outside jamb. Thus we were, in theory, locked safely away for the night. Luckily that nail too fell out when Nature called.

Nature's call was but one of many factors inhibiting repose. The floor felt tolerable, once ribs and hips had been adjusted to its corrugations, but by midnight the Indian Ocean's celebrated trade wind had reached gale force and the rattling of the loose roof made sleep impossible for over two hours. Then came a deluge, and efforts to elude various leaks left my head only inches from an icy draught blowing under the controversial door. On such occasions it was hard to believe that Madagascar lies so near the equator.

Unlike most peasants, the Malagasy do not rise with the sun – at least not on cold winter mornings – and there was no one in sight when Brother and Augustin led us out of Ambohinahavony-Ambonirohitra's territory. (As Rachel feelingly remarked, 'It's the last straw when they're double-barrelled.') For guests to offer money is *fady* so we had left behind a selection from our gift-box: razor-blades, pocket-combs, hair-slides. As we said good-bye Augustin presented us with provisions for our journey: two kilos of uncooked rice and three raw eggs. To avert a nasty calamity I soon ate the latter. (This was not a reprehensible example of child-neglect; Rachel is unenthusiastic about raw eggs.)

Already the sun felt gently warm and the sky's deep blue was emphasised by gauzy veils of high white cloud. A strong wind made loud sad music in the tassels of roadside pines and tossed the glistening silvered leaves of swaying eucalyptus saplings. As we walked uphill between banks of red earth, plump brown and grey thrush-sized birds ran along the track ahead of us, then briefly flew, then ran again. We saw dozens of these during the next few days but could not identify them for lack of a book.

Beyond this ridge lay an oval valley, its brown floor scattered with reflected blue where tiny fields had been irrigated. A narrow river raced between long whale-like boulders and a few men were repairing dykes and channels, or hoeing rhythmically together to aerate the heavy soil. Their friendly hamlet stood on a spur in the valley centre. We paused there to refill our water-bottles, then again climbed steeply past skinny zebu grazing on the coarse grass that grew between deep red gullies, known as *lavaka*.

Here we could see exactly how erosion works. *Lavaka* are not what we think of as 'gullies' – permanent features of a landscape created in ages past. They are, as it were, gangrenous wounds. Every year they become not only deeper but much wider as the hard laterite clay along their edges collapses by the ton, exposing the softer base which is even more rapidly washed away. Nowadays the air is so full of statistics that we scarcely notice them any more. But walking by the fragile rim of a *lavaka*, looking down at the maimed earth, one is almost brought to tears by the tragedy of Madagascar's most significant statistic – *three-quarters of the island's surface is officially classified as 'severely degraded'*. And each rainy season inexorably brings about a further deterioration. By now the grassy patches on which those skinny zebu were grazing will have disappeared.

Rice-fields occupy eight-five per cent of Madagascar's irrigated land; the remainder produces taro, maize, manioc, sweet potatoes, potatoes and – in one small area near Antsirabe – newfangled wheat. Some *vazaha* experts believe that the island could produce a wide variety of crops, but only rice is taken seriously – so seriously that one senses an almost mystical link between the Malagasy and their paddy-fields. The Reverend Ellis noted: 'Apathy, want of decision, and excessive indolence, characterize, very generally, the natives of Madagascar . . . The mass of the people seem alike destitute of forethought and enterprise . . .' These criticisms have since been oft repeated, though they are so blatantly unjust. 'Excessive indolence' and the successful cultivation of irrigated rice are incompatible. For ten months of each year rice-farmers and their families have to work long hours with a thoroughness and skill demanded by few other crops. There is much evidence that *only* rice-growing conquers Malagasy indolence, but far be it from me to censor anyone for not working hard at uninspiring tasks. I only work hard at writing, leaving the other compartments of my life in a state of irredeemable confusion –

which is perhaps why I feel such a strong affinity with the Malagasy.

The relationship between the rice-growing peasants and their fields, and the other tribes and their herds, partly explains why Communism is a non-starter in Madagascar. Family property is of prime importance when generations of toil have gone to the creation and preservation of a few fertile fields or a numerous herd. Incidentally, paddy-culture also explains why Merina marriage partners are chosen, if possible, from within the compact group of hamlets that makes up the Merina version of the 'extended family'. A suitable match is described as 'closing the breach', or 'inheritance not going away'.

The oddly European sound of distant church bells reminded us that this was a Sunday morning. Soon we were meeting church-going groups equipped with slim black prayer-books: usually half-a-dozen women and children, sometimes with a man or two walking ahead. Far away on other hillsides similar groups could be seen converging on a church invisible to us; so many rural churches have closed that some families walk ten miles or more to worship. Everyone wore clean colourful garments and a few carried plastic sandals to be slipped on at the church door. Obviously Saturday night is bath-night, as it was in rural Ireland before mod cons arrived.

The next hilltop overlooked miles of golden grassland leading to a still higher ridge, its crest fringed with mature eucalyptus. There was not a house in sight but using our binoculars we counted eleven tombs on the surrounding slopes. These isolated grey stone cubes, looking from a distance not unlike military pillboxes, give the Imerina countryside a faintly uncanny atmosphere. Who is to say that the ancestral spirits are not still around, when their descendants' relationship with them is so emotionally charged? *Razana* ('the ancestors') play such a singular part in the lives of the living that family tombs are built with much more care, and at far greater expense, than family homes.

These tombs may be seen as the visible expression of a form of *razana*-worship, though the Malagasy attitude to 'the ancestors', like everything else associated with their religious life, evades precise definition in our terms. Without formally ancestor-worshipping in the Chinese way, they obey what they believe to be ancestral rules and feel totally dependent on ancestral protection. Burial with *razana* is of immeasurable importance to even the most sophisticated Malagasy – who, if he goes abroad, likes to take with him a handful of earth from his future grave. That earth will always wish to return to Madagascar and should he die abroad its possession will increase his chances of burial in the family tomb.

This whole 'cult' (for want of a better word) is inextricably bound up with the deep love felt by the Malagasy for their Great Red Island. What we describe as our country, or nation, they describe as *tanindrazana* – 'the land of the ancestors'. The entire island is *tany masina* – 'holy ground' – because it is thought about (or felt about) primarily as a vessel holding all the ancestral bodies. Hence some educated Malagasy believe in the feasibility of training peasants to combat erosion and forgo the indiscriminate felling of rain-forests. But so far the ancestors have shown no interest in ecology.

The *razana* element in Malagasy culture coincides at many points with the beliefs of animist black Africa, where tribal ancestors have always been ceremonially honoured. But it also coincides with Toraja traditions. In the humid forested hills of Indonesia's Sulawesi, the proud, intelligent Toraja tribe still retains its ancient culture, despite intense pressure from Muslims and Christians. Toraja beliefs are centred on buffalo-sacrificing and death festivities, and their attitudes to both ritual cattle-killing and 'the ancestors' in many ways resemble Malagasy attitudes. But – as any Malagasy will tell you – whatever the origins of the *razana* cult it is now a distinctively Malagasy phenomenon, without exact parallel elsewhere.

Innumerable *fady* surround *razana*-worship (or dependence). For instance, a dog who lifts his leg near a tomb must immediately be killed. A human who does likewise (presumably this could only happen if he/she were drunk) must be fined one zebu, to be sacrificed at once on the scene of the crime. To point at a tomb is *fady* and anyone who accidentally does so must count their fingers aloud, from one to ten, beginning with a little finger and simultaneously spitting on each fingertip while saying, 'My hand is not leprous, it is not leprous.' A failure to do this may result in the hand becoming leprous. All such *fady* vary somewhat from region to region – and, nowadays, from family to family.

Any Malagasy who has to choose a tomb-site (which should be south-east or south-west of the village) is faced with a major decision because so many crucial *fady* are involved. A wrongly placed tomb may lead to early deaths in the family so the *ombiasa* has to advise on the exactly right spot. The tomb door must face west but not due west, to avoid giving it the same *vintana* (destiny) as the family home; because the dead have a stronger *vintana* than the living, a shared alignment would put them in a dangerously powerful position. No tomb must be built at the end of a valley, or where it can be seen from a village, and the building of it must take more than one year.

Not all these *fady* are still heeded, especially in Imerina where Christianity's influence is most pervasive. We saw many family tombs built within sight of the home, or of a village – though none faced due west. As one cannot possibly know which *fady* is still operating where, we always looked around carefully to make sure there were no witnesses before photographing a tomb, or closely examining it. Most of the newer Merina tombs had an incongruously suburban aura utterly unlike those of the southern tribes or of the east coast fishermen. A lot of concrete had gone to their making, they were surmounted by small carved granite Christian crosses, and their coloured stone motifs would not have surprised on the gate-posts of a Bexhill bungalow.

It would however be a mistake to deduce from those crosses, or from the sight of villagers proceeding decorously to church, that Christianity has even partially eclipsed the ancestors in Imerina. For most people it remains essentially an ancillary cult, though their Christian fervour may be totally sincere. During the regular Merina exhumation ceremonies, Christian blessings are sought and gladly given; no one questions the theological propriety of their juxtaposition to the immemorial rites of *razana*-worship. Similar mergings of Christianity and more ancient religions are of course quite common in Africa; the Zulus have their Zionist Church, the Congolese their Kimbanguist Church – and so on up and down the continent. But Malagasy syncretism seems to work better than most, no doubt partly because the Malagasy are an exceptionally subtle people and partly because the missionaries arrived in Madagascar some eighty years before the colonists – and were, originally, of a different nationality.

That afternoon we looked for a campsite far from the local *razana*. Eventually we chose a glade amidst young eucalyptus, reasoning that a government plantation was almost sure to be neutral ground, free of sacred rocks and springs and invisible Vazimba graves. By then the wind was so strong that we had some difficulty getting the tent up and it flapped noisily all night.

Next morning Ambatolampy began to plague us and it continued to do so for three days. Ambatolampy is a town on Route Nationale No. 7, midway between Tana and Antsirabe, and whenever we asked the way to Antsirabe (due south) we were directed towards Ambatolampy, to the east. Clearly nobody now walks from the heart of the Ankaratra to Antsirabe; they go instead to this wretched Ambatolampy, and there take a bus, and everyone assumed the *vazaha* must wish to do likewise. So – having been unable to find a detailed map of the region – we were dependent on our compass and Rachel's sense of direction (I do not have one).

We first heard of Ambatolampy when we stopped for breakfast in a village near our eucalyptus-glade camp. At 7 a.m. it was still cold and the thatched, low-ceilinged café-shack had just opened. House-flies covered the smoke-stained mud walls and were swarming inside a rusty bucket from which a beautiful and charming young woman was ladling grey-brown batter into a frying-pan on a charcoal stove. Meanwhile her husband (handsome and charming to match) was lighting a mud stove in one corner, to boil the coffee-water, and three small filthy children – sensationally good-looking, with huge eyes and happy smiles – were balancing on an unsteady bench eating bowls of rice-gruel, the standard Malagasy breakfast. As no one spoke French our conversation was limited to my asking, 'Antsirabe?' and the young couple chorusing, 'Ambatolampy!' while pointing to the rising sun. But their kindliness glowed through the language barrier and warmed us long before we were handed dirty mugs of black coffee – hot, strong and sweet.

Four mugs of coffee and seven delicious crisp pancakes cost the equivalent of 35 pence, according to Rachel's calculation – she was the expedition's treasurer. I have no head for figures and the Malagasy coinage is grotesquely complicated. The official monetary unit is the Malagasy Franc (FMG) but you also have to cope with the *piastre*, known variously (depending on denomination) as *ariary*, *drala* or *parata*. As far as I could make out (not very far), the substantial 5-ariary coin equals 100 FMG, which I found intolerably confusing; in any rational country it would equal 50 FMG. Moreover, people use all sorts of coins (ariary, drala and parata) in a single transaction, so that only a computer (or Rachel) could work out the value of a handful of change.

This chaotic system addles the average *vazaha* shopper. In markets and eating-houses I often overpaid – then felt a joyous lift of the heart when surplus coins were handed back. Such experiences remind us that money-making is not the inbuilt mainspring for all human activity everywhere. A ragged woman selling bananas by the roadside, who returns coins that would have trebled her profit, undermines the argument that 'it's only human' to give material gain precedence over every other consideration. Somehow we in the West have been persuaded that greed is a *natural* motive for every sort of perfidy. 'You can't do anything about it, it's human nature' – so people say when multinationals inflict extra hardship on those already grossly deprived. Or when a tycoon's sharp practice causes the draining of irreplaceable wet-lands, or the bulldozing of beautiful buildings, or the pollution of a lake or vandalising of an archaeological site. Yet the honesty often found in remote regions proves that greed is not so 'natural' that we must surrender without a fight to the 'profit-motive' ideology now corrupting our civilisation – and spreading its contagion wherever it can.

I am not of course suggesting that the Malagasy are like something out of a Rousseau fantasy. They have their share of urban cheats and predatory peasants and one of the latter joined us in our café-shack as we were paying the bill. He was that rarely seen animal, a surly Malagasy. Elderly, stooped and slightly cross-eyed, he exuded xenophobia and urged the young man to ask us to give our change to the children – using sign language as well as words, so that we too would get the message. But both our host and hostess rejected this idea, showing some irritation. (He was, I think, the father of one of them.) As they argued, our host caught my eye and we both smiled; and that moment became one of those strange little examples of perfect understanding without benefit of speech. The young couple knew how much we appreciated their endearing trio, who had been fascinated by our map – the youngest had ended up on my knee. And I knew they knew my not tipping the children was a sign of respect rather than meanness. And we each knew the other felt a tip would have spoiled the quality of the relationship we had enjoyed during our forty minutes together.

We saw no other surly expressions in that neat, clean, substantial village of two-storeyed thatched houses. Like most Merina villages it seemed relatively prosperous though there were no shops: instead, wandering traders set up stalls. Behind the 'main street', and on the outskirts, were many ruined dwellings, their rain-melted mud-brick walls giving them the appearance of some recently excavated archaeological site.

Walking up the rough street, we savoured the incense-like eucalyptus smoke of breakfast fires as it came drifting through windows and doors; the rural Malagasy consider chimneys an unnecessarily complicated addition to their homes. Shutters were being opened and bedding shaken from handsomely carved balconies – women with battered tins were queuing at the communal tap – loquacious hens were leading broods of belligerent chickens to the nearest dump-heap – yawning men sat on doorsteps, wrapped in bright lambas, awaiting their rice-gruel. Our progress caused much subdued excitement. Women called the rest of the family onto balconies to view us, most people waved and smiled shyly in response to our greetings, and when we paused outside the last house to ask – 'Antsirabe?' everyone in sight shouted 'Ambatolampy!' and pointed east.

The amiability of Malagasy village dogs is remarkable. Several large silent mongrels either ran away from us or tentatively wagged their tails when spoken to, instead of barking threateningly at the intruders as their counterparts do in every other country I know. The Malagasy are on the whole a gentle people and seem never to have encouraged that savagery essential for an efficient watch-dog system. This aspect of local life may seem unimportant from a distance. Yet not having to be ever on the alert to ward off slavering hounds contributes more than a little to the welcoming atmosphere of Merina villages.

The Malagasy canine/human relationship is what we think of as normal – i.e. loving, which is not at all normal in most peasant societies. This must partly explain the evolution of animals who are well-disposed even towards *vazaha*. Later I came upon a deplorably tendentious American missionary tract which listed the humane treatment of Malagasy dogs as yet another triumph for Christianity, though the various *fady* associated with dogs – which are mainly in their favour – antedate by centuries the arrival of the first missionaries. Unlike many taboos, these tend to have a known historical basis. For instance, to sell a dog is *fady* because long, long ago An Ancestor sharing property between three sons gave the youngest only a dog, who became the youth's sole help and comfort as he travelled through wild country on the way to seek his fortune. Years passed, and he prospered and became powerful. (Hence his status as an ancestor influential enough to establish a *fady*.) On his deathbed he summoned all his children and said, 'My dog was always my faithful friend during the difficult years. Cursed be the one of my children or descendants who sells a dog.' For some families it is also *fady* to kill a dog. In the village of Ambatomiady, near Ambatolampy, a man fell from a cliff, many generations ago, and was too badly injured to move. His dog hurried home – a three-hour journey – to fetch rescuers, and eventually the man recovered. When he realised that he would predecease his dog he requested that after its death it should be wrapped in a red silk *lamba* and buried beside his own tomb. And he made it *fady* for any of his descendants to kill a dog. I could not find out what happens when two *fady* conflict. If this family had a dog who peed on a tomb and should therefore be killed, which *fady* would win?

Cats, I should perhaps explain, are another matter. Rachel has not yet fully recovered from the shock of discovering that in most parts of Madagascar baked cat is a delicacy – though among the Sakalava tribe to eat them is *fady*. On this topic Hilary Bradt wrote to us: 'We were having a conversation with a tribal family in the eastern rain-forest and after we'd talked for quite a while about conservation and lemurs the father said, "Yes, and they certainly taste good!" "*Taste?* – what do they taste like?" "Oh, rather like cat." End of conversation. End of conservation.'

According to our feeble map, the track we had been following here turned south-west, away from Antsirabe. (The map classified it as 'motorable' but the Malagasy know better and it was vehicle-free.) A faint alternative path along the edge of a *lavaka* eventually petered out on high savannah swept by an easterly force-ten gale; had we been seeking Ambatolampy we would not have not got far that day. From this 7,000-foot plateau we could again see the pudding-mountain, some thirty-five miles behind us. The few villages we had passed were just visible through binoculars; their improbable little churches gave that rugged landscape a tinge of cosy domesticity. Along the horizon, in three directions, stretched distant contorted mountains – volcanic formations recalling Ethiopia's Simien range, as did the rich pure colouring of that high bright world, silent all day but for the endless song of the savannah wind.

Directly ahead of us, beyond the red, brown and green of nearer ridges, rose the weirdly misshapen granite summit of Madagascar's third-highest mountain: Tsiafajavona, 'place of standing mists'. This is a mere mini-mountain – just over 8,000 feet – yet it did not seem so as we walked towards it over flat miles of golden grassland, with a narrow cultivated valley far below on our right, half-hidden by a line of wind-demented eucalyptus planted on the escarpment edge. We found a path only when a solitary figure, bare-legged below his *lamba*, appeared in the distance carrying a bundle over his shoulder on the end of a long stick. Turning east, we bent to fight the gale and joined this path where it dipped into a sheltered gully. There we sat in the warm noon sun to eat our lunch of peanuts and glucose tablets and attend to Rachel's foot-blisters. These were coming along nicely, in my detached view – almost ready to burst and free of complications. Rachel was less appreciative of their orthodox progress. Neither of us had ever before carried camping-equipment on trek – usually we have a pack-animal – and our feet were reacting accordingly.

As we continued, two young men came running towards us at a steady pace, on spindly yet muscular legs, each bearing half the carcass of an enormous black pig split exactly down the middle from snout to tail. Their head loads prevented them from turning to stare at us but when we passed two pairs of unmistakably startled eyes rolled towards us, showing the whites like nervous horses. Some way behind came their wives, glossy-haired and golden-skinned, wearing new turquoise and canary skirts and shocking-pink and lime-green cardigans. They carried empty raffia baskets, to be filled with household goods when the pig had been sold. Their wordless beams encouraged us to try to check on the path's destination, but at the sound of my voice they were too overcome by giggles even to attempt a reply. Which, as Rachel observed, was better than being told to go to Ambatolampy.

We lost the path again while descending from the savannah around the grassy flanks of two steep mountains. Our objective was a flat-topped ridge beyond a mile-wide valley which, unluckily for us, had already been irrigated. Every square foot was flooded, and high, narrow, loosely built dyke-tops provided the only paths. We zig-zagged along these with arms outstretched, like tight-rope artists, feeling guilty each time our heavy boots sent chunks of dyke crumbling into the water. Thrice we had to change course because of open dykes through which flowed brown cascades. And twice we had to cross swift, broad streams by leaping from one smooth spray-slippy boulder to the next. None of this would have mattered but for our rucksacks, which were destabilising – especially mine, with its nonsensical complement of hardback books. Several split-level obstacles required long jumps down or scrambles up and the team-manoeuvre of removing rucksacks and handing them up (or down) to each other was not easy on such narrow dykes – often no more than six inches across. We spent over an hour negotiating that mile.

A few crudely built houses were scattered on the lower slopes of our ridge, but as the *vazaha* approached to seek guidance everyone took fright and withdrew to the shadowy interiors. Then suddenly we were on a clear path, winding level around the mountains above the valley floor. As we debated whether to follow this, or continue due south across the pathless ridge, a young man – bolder than his neighbours – emerged from the nearest shack followed by an aggressively strutting turkey-cock. He had the unorthodox good looks of many of these village men: a broad bronze face, high cheekbones, a wide nose, a jutting square chin, thick wavy hair. Over filthy frayed trousers he wore a brand-new pale blue cotton shirt. Gazing at our packs with a sort of horrified fascination (which was rather how we ourselves felt about them, at that stage) he declaimed dramatically in French – 'Here there is *no* tourist hotel!' Rachel assured him that we were not seeking any sort of hotel and asked the way over the ridge. The young man frowned and advised us to take the path instead: eventually it would lead us safely to Manalalondo. The ridge route is never used nowadays, he said, and we would find no path, people, houses, food or warmth. At that I felt a surge of adrenalin; uninhibited pathless mountains are what travelling is all about . . . 'You look like an aged war-horse scenting battle,' observed Rachel sourly – she had fancied the level path. We were touched by our friend's worried expression as he watched us scrambling through a débris of massive boulders on the lower slopes of the ridge.

This tough climb ended on a ledge where five inferior zebu with undeveloped humps and unprepossessing horns lay around under a few stunted pines despondently chewing the cud. In these grassland regions the lack of livestock surprised us. Perhaps intensive rice-cultivation leaves neither time nor energy for cattle-tending?

The flat-topped ridge (savannah again) ran north–south for many miles but was scarcely a mile wide. When the wind suddenly dropped we realised how tiring it is to be buffeted all day by a gale – even a cross-gale. It was now time to look for water and a site; the short days – only eleven and a half hours in winter – are a major snag for campers in Madagascar. Another snag is the impracticality of camp-fires; one stray spark could cause disaster.

Soon our tent was up on the soft golden grass of a wide ledge semi-encircled by graceful tamarind trees. Below us a clear amber stream raced through a glen and beyond rose another ridge, higher and sparsely wooded; the nearby head of the glen was dominated by a knot of stony mountains.

Rachel's blisters had burst satisfactorily during the afternoon and having replastered them I sat for a moment to relax my throbbing shoulders before cooking a dehydrated 'Nomad Supper' on our minute pocket-stove, fuelled by pellets. All around us the savannah glowed copper in slanting sunlight, while overhead tamarind leaves shivered against a sky still vividly blue. A pair of dark brown birds with fierce beaks (Malagasy buzzards?) glided slowly in wide circles, observing us. Their loud harsh calls – like a raven's much amplified – and the distant whisper of the stream, were the only sounds. To the west, as I stirred our supper, high streaky clouds flared to crimson and a strange carmine radiance briefly filled the valley. Then the sun was gone: and instantly, as though a switch had been pressed, the brighter stars were out. We ate gazing upwards, watching the constellations swiftly taking shape.

During that magical evening, far from the distorting pollutions of Technological Man, it was easy to understand the link between the Malagasy and their Great Red Island. There must still be an animist in each of us, however respectably inaccessible, and such experiences of beauty and solitude restore animist reverence to its proper place in the scheme of human emotions.

4

Among the Merina

Light frost lay on the savannah next morning – 'We might as well be in the Andes!' muttered Rachel, struggling to fasten her rucksack with numbed hands.

Ten minutes later we had to remove our loads while climbing down and up the high steep banks of the stream in the glen. A strenuous ascent on rocky, erosion-ravaged mountains led to another red-gold plateau, broken only by three isolated, symmetrical 'pudding-hills'. One would have assumed these to be man-made in a country with a longer history of human habitation. Here Tsiafajavona seemed close, beyond a grassy mountain at the far end of this plateau. Soon the cold wind was blowing again, stronger than ever. All morning we had to shout at each other above its steady howl.

By noon we were on the grass mountain, gazing into a dramatically deep and dark-walled ravine – all that now separated us from Tsiafajavona. Following an old cart-track, left over from the days before everyone took the Ambatolampy bus, we were astonished to hear confused shouting and the unmistakable creaking of wheels. We had seen nobody, and no stock or cultivation or dwelling, since leaving Blueshirt's hamlet.

Around the next shoulder they appeared – four wild-eyed, ragged, yelling men, their faces weather-toughened and their hair shaggy, escorting a flat zebu-cart loaded with a granite slab measuring some four feet by fifteen. This explained why we had just passed a mysterious newly dug hole, at least eight feet deep and twelve feet square. Clearly this was a tomb-building team; there could be no other conceivable reason for dragging tons of rock to one of the highest points in Madagascar.

Several thick grass ropes had been tied around the slab and burn marks along its side showed that it had been quarried in the traditional way. For centuries the Malagasy have been detaching grave-slabs from mountains by burning dung along the length they wish to remove, then pouring cold water on the hot rock. Before Europeans brought the wheel to Madagascar, five hundred men were commonly employed to drag one stone up a mountain; these two zebu looked as if they could have done with similar reinforcements as they strained and heaved, pausing every few yards to gain breath. Their escort continually shouted hoarse abuse but never struck them. Sometimes a wheel stuck in a particularly deep rut and had to be dug out. All this fascinated the expedition's photographer but we agreed it might be unwise to produce a camera; it seemed possible (even probable) that then and there *vazaha* were *fady*. The customary Malagasy smiles were missing and the men looked tense, distraught and curiously apprehensive. They also reeked of 'ardent spirits'. As we scrambled off the track to let them pass they scarcely glanced at us, so absorbed were they in their evidently traumatic task.

Around the next corner we came on four more men, two sitting by the track swigging from a grimy bottle and two using crowbars to prise another gigantic slab off the mountain. The latter pair were dripping sweat, yelling at each other breathlessly and working with frenzied vigour – an approach to manual labour uncharacteristic of the Malagasy. The sitting men shouted at us questioningly (to shout was unnecessary, as we were passing within a yard of them) but we did not linger to chat. Obviously this tomb was not being built because someone had recently died; if a corpse is awaiting burial it is *fady* to make any noise while preparing the grave.

Soon after, we could see, some 1,500 feet below, the head of that long valley to which we had been walking parallel all morning. Sections of the track were visible, coiling steeply down to a hamlet on a half-way ledge; and an empty cart was slowly approaching to pick up the second slab. We would have liked to watch the loading process since it was impossible to imagine it – this whole operation recalled the feats of the pyramid-builders – but the five scowling men with the second cart strengthened our feeling of being *de trop*. The mere getting of an empty cart up that steep broken mountain was in itself a feat. We were to see many more carts, often heavily laden, travelling on preposterous tracks: but never again anything comparable.

The zebu reins consist of a rope tied around the base of the horns and passed through the nostrils, which sounds cruel but seems to cause no distress. Normally zebu-carts have four high wooden sides, gaily painted in the more prosperous regions, and some are covered wagons in which whole families travel from market to market. I do not understand why Malagasy carts can negotiate terrain that no Irish cart could possibly tackle. For some arcane reason their two huge wheels can act independently of each other, one happily rolling along in a rut three feet below its companion. (A Malagasy rut is like none other; not unusually, a so-called 'rut' in a motor-road will be four or five feet deep.) Meanwhile the two zebus often seem to be pulling in different directions, which plainly is not the case since the whole dotty equipage almost always arrives at its destination with load intact.

Our cart-track ended on a small half-moon ledge supporting the ruins of three hovels. Beside them were the foundations for two new houses; doubtless the new tomb was part of this same enterprise. Nearby grew rows of an attractive podded plant, about the size and shape of a mature gooseberry bush, with foxglove-like yellow blossoms. The dark green, shiny, stubby pods – about three inches long – contained presumably edible beans; we took a specimen to Antsirabe but no one there could identify it.

The tomb-builders were darker-skinned than most Merina and the hamlet to which we now descended also seemed un-Merina-like. Its cramped dwellings, surrounded by low trees and scrub, had ill-fitting shutters and dishevelled thatches. On this ledge – some two miles by half a mile – potatoes and maize grew in fields of rich volcanic soil, but there were only a few ill-maintained rice-fields.

Our descent was watched by a few women and children, carrying long sticks. They were herding four zebu, eight small brown sheep (the first we had seen in Madagascar) and two hulking spotted black and white pigs – possibly relatives of that carcass we had met on its way to Tana Zoma. Two dogs fled on seeing us and the humans did likewise when we turned towards them to ask the way. In a communal farmyard numerous toddlers and crawling infants were playing amidst chicken-shit, zebu-dung and vegetable refuse. Despite the region's many springs, these were the filthiest children we saw in Madagascar. But we only glimpsed them: on our approach they disappeared like rabbits into burrows. A few frightened female faces then peered through doorways, before firmly shutting the doors.

Beyond a windbreak pine-grove we were overtaken by a middle-aged man with Merina colouring but slightly negroid features. He had observed our hesitant wanderings and felt it his duty to guide us to the valley floor – and to carry our full water-bottles. He also wished to carry both our rucksacks, the carrying of luggage being one of the courtesies traditionally extended to strangers. This benevolent character was probably a member of the village council; for all his destitute appearance, he had an air of authority. His guidance was invaluable. The going here got very rough, including a few *lavaka* which would have baffled us, so unlikely did it seem that a path to anywhere could traverse them.

Usually such help would prompt a reward but in Madagascar one does not offer money or a gift in exchange for guidance. A Malagasy proverb says, 'He who shows the right way saves life', and it is *fady* to show a stranger the wrong track or refuse to show him the right one. The Ancestors taught that travellers in unfamiliar country have Andriamanitra (God, or the chief creative spirit) on their side. A stranger disappointed by his reception in a village is entitled to curse the inhabitants, causing Andriamanitra to punish them. Some *vazaha* are discomfited to think that Malagasy helpfulness may be rooted in fear – a possibility stressed by mean-minded missionaries in an attempt to explain away the fact that for centuries the Malagasy have been, in certain respects, more 'Christian' than many Europeans. Their argument is of course absurd. Fear has always played an important part in popular religions – Christian or otherwise – as a blunt instrument with which to enforce the rules. But why do the Malagasy have so many rules concerning hospitality, generosity, courtesy and consideration for strangers? The *razana* who established this code were obviously inspired by qualities deep within the Malagasy nature rather than by superstitious fears. Hence these particular rules are still being kept, long after many other *fady*, once equally powerful, have been discarded.

On the valley floor our guide pointed to a grey track ascending a red-brown mountain on the far side of the valley. Then – lest we might get lost again – he sat in the shade of a tamarind tree to observe our progress. This involved fording a river, undergoing another trial by dyke-ordeal and struggling up a steep slope where long tangled grass concealed small boulders with jagged protuberances. We turned occasionally to wave to our guardian-angel, who began his tough climb home only after we had reached the track.

Half-an-hour later we paused to ponder a ten-foot-deep chasm extending across the track's entire width; even by the standards of Malagasy pot-holes this seemed excessive. Then we met an empty zebu-cart, escorted by cheerful youths carrying spades, and realised that earth was being taken from the chasm for brick-making. We still thought it odd to bisect the valley's only track for this purpose: but Madagascar is rich in such oddities.

Winter is the building season – for sensible reasons it is *fady* to build at other times – and we passed several houses at various stages of construction. Bricks were being dexterously shaped and laid out to dry, thatching grasses were being sorted, cart-loads of stones were being collected for foundations, new walls were being plastered with zebu-dung, red-brown roof-tiles were being stacked, doors and shutters were being carved. Apart from one tin roof, we saw no non-local materials in use.

In traditional Malagasy villages, built without colonial interference, the houses stand at odd angles to each other. But this unplanned look is a result of meticulous *vintana* (destiny) calculations, determined by the ancient Malagasy belief that the world is square and horizontal. (In other contexts this cosmology has, we were often assured, been discredited.) The design and siting of houses are influenced by the points of the compass and the months of the year, according to the calendar which remained in general use until the French came. This provided twelve moons of twenty-eight days each, plus eighteen intercalary days – one at the end of each month as its *vintana*, one added to each of four months of the year and two set aside at the end of the year for a great annual festival: *fandroana*. As the resulting total leaves eleven and a half days over, the year began again on the same date every thirty-three years. The pre-colonial Malagasy were vague about birthdays and used this thirty-three-year cycle to guess approximately how old a person might be: if he could remember three cycles he must be about seventy-three.

Some building *fady* have common-sense origins, though alternative or additional explanations may be given by *ombiasa*. You must never build at the head of a valley if there is only swampy water available; or at the mouth of a valley where you are exposed to cold winds; or near a new landslide. Other *fady* seem purely animist, like those against building in the shadow of a steep dominant mountain peak, or near a waterfall or lake, or where a river forks. It is also taboo for a son to build a bigger house than his father's and the digging of the foundations must be done by someone whose father has died. In a new house the owner's father (or some other elder, if Father has gone to The Beyond) must light the first fire, from the fire burning in his own home. And neither the new householder nor his wife may prepare the first meal; that too Father must do, to give it a sacramental quality.

Winter is also the corpse-turning season and there was much activity around two large tombs, built on scrubland not far off our track out of sight of any dwelling. The men and women thronging around their *razana* paused to gaze at us and a few called friendly greetings. I longed to snoop but good manners prevailed. Although there were no warning-off vibes, it would have been crass to intrude on any stage of the profoundly significant *famadihana* ritual.

During these exhumation ceremonies corpses are removed from their tombs, wrapped in new shrouds and often made guests of honour at jolly parties in their descendants' homes, before being returned to the spring-cleaned tombs with gifts of money and alcohol. This custom may startle when first encountered, yet to condemn it as 'morbid' is to miss the point. The Malagasy experience such a vivid sense of unity with the dead that maintaining contact with their corpses seems only natural – a recognition of their being alive and well and very powerful in the *Ankoatra*, 'the Beyond'. This view of physical death as a transition to another form of life, in which one enjoys increased wisdom and power, is not a million metaphysical miles from the Christian concept of unity with God in Heaven and participation in the Beatific Vision. To the Malagasy our apparent forgetting of dead relatives after the funeral, while we concentrate on how to live happily without them, is incomprehensible. Thus they appreciate the Catholic custom of celebrating memorial Masses on death anniversaries, and setting aside one month of the year during which the dead are specially remembered. But they never could accept the barbarous doctrine of eternal punishment – a doctrine as illogical in concept as it would be unjust in practice, since no sin committed by a mere mortal, during his brief life-span, could possibly deserve a punishment without end. Many Malagasy laws and beliefs seem to us equally illogical and unjust: but they were accustomed to those.

Famadihana rituals take place every few years, according to a family's wealth or its needs. A dead relative returning in a dream – an alarming event for the whole family – is a sign that the deceased

feels cold, hungry, thirsty, bored and generally neglected; so a
'turning' must be organised as soon as possible. Other motives are
a decline in family prosperity or general health, or a young wife's
infertility. The role of *razana* in conception is believed to be far
more important than the husband's role and during turning
ceremonies the infertile wives bite off fragments of a parent's or
grandparent's old shroud and eat them. Unless some such crisis
demands an immediate *famadihana*, longer intervals are now being
allowed between turnings because of the expense involved,
though it is *fady* to let too much time elapse. *Razana* need to be kept
in touch with their families and the families need to placate them
so that they will use their enormous powers constructively; the few
who neglect ancestral corpses are considered stupid, rash and
dishonourable.

Each *famadihana* enhances a family's reputation and often three
or four hundred people (the extended family) are invited. Many
zebu – which must be monochrome – are killed; incalculable
quantities of rice and innumerable gallons of 'ardent spirits' are
provided. Much money is also spent on new clothes, particularly
for the women of the family, and on new bed-mats for the guests
and other new mats on which to lay the corpses outside the tomb –
and, if you want to keep up with the Joneses, on new *lambas* of
hand-woven dark red silk for each corpse. (No living person may
wear such a *lamba*.) In these hard times few can compete with the
Joneses; at Tana and Antsirabe markets we saw only undyed
cotton *famadihana* shrouds.

For three days and nights musicians play, sing and dance
non-stop and the fees they demand are in proportion to the energy
expended. These fees are not however considered an extravagance; the thunderous drum and shrill bamboo flute are needed to
summon back to base any *razana* who may be away on a spiritual
business trip. If the soul is out of the corpse during the festivities a
lot of money is wasted as it will not ever know how much has been
done to make it happy. Even today, many families spend most of
their cash income on these feasts, just as they spend far more on a
new tomb than on a new house. Everyone economically responsible for the *famadihana* must pay his fair share or incur
excommunication from the family, from the home and – most
devastating of all – from the family tomb. Andriamanitra, too, will
punish the miser (or, nowadays, the sceptic), either with leprosy
or lightning.

Rounding the base of a hill we were shocked to see our track crossing a narrow river by an ugly new concrete bridge. Further experience taught us that such irrelevant 'communications improvements' are a not uncommon feature of the Malagasy landscape. More poignant were the brand-new, never-opened schools to be seen throughout Imerina. We paused that afternoon to admire a handsome single-storey building, well-finished, with a roof of flat local tiles and a sports ground of beaten earth. Many such schools have been built by voluntary labour on the understanding that once the people had provided a building the government would provide teachers and equipment. But now there is no money for educational expansion.

Beyond the bridge straggled another hamlet and we rejoiced to see, by the side of the track, a wooden crate supporting a row of chipped enamel mugs and a few stale rice-flour buns in a glass jar. This coffee-stall was unattended; it must depend chiefly on market traffic. But an unkempt young man soon appeared, carrying an even more unkempt but beautiful baby and followed by his wife bearing a tin kettle of weak coffee. Wife quickly scuttled away while husband greeted us with the characteristic Malagasy blend of friendliness and formality. Then, still holding the infant, he filled two mugs, having first rinsed them in a shallow basin of opaque water standing nearby. (Eventually we were to have cause to ponder such washing-up methods with clinical interest.) Flies swarmed as we ate, pursuing the buns to our very lips. Cold, grease-sodden, sweetish rice-buns must be among the least appetising forms of sustenance known to man; but we were too ravenous to notice. On the opposite embankment several small children, shy but fascinated, stood observing us in a typical pose – legs apart, hands behind backs, heads slightly to one side. When I overpaid by 50 FMG the young man smiled as one smiles at a foolish youngster and returned the coins. As we were loading up, he tried to send us to Ambatolampy.

Soon after, we found a tomb-free campsite between a pine plantation and an expanse of feathery bushes stretching to the foot of a nearby ridge. There were no dwellings in sight – but suddenly, as we struggled with the peg-resistant ground, a man emerged from the bushes. He greeted us politely, in French, showing none of the surprise he must have felt on seeing and hearing two *vazaha* females swearing over tent-pegs. Coincidentally, he was the local Chief; when he had read Samuel's letter he gave us permission to camp, if we insisted, but said he would much prefer us to be his guests.

On the way back to the hamlet Joseph (all we can remember of his name) carried our water-bottles and wore Rachel's rucksack; he offered to carry mine, too, but that was a burden I would not have inflicted on my worst enemy. As a youth Joseph had served with the French army and in 1970 he was appointed a secondary school teacher in the nearest town, a few miles down the valley. This explained why he was, most unusually, wearing shoes – real shoes, made by BATA in Madagascar. He also wore a faded purple jersey, neat navy-blue trousers and a fashionable straw Homburg.

Joseph's home was new, a posh six-roomed mansion of pale gold brick, with large windows, blue shutters and doors, a tin roof and wood floors – something rarely seen in the newer village houses of deforested Madagascar. All the floors, including the verandah, were highly polished; those Malagasy who can afford wood floors cherish them obsessionally, which explains why so much home-made beeswax is on sale in the markets. The whole house was Swiss-clean but sparsely furnished as compared to the same grade of home in most Third World countries. Its inexplicably cramped entrance made us aware of being much bulkier than the average Malagasy. A narrow doorway under the verandah led to a cubby-hole hall where turkeys roosted at night in two alcoves. Here one had to turn sharp left to ascend a steep ladder to the broad unrailed balcony; it would have been impossible to squeeze through the hall and climb the ladder wearing our rucksacks, which had to be held sideways.

Mrs Joseph came to greet us as we relaxed on a bench against the wall of the verandah-cum-sitting-room. She spoke no French but was as self-possessed as her husband. Her thick straight hair was parted in the middle and drawn back in a bun; she was barefooted and wore a neat, self-made brown and white check dress.

When Grandad appeared I stood up to be introduced; it would have seemed monstrous for a youngster of fifty-one to remain seated while being welcomed by a venerable gentleman of eighty-eight. (In Madagascar most old parents live with one of their children, preferably the eldest son, and like all non-Westerners the Malagasy are shocked by what they see as our callous neglect of the old.) Grandad was physically agile but very deaf. He had lost all his teeth while fighting in the trenches during the First World War and was equipped with exotic dentures made entirely of *tin* – including the palate. If one had met him in the street, one might have mistaken him for a Chinaman; in infancy and old age the Merinas' Asian origin is much accentuated.

The balcony overlooked four smaller and much older thatched dwellings, and a neat clean communal farmyard. Outside two doorways women were husking the supper rice, steadily pounding the grain in ancient stone mortars with three-foot bamboo pestles. Directly below us the younger two of Joseph's three sons – aged thirteen and eleven – were husking together with shorter pestles, their rhythmic movements marvellously co-ordinated, their double-thud blending with the women's single thuds to create fitting background music for a fiery-gold sunset. Meanwhile Joseph's two glossy zebu were being secured in their stockade and thrown a few armfuls of hay. And innumerable hens, ducks, turkeys and their young were being rounded up by small children and shooed into their respective shelters. Under the balcony Joseph's youngest child, a girl of ten, was feeding three turkey hens and their much-loved, cheekily tame chicks. As she draped sacking over the roosts, her father summoned her to be introduced to the *vazaha*.

The strong current of affection running through Malagasy life is especially noticeable in father/child relationships. In many countries, the more procreative the menfolk the less interest they take in the results of that activity; but Madagascar seems to have an astonishing proportion (it looks like ninety-five per cent) of doting fathers. Two specimens were visible from the balcony, each cuddling a baby enchanting enough to melt even my non-baby-centred heart. (If, which Andriamanitra forbid, there were a baby competition analogous to Miss World, Malagasy babies would win it annually.) And this paternal interest does not stop at cuddling; Malagasy fathers are so good at practical child-care that not even the most extreme feminist could fault their role within the family.

The temperature dropped abruptly as that red-gold sunset melted away into darkness. Our host then led us by candlelight through the main bedroom, furnished only with a double bed, to the guest-room. This was both Joseph's office and the eldest son's bed-sitter; a narrow plank-bed occupied one corner near a window, with a low trunk beside it serving as table and wardrobe. An umbrella and a storm-lantern hung on one freshly white-washed wall and the ceiling was of rough-hewn planks.

Having closed the shutters, Joseph went to a small table (his 'desk') and for some unimaginable reason carefully copied into an exercise book our passport details and every word of Samuel's letter. On the table stood a faded snapshot of Mrs Joseph as a plump little girl in startlingly familiar First Holy Communion clothes – no different from those worn in Ireland for the occasion. Her family, unlike most Merina, was Roman Catholic. But Joseph later explained that neither of them goes to church now, preferring to base their religious lives solely on *razana* traditions. Some Malagasy have come to see the abandonment of Christianity as an affirmation of patriotism, which reaction perhaps betrays a mild version of the feeling behind American Born Again-ism and Islamic fundamentalism.

As we unpacked, a singular odour prompted Rachel to whisper, 'Drains!' But alas! it was not drains. It was our supper.

Joseph carried a mountain of soggy rice; his wife followed with a hill of peeled boiled potatoes and two duck eggs. Moments later Joseph was back with the *pièce de résistance*, a huge oval dish of rotten fried fish. Their eyes, fins, tails, bones and entrails were gradually revealed as one pushed aside a glutinous greyish sauce. We were reminded of the day our dog rolled on a long-dead hedgehog.

Rotten fish is a Malagasy delicacy, reserved for Festive Occasions or Honoured Guests, and this pungent compliment could not be discreetly smuggled away in a plastic bag or disposed of otherwise than by ingestion. I was hungry enough – just – to cope. But the sight of her mother filleting and swallowing those stinking chunks made Rachel retch and she insisted in a paranoid way that the potatoes had been cooked with the fish and were tainted. She ate only the eggs, undefiled within their shells. Poor Joseph was disappointed when he returned to collect the dishes.

Soon our host and hostess were back with Pierre, their handsome eldest son aged fifteen and by Merina standards tall. He was studying English and his mother persuaded him to read aloud so that we might correct his pronunciation. As he miserably negotiated a long list of difficult words his siblings giggled in the shadowy background and his parents gazed at him proudly, while Rachel sent him sympathetic glances of adolescent fellow-feeling. He did quite well in his struggle with the crazed illogic of the

English language, once described to me by an Amhara student as 'a crime against humanity'. We may laugh at people with kings called Andriamandisoarivo, Andrianamboatasimarofy, Andriantsimitoviaminandriandehibe – and so on. But the Malagasy can laugh louder at people who think about what they have thought but do not brink what they have brought.

At intervals during the evening barefooted men appeared silently in the doorless doorway, seeking chits from Joseph – the President of the local People's Executive Committee. Apart from a worn rubber date-stamp, this decentralised government office had no official equipment, only a biro and an exercise book from which Joseph carefully tore half or quarter pages, as required.

By 8.30 Mr and Mrs Joseph had shaken hands and gone to bed in the outer room. Our lullaby was the sleepy cheeping of turkey chicks and Joseph's gentle snoring. Lying beside Rachel on Pierre's plank bed, I wondered about the observance of domestic *fady* in such a family. Would the conspicuously tall Pierre be expected to 'buy' his extra inches? The ancestors decreed that a boy taller than his superiors must 'buy' that advantage by presenting a fine *lamba*, or a zebu or cash-gift, to prove that despite his unseemly physical advantage he *feels* correctly submissive. The stability of Malagasy society still largely depends on a genuine respect for superiors. To a remarkable extent, civil order has been maintained throughout most of Madagascar's history by individual family heads rather than by tribal chiefs – not many of whom ever got their law-enforcement act together – or by any centralised authority.

The dawn noises were creaking and jolting zebu-carts, and a mixed poultry chorus, and Joseph sweeping the balcony with a rush broom. Opening the shutters, I saw his old father already pottering about the yard: inspecting the zebu fodder, collecting turkey eggs, still happily involved in the daily routine. Beyond the houses a long line of pure white egrets was flying ritualistically up the river valley, caught in the earliest rays of the sun while the land below was still mist-veiled. Then suddenly it struck me that Grandad, being eighty-eight, was born *before* the French conquest of Madagascar. He was a living link with the Merina monarchy, a Malagasy who had started life as a subject of Queen Ranavalona III and, having spent sixty-four of his years under a colonial power, seemed likely to end it as a citizen of a Marxist-Christian

Republic. I gazed down at him as he paused to converse with a toddler sitting on a doorstep eating a bowl of rice-gruel. If that toddler lived to be eighty-eight, he could boast in the year 2070 of having talked with a subject of the last Merina monarch, deposed in 1896 . . .

'Why have you gone into a coma?' asked Rachel peevishly. 'Where have you put our pens? Why did you add so many of those beastly tablets to *my* water-bottle?' She is never at her best before breakfast.

Soon we were confronting the statutory mound of rice, two hard-boiled eggs and two mugs of hot rice-water. I asked Joseph, 'Your father was born in 1895?' He smiled, 'Yes' – he pointed to a thatched dwelling on the far side of the yard – 'he was born in that house, the year after it was built. We are Hova. We were never slaves, until the French came. But they did some good things, and many of them liked the Malagasy people.'

Pierre appeared then, shyly apologising for having to take a garment from his wardrobe trunk by the bed. When he is eighty-eight, how important will their brief colonial experience seem to the Malagasy? Not very, I suspect. Modern Madagascar is a very French ex-colony, in superficial ways. Yet the European intrusion, both British and French, seems already to have been absorbed and transformed.

Before we left, Joseph showed off his *lavabary*, the cellar below the house, clay-lined and waterproof, where last year's abundant paddy was stored and Pierre was measuring ten kilos into a cotton cloth to be carried to market on his head. He and his mother accompanied us to Manalalondo (our first town since leaving Arivonimamo) and we had covered a few miles when one of the younger boys breathlessly overtook us, clutching two discarded Irish biros – presumed forgotten by Joseph.

Apart from our own equipment, we might, that morning, have been travelling in the reign of Queen Ranavalona III. As we walked along the market-busy wide red track, beneath a wide blue sky, green-flecked grey hills stretched for miles on our left and neatly ditched paddy-fields lay below on our right – some just ploughed, a few newly irrigated and borrowing blue from above. The sun was warm, the breeze cool, the light brilliant, the silence broken only by quiet greetings as friends met and by the groaning of traders' wagons – brightly painted, with arched covers, like gypsy caravans. Most of the gaily dressed women were carrying loads on their heads and, if alone, babies on their backs suspended in a *lamba*. If father was present he usually carried the baby.

Manalalondo has seen better days; it is a memorial to the social upheaval caused by colonisation. Although a small town, it was prosperous in times past. The main street boasts an impressive double triumphal stone archway, vaguely Moorish and sprouting tufts of pale gold grass. Several fine houses, now decaying, still belong to *Andriana* or *Hova* (aristocratic or gentry) families who deserted the countryside after the conquest. The abolition of slave labour, and the introduction of taxes, made a career in the administration, or in the new expanding business world, more attractive than the life of a rural landowner obliged to pay both wages and taxes. Most such houses have a massive family tomb nearby, which is one reason for their not being sold. It is hard to obtain the necessary consent of the original owner's many and perhaps widely scattered descendants, who by now may have divergent views about the ancestral property. Yet few mansions stand empty; *Andevo* (peasant) families occupy them and we were assured that in the new Marxist-Christian state such tenants no longer have to pay rent. The *Andevo* Merina are often a shade or two darker than their 'betters', with suspiciously crinkly hair. African slaves were not unknown in this region, and many women and children were captured and enslaved after battles against the Bara, Antandroy and Mahafaly – the main tribes of southern Madagascar.

Manalalondo's shops – some quite large – were either closed or almost empty. In the market-place the few occupied stalls sold little more than rice, onions, eggs, rotten sardines and unidentifiable wizened objects – probably traditional 'cures' and *ombiasas*' charms. Here, as in other areas during the weeks ahead, we got the impression that the rural Malagasy have reverted to a subsistence economy. Families depend on their own and their neighbours' produce, often exchanged rather than bought, and the flow of imported foodstuffs and consumer goods, stocked in colonial and immediately post-colonial days, has dried up.

On the edge of the town we sought refreshment in a thatched 'café' so tiny that our heads touched the ceiling and we had to leave our rucksacks outside. The young couple crouching in the smoky interior, and their four children, looked wretchedly unhealthy and seemed half-afraid of us. Husband sat slumped in one corner, his eyes dull, holding a whimpering filthy baby. We shared his unsteady bench while wife cooked rice-buns on a grass-burning mud stove. Suddenly he was overcome by a paroxysm of coughing and the baby howled in sympathy; he handed it to a toddler and lay on the ground at our feet. In the firelight I could see sweat glistening on his forehead before he drew his *lamba* over his head.

Wife had ladled the rice-bun batter from a rusty tin at Rachel's feet and was cooking two dozen at a time in a patty-tin used as a frying-pan. The eldest child, a girl aged perhaps six, continuously stuffed twists of grass, taken from a stack outside the door, into the flames. An even smaller boy was boiling coffee on a minute wood-fire in another mud-stove. Every few moments wife deftly turned the buns with a special wooden implement, adding a drop of grease to each 'cup' at each turn. We admired the skill with which she overcame all the limitations of her kitchen; the twenty-four buns were uniformly brown and crisp when she slid them onto a wooden tray. But hot rice-buns are only marginally less revolting than cold rice-buns. And the coffee was not coffee, though coffee coloured. If you use grass as fuel, you must know which berries serve best as a coffee-substitute.

Not far beyond Manalalondo a young couple, shy but smiling, caught up with us. When we had convinced them that we were *not* going to Ambatolampy they invited us to follow them on a cross-country short-cut and the next two hours had an endurance-test flavour. Our guides were a handsome pair, small and light-skinned, with compact muscular graceful bodies. Whether going uphill or down their pace never varied and we enviously compared their loads with our own. Husband's was a zinc bucket containing a litre tin of kerosene and an earthenware jar of honey; wife's was a head-basket containing two dozen oranges, one packet of biscuits and a small bar of soap.

We crossed three high grassy ridges, separating broad valleys. On the more precipitous slopes the narrow path was treacherous, its outside edge blurred by bushy red grass; a misjudgement here would have meant falling hundreds of feet. On the valley floors mini-chasms were spanned by dicey little bridges of thin sticks supporting loose sods of earth. From a distance we saw an isolated hamlet, on a hillside far above, and hoped for a brief pause. But our friends pressed relentlessly on, calling cheerful greetings to the inhabitants as we passed between hedges of tall sword-cactus. We glimpsed a six-inch orange and green chameleon while scrambling up long steep slabs of smooth rock, hot to the touch beneath the noon sun. Soon after we met a two-foot brown and green snake and the young woman shrieked fearfully, though no Malagasy snake is dangerous. At the base of another rock-slab mountain Rachel and I admitted defeat and let our guides, who were so evidently in a hurry, go ahead without us. We collapsed under a bush, our arms glistening with crystallised salt. Even in mid-winter, and even in the mountains, it is hot at noon around the Tropic of Capricorn.

Five minutes later our friends were back, looking worried. No words were needed to explain the situation. They smiled at us, gently, and when we gestured to them to keep going they sat down instead and insisted on our eating two of their precious oranges. Again the young man offered to carry my rucksack. When I shook my head he picked it up, testingly, and registered comic dismay. On the next stage our pace was greatly reduced.

The granite summit of that mountain overlooked a deep valley holding an ochre track, a green river, many paddy-fields and our friends' home. Beyond their village the track was a continuation of the motor-road we had followed out of Manalalondo, without then realising that it was meant to cater for the internal combustion engine. Had we not taken photographs, I would now doubt my recollection of this highway. Where it had been bisected by years of flood-damage, never repaired, the two-foot-wide central rut was four feet deep and accompanied by numerous relatively minor side-ruts. When it abruptly disappeared on a sloping ridge, amidst evergreen bushes and hummocks of brown grass, we circled the area in search of any kind of path – and then, incredibly, found smudged tyre marks between bushes and hummocks. An hour later, in the next populated valley, we were fascinated to see rafts of vegetation, some twenty yards by thirty, floating on a jade-green river – anchored with stones in mid-stream. These are artificial paddy-fields, created where there is an urgent need for extra land.

During the afternoon we swam in a tingling cold pool, between high grassy mountains, watched by a pair of ceaselessly circling buzzards. An hour later we were back in fertile country – too fertile, for the sun was declining and we could see no possible campsite amidst the paddy-fields. Snatches of song came from substantial houses above the track, groups of men were sitting around playing the Malagasy version of violins or guitars, children's laughter sounded loud in the windless evening air. Not everyone greeted us and some chatting neighbours fell silent as we approached. But their reaction was understandable; few *vazaha* pass that way.

At last we spotted a low scrub ridge; the sun set as we pushed upwards through dense bushes, seeking tent-space. Suddenly an enormous ancient tomb loomed out of the dusk. Obviously it was no longer in use; equally obviously it housed *razana* of some consequence and *vazaha* camping in its vicinity might not be amiably regarded. We hastened on and five minutes later – it was then dark – reached a level site carpeted with some powerfully scented herb. But the *razana* were still too close for comfort; a zebu-cart on a nearby track prompted us to switch off our torches and (feeling more than slightly foolish) lie doggo by our half-erected tent. 'Better to be undignified than got at by some *ombiasa*,' remarked Rachel as we stood up. For supper we enjoyed Nomad Soup, poured onto surplus breakfast-rice smuggled away in our plastic bag.

A new two-(wo)man tent for the Malagasy expedition had cost only £15 but was alleged to be waterproof. However, within an hour of the rain's beginning at 9.30 p.m. pools were accumulating all around us. It was heavy rain, and steady. Rachel slept until midnight, muttering and squirming miserably as the chilly lake deepened. After that neither of us slept. My companion expatiated on the folly of parsimony at great length and with bitter eloquence. I curled myself into a soggy shivering ball and listened humbly, making occasional penitent noises. Wistfully I remembered the good old days when Rachel uncritically accepted the vicissitudes of travelling with a not very practical Mamma.

Towards dawn the rain dwindled and soon there was silence, apart from nasty squelchy noises caused by our slightest movement. As I unzipped the entrance the herbal aroma, intensified by the rain, acted on us (or at least on me) like a strong stimulant. Crawling out, I saw that we were in a slight hollow on the ridge-top, which restricted our view of the immediately surrounding terrain and emphasised the immensity of the sky. I stared in wonder at the still starry purple-violet zenith – a tinge belonging to neither night nor day. The stars vanished as I gazed. To the east lay distant chunks of mountain darkly colourless below a magnolia glow. To the west drifted royal-blue banks of broken retreating rain-cloud. I held my breath, waiting. Then the sun was up, behind the chunky mountain, and purple-violet changed to powder-blue – magnolia to the palest green – royal-blue to gold and crimson.

That was, I think, the most magical dawn I have ever attended. But when I remarked to Rachel that one wet night was a small price to pay for such an experience she merely grunted and went on wringing out her flea-bag. Perhaps at fourteen one's aesthetic sensibilities are still latent.

We set off at 6.15, our loads perceptibly heavier, sucking glucose tablets for breakfast. Pathlets on which we met nobody led us for four hours through pine-woods and eucalyptus plantations, around bare red hills, over grassy ridges and across a wide cultivated bowl-valley where the soil seemed poor and the few inhabitants were timid and illiterate. Their illiteracy emerged when we produced Samuel's letter as a preliminary, we hoped, to acquiring food by purchase or barter. It did not work in this area, serving only to increase the local fear of tough-looking *vazaha*.

While we rested in a tamarind glade, lying on feathery green-gold grass, the sun undid the rain's damage. Its power astonished us; within thirty minutes even our thick flea-bags were dry. Here I heated our last Nomad Soup for Rachel and refuelled myself with our last fistful of peanuts.

'How are we getting out of this valley?' asked Rachel as we repacked.

Through binoculars I studied the apparently pathless southern mountain-wall. 'There must be a way over,' I decided, 'even though we can't see it yet.'

'Why must there?' demanded Rachel. 'Who in their right mind would ever walk over *that*?'

'People have to go from here to Antsirabe,' I pointed out in my parent-being-patient-with-silly-child voice.

'I'll bet we passed the Antsirabe track ages ago,' said Rachel, 'at the junction where you *would* take this dotty little path. Maybe you thought your day would be spoiled by meeting one vehicle if we took the right track.'

I ignored this deserved taunt and persisted, 'I'm sure there's a path – we'll ask.'

'Ask who?' enquired Rachel, sweeping the deserted valley floor with her binoculars. 'Even if we do meet someone we won't be able to understand them.'

Luckily this prediction was wrong. At the next hamlet a group of laughing women retreated into their hovels as we approached, then cautiously peered out when they heard me rather desperately shouting – 'Antsirabe?'

'Ambatolampy!' yelled the eldest woman, pointing to the north-east. (Behind me Rachel muttered a word that was not in her vocabulary before she went away to school; is it for this that we court destitution to pay school-fees?)

Again I shouted 'Antsirabe?' The women conferred, then summoned a youth from within. He reluctantly advanced a few yards, pointing to a steep bushy slope rising above the hamlet. 'Antsirabe!' he affirmed, repeating the word while gesturing towards a distant cleft in the mountain wall directly behind the steep slope. There was no mistaking his meaning; to get to Antsirabe we had to climb that escarpment.

We found no path until reaching the top. Evidently those who use this route (perhaps not many, as Rachel suggested) have their own favourite ways up and down. One would not have chosen to tackle such a gradient on an almost empty stomach after a sleepless night and we often rested, collapsing where there was some boulder or ledge on which to lean our loads. At each halt the view was more spectacular, encompassing all of Imerina – and much more besides.

From the top we could see miles of undulating golden savannah unbroken by bush or tree or boulder, with mountain summits peering over the distant edges to remind us that we were, by Malagasy standards, at a great height. The faint path divided occasionally and sometimes an even fainter branch path seemed to be going more directly south. But we were following a trail of 'ecological litter', as Rachel called it – white wads of sugar-cane fibre spat out by villagers returning from market. At the far side of the plateau, after two hours fast walking, we might well have gone astray but for these clues. Here pathlets proliferated bewilderingly amidst hills, glens, spurs and ridges, some thinly forested, some entangled in thorny scrub, a few supporting potato-patches.

In the deepest glen we filled our water-bottles and bathed our feet in a rapid sparkling mountain stream that might have been Irish. Before replacing her boots, Rachel wordlessly extended her feet towards me. I looked – and recoiled. Uncooked steaks is the obvious simile. None of our plasters would cover the affected areas.

'Why didn't you say something earlier?' I demanded, as though the whole thing were somehow her fault.

'Well,' said Rachel, 'you can't piggy-back me any more and we couldn't just sit starving on a mountain.'

I gave minimal medical aid while repenting my earlier bitchy thoughts about the feebleness of modern youth. You have to be tough to carry a load for twenty miles on flayed feet. Luckily we did not then know how many more miles lay ahead.

Beyond that glen, several isolated houses and tombs stood out against the sky on far-away ridges. Fat-tailed sheep, small and dark brown, nibbled unattended beside the path in the shade of ancient, tall, unfamiliar trees: a sad fragment of Madagascar's primary forest. Soon we had to cross a tricky, unexpected marsh and then came an anxious fifteen minutes; our fibre-trail disappeared, leaving us to the mercy of our compass on pathless green grassland – the only green pasture we saw in the Ankaratra. Here zebu were being tended by two small boys wrapped in *lambas* and holding sticks twice as long as themselves. They fled from us, abandoning their herd, and hid in bushes.

Sullen clouds filled the sky as we climbed to a broken plateau covered with brown scrub, like winter heather. Our spirits rose when we saw a café-shack in the distance – but it was deserted. Then, without warning, we were on a wide cart-track, deeply eroded yet unmistakably going somewhere of importance. It began (or ended) just like that, in the middle of nowhere, for no particular reason. 'This is the maddest country I've ever been in,' reflected Rachel, intending no pun.

Moments later we met three men returning, as we later realised, from Ambohibary market. One carried a new iron blade for his plough, another carried a can of kerosene, the third carried nothing but was wearing a pair of brand-new blue jeans. Rachel deduced optimistically, 'If they sell jeans it's a big town, with lots of food!'

Soon the track could be seen for miles ahead, dropping into a broad valley before climbing high on the flanks of a long, multi-spurred mountain. The whole wide expanse of countryside beneath us was thronged, as people turned off the main track to go to their hamlets in the fertile valleys to east and west. After walking in solitude for ten hours, this bustle of humanity seemed quite urban.

We developed a guessing-game: identifying various improbable head-burdens from a distance. An empty tar-barrel – a pair of new shoes – a wooden bench – a ten-foot roll of raffia matting – a tower of dried tobacco leaves – a Scotch whisky crate full of vociferous fluffy ducklings – a basket of long French loaves. (Our mouths watered as we caught a whiff of that fresh crustiness.) Only cocks and hens were not carried on heads but tucked under arms. We were moved by the number of poultry-owners who were talking soothingly to their burdens, sometimes stroking them gently with one finger. Even more moving was the fact that almost everyone stopped to shake hands with us and murmur a greeting. They were all chewing cane and soon our hands were as sticky as theirs. No one tried to question us about our identity or destination; those greetings were brief, gracious – and unforgettably heart-warming. Apart from the Tibetans, I have never travelled among a people as endearing as the Malagasy.

While ascending the multi-spurred mountain we met many descending zebu-carts, which frequently left the track because the ground on either side was less difficult to negotiate; they were covering not more than half-a-mile per hour. The introduction of the wheel to this region was perhaps a mistake. Why, since horses flourish around Tana, has equine transport never become popular in Imerina? A similar returning-from-market scene in Ethiopia's highlands would have contained many speedy horsemen and nimble pack-mules.

At 4.30 Rachel rejoiced to see Ambohibary in the centre of a wide flat paddy-plain far below. But mountain distances are deceptive and I had my doubts about reaching it before dark. Three linked wooded hills still stood between us and the plain and our progress was being slowed by all those pauses to exchange courtesies. Yet the traffic also helped; we took several short-cuts that would have seemed imprudent, or impossible, had we not seen people using them. On such severe slopes, tiny children were carried up or down. Otherwise they walked sturdily for miles, hand-in-hand with a parent or older sibling. It was an odd sensation, being the only people – among all those hundreds – going *towards* Ambohibary.

As the foot-traffic thinned the slower cart-traffic increased and our imaginations boggled wildly at the thought of zebu-carts crossing these mountains by night. The town still looked very far away when sunset came as we were descending the third hill. In the twilight we passed an elaborate tomb on the edge of a pine-wood; its porch-like façade offered shelter from the probable nocturnal downpour but Rachel declined to share accommodation with corpses. I did not argue, her feet being my only reason for proposing this risky intimacy with the local *razana*. Here we were briefly able to follow the glimmer of wheel-marks, where the earth had been compacted and polished. Then total darkness came. Not a star shone through the heavy clouds and as all our batteries had been victims of the tent-flood we were reduced to cart-speed by the deep ruts and high tufts of grass. The blackness of the plain puzzled us; even from a non-electrified town one expects some faint glow after dark.

Without warning we were in a hamlet, astray amidst houses and trees occupying various shelves on the hillside. As we stumbled between the dwellings, none showing a light, one door opened and the oil-wicks flickering within seemed brilliant. Three men emerged, laughing loudly, and we decided to show them Samuel's letter. Unfortunately they were drunk; not very, but too much so for us to communicate in sign-language in the dark – not a particularly feasible scheme, when you come to think of it, even had they been sober. My query – 'Ambohibary?' – loosed a torrent of Malagasy from all three simultaneously. Then an elderly man appeared at the open door, shouted, 'Route Nationale No. 7!' and pointed downhill. This was not helpful; we already knew our way led downhill. As the door was closed, and firmly bolted, the trio surrounded us, exhaling fumes reminiscent of the cheapest grade of Russian petrol. Gripping our arms, they led us down a twisting path apparently criss-crossed by tree-roots, all the while continuing to address us animatedly in Malagasy. On level ground they triumphantly chorused, 'Route Nationale No. 7!' Then they groped for our hands, regarding impenetrable darkness as no excuse for a breach of etiquette, and having completed their farewells left us to make what we could of Route Nationale No. 7.

'This *can't* be a national highway!' said Rachel ten minutes later. Already she had tripped over three chunks of rock and I had turned an ankle in a cavernous pot-hole. We continued with linked arms, for mutual protection.

The clouds parted slightly at an opportune moment. We were only ten yards from a rubble-filled chasm that had to be climbed into and out of – an exercise for which meagre starlight provided unsatisfactory illumination. By this time we had covered at least twenty-eight miles and I suggested sleeping by the wayside. Rachel however was determined to make Ambohibary, and food, though she admitted to needing a rest. I pointed out what seemed a suitable boulder-seat but unhappily it proved to be a prickly-pear cactus. For some reason (unclear in retrospect) this provoked us both to uncontrollable mirth and we sat in the middle of the road and laughed until our ribs ached as much as our shoulders.

The cloud gap closed as we continued and instinctively one listens more keenly when unable to see; otherwise we might have ended up in the wide, fast irrigation channel that soon after crossed the road. It took time to find a bridge of wobbly planks in an adjacent field.

Fifteen minutes later we became aware of tall houses on both sides of the track – Ambohibary, we presumed. It was only 8.15, yet there was no sound, no light, no movement. A Merina proverb advises: 'Do not arrive in a village after dark for you will be greeted only by the dogs.' Here not even dogs were registering our presence; the place might have been abandoned a century ago. 'Let's keep going,' said Rachel, 'this is just a suburb.' As she spoke five men materialised nearby, their leader's flaming resin-torch swaying like the mast-light of a ship on a stormy sea. They were much drunker than our three guides. When I asked, 'Hotely?' the leader belched (more Russian petrol fumes) and the others began to giggle and sing. 'We'd better push off,' said Rachel impatiently, 'before they all feel they must shake hands.' But she was at the end of a tether that for hours had been stretched to breaking point. Although the spirit was still willing the flesh had to be supported by me as she hobbled the next few hundred yards – which took us back into open countryside. We had merely passed through a village.

'That's it,' I said. 'Here we sleep, come hell or high water – probably high water. Even if we could get to Ambowhatsit, it's too late to find food.'

Starlight revealed a roadside trader's stall: four crooked branches supporting a sheet of corrugated iron. Beneath it I cleared a space of loose stones and spread our flea-bags on the bumpy iron-hard ground. Less than five minutes later Rachel was asleep.

I was too hungry to sleep; the lack of food for sale en route had taken me unawares. I reproved myself for being so illogically inhibited by the peasants' refusal to *sell* food to travellers – I often enough condemn the transfer to other societies of the standards and principles of our own. On the previous evening we should have sought hospitality instead of camping; we could then have eaten our fill and started the day with substantial breakfasts. Again, at the foot of the escarpment we should have explained that we were very hungry; no Malagasy peasant would have to go without to feed us. Yet my inhibition was not entirely based on a reluctance to cadge. Another factor was the extent to which, in rural Madagascar, daily life has a fixed and formal pattern governed by *fady*. It is a friendly and generous but not a relaxed or spontaneous society. And the complexity of local inhibitions about *vazaha* reinforces the *vazaha*'s own inhibitions.

To outsiders the Malagasy submission to ancestral decrees can seem absurd – even neurotic – yet that afternoon we had been impressed by some of its effects. If an old man is heavily laden, any young man catching up with him insists on carrying his load for some distance, though they may be total strangers. And young people ask permission before overtaking their elders on the track. Is it a measure of the uncouthness of the modern West that we marvelled so to observe these courtesies?

At that point in my ruminations a dog approached, sniffed curiously around us, then took fright at the *vazaha* smells (as anyone might have done, that evening) and ran away yelping shrilly. Otherwise nothing moved until 4.50 a.m. when two men passed, chuckling and chatting. They did not notice us. It rained lightly for a few hours: harmless straight-down rain – we were only dampened around the edges. I might have slept eventually but for the decibels of a corpse-turning party obviously intended to summon ancestors from Outer Space. This ceremony began at 8.45 p.m. and was still going loud and strong when we left the area. Luckily Malagasy music is pleasing to the ear, if a trifle monotonous.

An overcast dawn showed Ambohibary scarcely a mile away. Most windows were still tightly shuttered as we hastened towards the town centre, through lanes piled with morning-after-market refuse. Malagasy litter is ninety per cent edible and scores of truculent ganders, pompous geese and bumptious goslings were on garbage-disposal duty. Never have I seen so many geese in one place; at that hour they seemed to own the town.

A few café-stalls were open in the market-square and we devoured so many rice-buns so quickly that the attractive young woman who was serving us called her mother to watch. As we ate, other stall-holders began to light their charcoal-stoves and display rice-buns – to be bought in bulk and taken home for breakfast, a habit perhaps picked up from the French.

A short-cut over a eucalyptus-planted hill took us to the real Route Nationale No. 7 and we realised why Ambohibary's market is so important. A link road that once was tarred is still capable of taking truck traffic to Ambohibary from Route Nationale No. 7, the Tana–Antsirabe highway. Our bizarre 'road' of the previous evening is a continuation of this link, going to Arivonimamo via Manalalondo. But it is not, as we had seen, conducive to a free flow of goods throughout the Ankaratra.

The junction is marked – and marred – by a pretentious new 'bar'-stall of pale varnished wood, designed to attract passing motorists. Sadly, the beer bottles lining its shelves were all empty. Here we relished a second breakfast of slightly sweet crisp fritters, fresh from the pan, while a plump gentle dog sat hopefully at our feet – his girth proving that his hopes were often fulfilled – and minuscule ducklings splashed ecstatically in a nearby puddle. Opposite the bar a barely legible kilometre-stone said 'Antsirabe 33' and we decided to walk on but take the first available bus out of consideration for Rachel's feet.

During the next four hours withdrawal symptoms afflicted me: inevitable on exchanging mountain-tracks for a motor-road, however light the traffic. I could not agree with our Air Mad guidebook – 'The Tananarive–Antsirabe road is bituminized, and the trip very nice.' But that was sheer prejudice; by normal standards the trip *is* 'very nice', as Route Nationale No. 7 undulates through miles of mature pine-plantations or densely populated farmland. Our guidebook explains:

> 'From the economic point of view, it must be stated that Antsirabe is at the centre of a rich agricultural region which produces: rice, beans, sweet potatoes, corn (maize), taro, soja, potatoes: all vegetables grow wonderfully. The vine-yards give 350,000 to 400,000 litres of wine. Let us mention that the harvest of wheat has begun. Also to be found is a very wide range of european and exotic flowers. For stock farming let us mention: cattle, sheep, numerous pigs, also poultry and horses.'

In the woods government foresters were manhandling trimmed trunks onto decrepit trucks. Private enterprise was also active. Youthful entrepreneurs had gathered small branches into neatly bound bundles for sale to passing city-dwellers. And larger branches were being loaded into motor-vans by Antsirabe fuel-merchants.

In the 'rich agricultural region' traditional Merina dwellings were interspersed with colonial bungalows or dainty two-storey residences half-smothered in flowering shrubs. Yet even along this motor-road there were symptoms of economic collapse: rows of recently abandoned wayside market-stalls (the local equivalent of a supermarket), and derelict petrol-pump stations, and two colonial restaurants now used as vegetable depots.

Light showers refreshed us during the early forenoon but by midday the sky had cleared, the heat was brutal and Rachel was limping very badly. We sat in a wooded glen, overlooking a narrow river in a wide river-bed, and waited for a bus. From afar we could see a ludicrously sophisticated skyscraper flour-mill, to cater for the 'harvest of wheat'; we later learned that it is having severe (though hardly surprising) problems to do with maintenance and fuelling.

During the morning three buses had passed us, all preposterously overloaded. The fourth was no less so but two men gave up their seats to the *vazaha*. Large baskets of vegetables and small children standing on laps restricted our view of the approach to Antsirabe. Most of our fellow-passengers were well-groomed, wearing clean, brightly coloured *lambas* over neat shirts and pants or blouses and skirts. Their appearance did not match the state of their conveyance; I have never travelled in a more beat-up vehicle. As there was no door remaining, and not much floor, the dust-intake from the 'bituminized' road was considerable and both conductor and driver wore scarves around their noses and mouths. The driver sat crouched and tense and frowning, using accelerator and brake equally violently. Every few hundred yards he swerved acrobatically to avoid either straying livestock or a mini-crater. Mere pot-holes he took as they came and each jolt jarred us breathless. At the end of that ten-mile journey Rachel mused, 'What are we going to feel like when we've covered a few thousand miles in Malagasy vehicles?'

5

Antsirabe Insights

There are many more *pousses-pousses* than motor-vehicles on the tree-lined streets of Antsirabe. What there is of motor-traffic – ancient French cars, trucks and buses – moves either very slowly, because of some lingering disease, or very quickly because lack of competition discourages caution. The *pousses-pousses* men are ragged, dirty, cheerful and of all age groups. They are most numerous during winter; when the rice-planting season starts many return to their villages. At first the more enterprising shouted questioningly to the passing *vazaha*, but that was a legitimate advertising of their function and they never pestered. After a day or so, we being the only visible tourists then in Antsirabe, they knew our pedestrian habits and either grinned broadly as we passed or made teasing remarks while rubbing their calf-muscles in simulated agony. They probably also knew where we were coming from and going to, so small and intimate is this odd little city.

The first *pousses-pousses* passenger we saw in Antsirabe was symbolic – a frail old Frenchwoman with a shrunken, ivory, smiling face, wearing a black scarf over white curls. She sat well back in her rickshaw, clutching three long French loaves and seeming very much a footnote to history. Our Air Mad guidebook explains – 'The French Government has subsidized a Home for his aged nationals who are without resources, which Home accepts paying boarders.' It adds, 'The climate is quite healthy so that numerous Europeans who did not have the possibility of going home, or who have sentimental ties in the country have settled there. It is environed with pine-trees, eucalyptus and mimosas, whence a vivifying air. Antsirabe is also a touristic town with beautiful avenues lined with European and Tropical trees, with nice villas amidst vegetation and flowers. It is clean and coquettish. Let us mention the 45 hectares of East Park with its ponds, its lawns and its courses for riders. The arboretum and its kilometres of alleys snaking amidst a rich and varied essence. The nice 9 Hole Golf Course is a delightful size, etc.'

Antsirabe is entirely a *vazaha* creation and remains the most European Malagasy town, both in appearance and atmosphere. A village was founded on the site in 1869 by two Norwegian missionaries, Rosaas and Borgen, whose compatriots still run a large, red-brown fortress-like hospital. In 1923 the Governor-General, Hubert Garbit, decided to develop the little town that had by then grown up around the hospital and the H&C mineral springs. A rest-resort was needed for the colonists, especially those posted on the coast. Where better than Antsirabe, set in the coldest accessible area of Madagascar? In winter, as we soon discovered, the night temperature regularly drops to freezing point or below; and even in summer the heat is never intolerable or the rain incessant.

Garbit declared an open-season for town-planners and architects – some of the latter, it would appear, amateurs. Space is no problem and from the commercial centre radiate wide, long boulevards, all with a suburban character so that you may wander for an hour in search of the city's hub and never realise that you are all the time criss-crossing it. Much architectural miscegenation took place along those boulevards and the shorter avenues leading off them. There are hints of Scandinavia, Italy, Switzerland, England and Imerina mingled with the Frenchness of the detached villas – none very large, some quite petite. Tall trees shade the gardens and flowering shrubs scent them. Creepers drape the walls and poultry sometimes scrabble in what once were ornamental beds or fertilise what once were formal lawns. Tin roofs and iron gates are rusting, doors need repainting and windows re-glazing. A vast rectangular army barracks – by far the ugliest building in Antsirabe – is more obviously occupied by hens than by soldiers. (Before Independence, French troops were permanently stationed there.) The many large shops are, as in Tana, almost empty. The grandiose semi-circular cream-washed General Post Office is now little used, though regularly opened. The hotels depend on a thin trickle of Malagasy businessmen and government officials. Here Madagascar's economic collapse seems much more obvious than in Tana; the Merina capital existed long before the French came and has its own soul. In comparison Antsirabe feels slightly forlorn – a place created to cater for a way of life that no longer exists. One is aware of unfulfilled potential, of dreams withering. Yet by Malagasy standards this is a big city (population about 80,000) and heavily industrialised, with a brewery, a cotton-mill, a tobacco factory, a fruit-juice and cider factory – and now a gigantic new flour-mill. It is also the preferred town of the Merina élite, who since Independence have moved from Tana in considerable numbers. Whether willing to admit it or not, the *Andriana* and *Hova* feel that their capital has lost tone since the French left and the 'coastal people' began to participate as equals in the government of the country. (The 'coastal people' is a wildly misleading euphemism for non-Merina. Imerina occupies a small area of Madagascar and millions of non-Merina have never laid eyes on the coast. The 'highland people' is a less misleading phrase often used nowadays to describe both the Merina and the Betsileo, who occupy the mountain plateau just south of Antsirabe and have much in common with the Merina.)

Nature has combined with man to give Antsirabe its European flavour. The immediate surroundings are pleasing but undramatic. An uneven fringe of blue mountains – average height 7,500 ft – encircles the plain. Low hills rise nearby, a few still pine-green, most deforested within the past decade and showing sad mutilated pale brown flanks. The plain is exuberantly fertile – both pasture and paddy-fields – and the many large nearby villages seem relatively prosperous even now, when the city itself is in decay. This region has always produced a surplus of food, some of which goes to the east coast via Tana.

In Antsirabe we fell among English-speakers. Our host and hostess both belonged to multi-lingual families: several of their siblings had studied in France, Germany and Britain. They were nonetheless proudly Merina and staying with them helped us to understand why 160 years of close contact with European culture failed to dilute the island's essential 'Malagasy-ness'.

We learned much during that week. When we remarked on the Independence memorial that dominates the main boulevard – a stela listing the eighteen main tribes of Madagascar – one of our new friends observed that although the Malagasy do use the word 'tribes' it gives *vazaha* a wrong impression. In his view this word suggests wider differences of ethnic origin, language and custom than exist in Madagascar. He pointed out that apart from a small Kishwahili-speaking community of Comorians (immigrants of Afro-Shirazi stock from the Comoro Islands), all the Malagasy speak mutually intelligible dialects of Malagasy and share a unique common culture. The many regional variations in custom are superficial, based mainly on contrasting natural environments and past political divisions. They are not, he insisted, marked enough to be properly described as *tribal* differences. I did not presume to argue; the Malagasy are sensitive on this issue, having learned the hard way that internal dissension invites *vazaha* intervention. They are well aware that at present both Moscow and Washington would welcome any excuse for directly influencing political developments within Madagascar. Nevertheless, as we travelled further and noticed the radical physical differences between the 'highland people' and the 'coastal people', we decided that the use of 'tribes' – however politically undesirable – makes ethnographic sense.

Our Antsirabe experiences also taught us that among the educated Malagasy – even those too young to remember colonial times – there is a persisting love–hate relationship with France. At first this seemed to me not unlike the ambivalent emotions aroused in many Irish people by their ex-rulers. But I soon realised my mistake. The French ruled Madagascar for only sixty-four years and the Franco–Malagasy relationship is far less tangled, even among the Merina, than the Anglo–Irish relationship. The Malagasy are not at all confused about their identity (not being white must help) and I could detect no trace of that crippling blend of deep-rooted inferiority feelings and ingrained resentment which handicaps so many Irish in their political and personal dealings with the English.

Only occasionally does the *vazaha* hear anyone explicitly condemning President Ratsiraka's régime, but one afternoon we met two outspoken critics in Antsirabe's most astonishing edifice. This hotel's name escapes me; the relevant pages of my diary came to a sticky end, in circumstances to be described later. By Malagasy standards it is colossal; Nigel Heseltine thought it resembled 'a late 19th-century Swiss mountain hotel, with huge gables and steep-pitched roofing'. It overlooks the 'Centre National de Crenotherapie et de Thermoclimatisme' (spa) and is vastly surrounded by the ghost of an ornamental garden. It is a *tour de force* of the woodcarver's art, with doors, shutters, balconies, banisters, cupboards and even walls of a richly grained, richly hued hardwood (name also forgotten) found only in the rain-forests of Madagascar. The ceilings are high, the corridors long, the staircases wide, the verandahs deep – and, when we were there, the many bedrooms were all unoccupied. So was the bar, apart from ourselves and two middle-aged Merina gentlemen – residents of Antsirabe, we gathered, though we never learned their names, nor they ours.

No doubt this mutual anonymity encouraged them to speak freely, deploring the fact that a misguided idealism, an impractical longing for a *truly* independent Madagascar liberated from all French influences, had induced certain politicians to upset the Franco-Malagasy applecart so carefully set rolling in 1960. They differed about whether the Russians had actually created this situation or merely been quick to exploit it. Certainly disengagement from the Western bloc had been vigorously encouraged. The Russians had promised generous 'altruistic' support, like the awarding of hundreds of Moscow University scholarships to Malagasy students every year and the sending of hundreds of Russian teachers to Madagascar. But the country would of course be left free to evolve in its own way – backwards, if it liked, to those happy days before English missionaries and French colonists messed everything up. Yet somehow it soon became necessary to spend astronomical sums on Russian fighter-planes and other sophisticated weaponry not ideally suited to a people who cannot even keep the sewage flowing. Then suddenly the notion of 'Christian Marxism' hove in sight and the Russians were left wondering if Madagascar had been worth the effort.

By then the modest prosperity of the immediate post-Independence period had evaporated. Industry – what little there was of it – lay at death's door, deprived of raw materials for lack of a normal export-import trade. For lack of maintenance the motor-roads – never great – had become a joke. The postal and telephone services had become a nightmare. The medical and educational services had become a tragedy. Black-marketeering was rampant. Either corruption or laziness, or both, had emasculated every government department. Politicians were despised and police feared. Agriculture was neglected or mismanaged. The embryonic tourist industry had aborted – because of official apathy, and rates of exchange on the Soviet model, and the absence (apart from Air Mad) of anything *vazaha* would recognise as a transport system. The movement of goods and people had become a major gamble. Acute shortages of petrol, tyres and spare parts, added to the state of the roads, meant that no one could guarantee when – if ever – a given journey would begin or end. Listening to these moans, we wondered how much our friends were exaggerating. Soon we were to discover that concerning transport they had understated the case.

We were offered, and accepted, another orange-juice: fizzy but genuine, made in Antsirabe. Madagascar is the only country I know where most nicely-brought-up people do not drink alcohol because they do not want to. Of course even if they did want to they could not legally obtain foreign drinks, yet even in households well supplied with duty-free liquor the bottles seem to be valued more for their decorative than for their stimulating properties. 'Having a drink' is just not it seems part of the middle-class way of life. Antsirabe beer, tolerable though expensive, is sometimes available in the bigger restaurants and hotels in the bigger towns; but there are no pub-substitutes, no small bars or cafés where you can drop in for a casual snifter with the locals. Wine is produced around Antsirabe and Fianarantsoa and is rumoured to be drinkable. We were never able to confirm that rumour; the liquid sold to us in wine-bottles was superlatively undrinkable. In some areas – particularly in the south and along the east coast – villagers make their own booze. But that painful story comes in a later chapter.

The two white-coated young bar-tenders (why two?) had been standing on chairs as we talked, doing things with wires in a hole in the wall. The sudden result was a blast of rock-music. They looked towards us, grinning triumphantly. They had done their bit to encourage the tourist trade. Our plump friend eyed me doubtfully. 'You like it?' he asked. 'Not really,' I admitted. 'But say nothing, they worked so hard to make it happen.'

I sympathised with our companions' shame about the present state of their country. They had listed Madagascar's shortcomings almost as an act of expiation. Again I sensed the mature quality of Malagasy patriotism; it is a sincere, dignified love of the homeland, as distinct from the ersatz, frenetic nationalism of so many young countries. These two, I suspected, had served Madagascar abroad; one of them spoke English with a faint American accent. Yet they were not condemning the mass of their countrymen from the detached, superior viewpoint of Westernised Third Worlders. Like our friend at Tana zoo, they gave an impression of somehow associating themselves with all that had gone wrong. And they had stressed the mistakes, rather than the wickedness, of the politicians responsible.

I suggested, tentatively, 'So European-style democracy has failed yet again in an ex-colony?' When no one contradicted me I decided to be bold and ask the obvious question – 'Would it have been better if the Merina could have kept more of the power, as Galliéni planned?'

'It might have been better, but it was not possible,' said our plump friend drily. 'The coastal people resented us, *because* it would have been better.'

His companion quickly contradicted him. 'No, they were *afraid* of us – afraid that we would take over again. They wouldn't, I think, have resented us if they could have trusted us not to look for more than our share. The coastal people have many able leaders – though Ratsiraka has made blunders for *emotional* reasons he's an intelligent man. Now he's learning a lot, though it's said that all our people have had to suffer so that one man could learn. There are good leaders in most of our tribes, clever, imaginative, hard-working men. But among the Merina the *average* level of energy and competence and – I really believe – of *honesty* is higher. So in general they make better administrators, better educators, better managers of industry. But we can't go back to the nineteenth century. Our task, as Merina, is to work to raise standards of all sorts throughout Madagascar. We must never again use our advantages to keep other people down. That's the road to civil war. It's not an easy task we have. Maybe it's not possible. But we must try.'

To cheer them up I pointed out that Madagascar's present state, grim as it must seem to those who can remember better days, is healthier than the state of ex-colonies which now are dominated either by the USA or by the USSR. The Malagasy are still in control of their own destiny. They may for the moment be making a mess of things but a home-made mess leaves scope for a home-made remedy. A Superpower mess, for as long as it benefits the Superpower, is irremediable.

As we walked home through the chilly dusk a solitary submarine-shaped cloud floated crimson in a blue-green sky just above the western horizon. By the roadside, under the tall winter-bare chestnut and lime trees, *pousses-pousses* men were exchanging jokes as they cooked their supper-rice on charcoal-stoves before curling up to sleep in their rickshaws. The tiny wooden coffee-stall near our friends' house was closing and on the grass verge beside it the owner's two small children scuffled and giggled – then were called to carry home on their heads a kettle and a basket of left-over rice-buns. In the middle of the road three pairs of legs stuck out from under a broken-down bus and chuckles mingled with the clanking of tools. For all their problems, the Malagasy remain a happier people than most. One fancies theirs is an indestructible sort of happiness – built-in, impervious to the slings and arrows of outrageous politicians. But that is a dangerous bit of sentimentality. The population is exploding, the land is eroding . . . However distasteful the thought, these easy-going folk must soon be made aware of threatening statistics and to some extent be regimented. The only alternative to forward-planning is famine. There is not unlimited time for sorting out the mess.

We found our hostess in the kitchen, her sleeves rolled up, doing inspired things with a casserole. All Zanoa's movements were quick and decisive – to match her mind. Like so many Malagasy, she seemed extraordinarily well-adjusted: to herself, her family, her demanding job and the world in general. (But why should being well-adjusted seem extraordinary? Does this mean that now, in the West, many of us are ill-adjusted?)

Gervais was in the adjacent living-room of the new brick bungalow, feeding their eighteen-month-old daughter and gently encouraging the three-year-old to feed herself. Among the Merina élite, no less than among the peasantry, Father joyously child-minds. Gervais was besotted by his two beautiful daughters, who were 'indulged but not spoiled' as Rachel aptly put it. They rushed to greet him, like exuberant puppies, whenever he came home from work; yet in her dealings with *vazaha* the three-year-old had already acquired the friendly-yet-formal Malagasy manner. Both parents showed endless calm patience with their children; Zanoa was the more effective when disciplining was required but Gervais – even if he could never quite bring himself to initiate tough action – unfailingly supported Mamma.

Gervais was tall, not dark and handsome. He always looked worried, partly because he had that kind of face and partly because the prevailing shortage of everything to do with machinery was having a deleterious effect on his livelihood. In the evenings his business-partner – an uncle not much older than himself – usually called to discuss what seemed to be a chronic crisis and the two sat hunched over a pocket-calculator, looking apprehensive.

On our arrival in Antsirabe we were relieved to discover that *haute cuisine* has survived Independence – and even Christian Marxism – among the higher reaches of Malagasy society. The customary mounds of rice appeared at lunch and dinner (and at breakfast-time, for an aged resident relative) but were accompanied by a delectable variety of cunningly seasoned soups, casseroles, grills, salads and stews, and followed by a wondrous range of fresh fruits and puddings. For breakfast we had herbal tea, French bread hot from the *boulangerie*, fried eggs and sometimes mashed buttered yams that had been boiled with a little sugar – a favourite breakfast and tea-time dish, though not many can now afford butter. Or the last course might be fluffy pancakes with home-made Cape gooseberry jam. We soon regained the weight we had lost in the Ankaratra.

Zanoa did all the cooking herself, Gervais often helping to chop the meat or prepare the vegetables. An elderly much-loved 'daily' arrived at 7 a.m. to wash up and launder clothes in a huge zinc bath under a tap in the garden. She also looked after the children, as she had once looked after Zanoa. Later, a handsome crinkly-haired youth arrived to wash and polish the floors. Zanoa did the gardening – more vegetables than flowers – and the arduous weekly shopping; *haute cuisine* does not happen effortlessly in modern Madagascar.

We were staying about 150 yards from the bungalow in a charming guest-annex simply built, many years ago, of brick and wood. It contained two small bedrooms, with the nightwatchman's quarters at the rear. (This temporary 'chowkidar' was needed only because Zanoa and Gervais were building a two-storey house near the bungalow and the piles of hard-to-come-by materials that lay around had to be guarded.) Our meticulously maintained earth-closet, in a tiny bamboo hut, stood twenty yards away beyond a line of flowering cactus. Several gigantic pines shaded the two scrubby acres that were soon to become a garden. Zanoa's vegetable plot was constantly threatened by neighbours' hens and at night an inordinate number of dogs gathered beneath the pines to fight noisily over the favours of a large black bitch of indeterminate ancestry but – it seemed – fantastic sex-appeal.

We accompanied Zanoa to the main weekly Zoma on high open ground at the far side of the town. It lacked Tana's atmosphere but offered a wider range of foodstuffs, including silk-worms whose cocoons a wizened little man was slicing neatly and swiftly with a razor-blade. The huge squirming auburn grubs are considered a delicacy by some.

Antsirabe's greater variety of goods was perhaps linked to the operations of the Black Market. The Government controls – or did then – all supplies of rice, sugar, tinned milk, kerosene, matches and so on. But officials sell only a percentage to the licensed shops at fixed prices; the rest goes to Zoma merchants. Hence the almost empty shelves; it is no longer possible for unlicensed shop-owners, representing private enterprise, to engage in normal trading. Yet things were improving we learned. A few years ago long food-queues were common, to the great alarm of those who saw them as a sinister symbol of Soviet influence. Now the queuing is over, though ration books for use in licensed shops are still issued. Those who can afford to do so boycott the government system, buy at higher prices in the Zoma and give their ration books to their servants. There is also growing and outspoken opposition to restrictions on private-enterprise shopkeepers.

We bought two kilos of peanuts to sustain us during our mini-trek in the Isalo lemur-reserve but could find no other portable food, apart from many tins of Malagasy corn-beef with labels so faded that we judged it prudent to avoid them – as, apparently, did all other potential customers. I tried to buy a skirt at one of the hundreds of clothing-stalls; but the female form divine is of quite different dimensions in Ireland and Madagascar. Zanoa advised trying a cotton-merchant's shop on the way home and there we found an elegant sarong-type garment such as is only worn nowadays by peasants. It depicted zebu ploughing and a legend around the hem exhorted all and sundry to – STOP TALKING AND WORK.

Unlike Antsirabe's other colonial amenities, the hydrotherapy complex is still well-run and much-used. We parted from Zanoa to swim in its health-giving, fifty-metre indoor pool. According to our guidebook, these waters give a lot of health:

'Antsirabe has been baptised the "Vichy Malagasy"; its waters (bicarbonated, sodic and to a certain extent calcic) allow complete cures for numerous diseases (liver, gall-bladder, rhumatism, hepatic insufficiency, etc.) After important researches made by eminent French professors a thermal establishment was built in 1924 in the residential quarter, on the spot of ancient marshes. An artificial lake has

been created in the neighbourhood. It is perhaps ornamental, but also helps to prevent the escape of the thermal
gases. The installations of the establishment include hydrotherapy and physiotherapy equipments, a swimming-pool,
showers and medical gymnastic rooms.'

At the crowded swimming-pool we were usually in a double
minority – female and white – though occasionally a few young
mothers arrived, escorting tiny children who already were confi-
dent in the deep water. One could not swim seriously amidst such
a mass of swift agile brown bodies accomplishing all sorts of
aquatic stunts. But just being there was tremendous fun, seeing
faces with bright laughing eyes and flashing white teeth popping
up on every side out of the murky warm water and shyly apologising if there had been a collision – as there often was. The
surroundings, however, were dreary; a high domed building, with
stone benches around tiled walls that displayed tattered French
Tourist Board posters.

Few Antsirabe households have baths and soon after daybreak
scores of people of all ages and classes begin to queue for a private
cubicle where, on payment of a few pence, they can soak in a deep
rectangular stone tub of very hot water – and then, if they wish,
have a cold shower. The average waiting-time, we found, was
about forty-five minutes. Sitting around in the foyer, with numbered tickets which established our place in the queue, we realised
what an important centre of activity the spa still is. White-coated,
stethescoped young doctors (male and female) wandered in and
out; Norwegian-mission-trained physiotherapists gave orders to
often bewildered-looking patients; nurses with kind smiles assisted disabled geriatrics to and fro between the various treatment-
centres. But there were, we noticed, no Hi-Tek 'aids' of the
sort one would see in similar surroundings in the West. Our
bath-time usually coincided with that of half-a-dozen obese Indians in padded dressing-gowns, who arrived in *pousses-pousses*
clutching bundles of clean clothes and bars of Palmolive soap – a
luxury undreamed of nowadays by the average Malagasy. Madagascar's many affluent Indian and Pakistani businessmen are not
popular. That little group always kept to itself, being greeted
coolly, if at all, by the locals.

A century ago Antsirabe was Madagascar's Balmoral – though
then a mere village, slowly growing around the Norwegian mis-

sion. Their Majesties, accompanied by thousands of soldiers and hundreds of courtiers, often stopped there for a few weeks rest, to take the waters, on their way home from 'unification' battles against the southern tribes. King Mahommed V of Morocco was also a 'royal tourist', though a reluctant one, when the French exiled him to Antsirabe in the 1950s.

Queen Ranavalona II is said to have particularly appreciated Lake Andraikiba, some five miles west of Antsirabe. We spent two lazy days by that dark expanse of mountain-encircled water, several miles long and a few miles wide. The French built a rudimentary water-sports-centre-cum-café, now little used. On Sundays a few rich Malagasy go swimming or water-skiing and a few pallid missionaries sit at the little café tables in decorous beach-attire, sipping fruit juices against a flaring background of poinsettia. Otherwise the place is deserted, but for a few herds-boys in charge of skinny zebu grazing along the bank, and a few fishermen in rough-hewn canoes, and a few villagers washing clothes. At the base of a steep brown mountain across the water we could see great patches of bright garments spread out to dry, looking from a distance like so many flower-beds. But there would be no silk garments among them; it is *fady* to let silk touch the sacred waters of Lake Andraikiba. And pork anywhere near the banks – never mind the water – is even more *fady*.

In Madagascar every remarkable natural feature has its cluster of *fady* and legends. Once upon a time a rich and powerful Merina official could not make up his mind which of two graceful girls to marry. So he asked them to race across Lake Andraikiba: he would marry the fastest swimmer. But alas! one was already pregnant and disappeared forever in the centre of the lake. To this day the local villagers insist that she may be seen every morning, in the brief pre-dawn half-light, sitting on a high rock above the water. But if anyone is bold enough to come near she vanishes.

This being a volcanic lake the cold clear water is instantly deep; one can dive in from the grassy bank. Between long swims we lay reading and writing for hours in not-too-hot sun on the fringe of a pine-forest so far (but for how much longer?) spared the axes of the poor. At intervals two chatty little cowherds came to sit close beside us – dark-skinned and bright-eyed and clad in what seemed to be the ragged remains of nightshirts. They scrutinised with amusement and amazement our white skins and my diary-writing. Hilarity took over when we tried to teach each other how

to count up to ten. A fisherman then intervened, under the
mistaken impression that they were being a nuisance to us. Soon
after they realised that their zebu had wandered too far into the
pines and away they scampered, waving their long sticks and
yodelling weirdly – evidently a satisfactory method of communi-
cating with zebu, for the animals at once returned to the grass by
the water. I thought then how horribly different our encounter
would have been in a 'tourist spot' – how those boys would have
begged instead of chatting, and whined instead of laughing, and
sniggered at our scantily clad bodies instead of stroking my bare
white shoulder wonderingly with small black fingers. The distor-
tion of human relationships, rather than the building of Holiday
Inns or the sprouting of souvenir stalls, is the single most damaging consequence of Third World tourism. And let no one believe
that those children's families would be better off if Antsirabe were
'developed'. They would not. But a lot of already rich Malagasy
would be even richer.

Going to and from Lake Andraikiba we used different footpath
routes across the densely populated countryside. Here the villagers, long accustomed to *vazaha*, were much less shy than in the
Ankaratra. But it was otherwise when we went to Lake Tritriva,
twelve miles from Antsirabe near the summit of a highish mountain; on the way several little children fled from us, their faces
puckered with alarm. An allegedly motorable track leads to the
foot of the mountain but few vehicles attempt to defy its dustiness.
For miles this floury red dust is more than a foot deep: we paused
to measure it. However, footpaths accompany the track, or take
precipitous short-cuts up rough hillsides past isolated straggling
hamlets and an astonishing number of churches.

By 10.30, four hours after leaving Antsirabe, we were suddenly
looking into the pellucid jade-green Lake Tritriva – hundreds of
feet below us, with vertical, lushly overgrown walls of rock rising
from the water on three sides. Those cliffs merged into almost
equally sheer mountain, still densely forested, its pines protected
from casual wood-cutters by the gradient. We ate our bread,
tomatoes and onions sitting on the ant-infested grass of the narrow
ridge that forms the fourth side, overhanging the remote still
waters. Once upon a time two very young lovers, denied parental
permission to marry, plunged despairingly into Lake Tritriva –
and we saw them on the opposite cliff in the form of two gnarled
freak trees that have been growing intertwined for centuries. But

we could not find the memorial plaque to a rash *vazaha* who laughed at the lovers' curse and made a bet that he could swim across the lake.

Rachel chose to be contemplative while I climbed on a ladder-steep path, slippy with pine-needles, to the summit of the mountain – where I was opposite Rachel, far below on the ridge. On the way up, near the top, I came upon a group of four men and two women sitting in a shadowy glade between the towering pines, talking in low voices. They had no possessions with them and had evidently gathered at that secluded (sacred?) spot to discuss something very special, probably connected with the *razana*. I saw them before they saw me and momentarily I sensed an odd tension in the atmosphere. When they did see me they stared, startled, and nobody greeted me, or smiled. Feeling quite exceptionally *de trop*, I hastened past. On my return fifteen minutes later they had disappeared.

The summit overlooked a magnificent turbulence of scarcely inhabited mountains – stretching away, ridge beyond ridge, to become hazy blue in the distance. These tempted me to go on walking for the next two months but I knew they would not have the same effect on my companion. During the descent I was overlooking an entirely different sort of landscape: a wide, calm farming scene, all red and gold and green and cinnamon, every detail distinct beneath a cobalt sky.

At the foot of the mountain we each drank a litre of fizzy orange, the last two bottles on the ninety per cent empty shelves of an isolated shop. Nearby a zebu had just been killed, in a butcher's stall raised from the ground on wooden stilts. We watched a dirt-ingrained little fellow of five or six, enveloped in a ravelling adult's sweater, buying a few pence worth of offal. Scraps of green tripe, mauve lights and other unidentifiable multicoloured innards were threaded on a length of grass-twine; then off the wee lad trotted, escorted by a swarm of flies. Rachel shuddered. I thought positive and pointed out that it was protein, of a sort.

Soon after we saw what can happen when the Malagasy are not teetotal. It was a Sunday, and a noisy festival was in progress near one large village, and at least half the men we met thereabouts were footless at four o'clock in the afternoon. The reek of raw alcohol was so strong one felt a lighted match might have caused a conflagration for miles around. We paused in three villages to drink herbal tea or pseudo-coffee and had the impression that the people of this area, where there is little trace of 'slave' blood, are for some reason (probably inbreeding) remarkably dull-witted. All these villages were handsome but decaying. In pre-colonial days, before the landowners and their extended families and upper servants moved to Tana, the social structure of such regions must have been much sounder, both culturally and economically.

When we reached the level plain surrounding Antsirabe the moral tone improved dramatically. Vesper bells were chiming in half-a-dozen villages and soon the still air was carrying fervent hymn-singing across the paddy-fields from churches lit by wavering oil-lamps.

Gervais had good news for us that evening. Within the next few days we might get a lift to Fianarantsoa – 255 miles further south – in a beer-truck. Bus and bush-taxi services are frequent on this comparatively good stretch of Route Nationale No. 7, but Gervais had long since resolved to get us a free ride. He was one of the kindest people we met in Madagascar, which is saying a great deal, and he grieved over our being ripped off by the Soviet-style rate of exchange – that bus ride would have cost more than £60. From then on we stayed close to base lest the truck might suddenly decide, as is the capricious way of Malagasy vehicles, that *now* was the time to move.

6

Lemurs and Things

Our truck-driver was a tall young man with wavy hair, darkish skin, almond eyes, a fine high forehead, slightly flared nostrils and beautiful manners. He wore threadbare jeans and a new white T-shirt and his name, disconcertingly, seemed to be Rosy. Although without a phrase of French, he hugely enjoyed the sign-language game. His two mates were small, wiry, rather unwashed and very ragged, with decidedly crinkly hair and quick smiles. We regretted being the causes of their having to travel outside, balanced on a high load of crates, protectively hugging our rucksacks. Two mates were needed not to unload or share the driving but to help cope with any of the wide variety of mishaps that may befall a Malagasy vehicle as it goes about its business.

We left Antsirabe at 11.45 a.m. and during the next ten hours only two trivial mishaps befell us, each remedied by the performance of strange rites with pliers and wires. Rachel calculated that we were moving for just over eight of those ten hours, at an average speed of thirty-two miles per hour. (Later, we were to look back on that as a breakneck journey.) We went much more slowly downhill than uphill; the truck was spectacularly overloaded with a towering excess of beer-crates and Rosy gestured graphically to convey that our brakes were not to be trusted. For the same reason he always stopped when another vehicle was either approaching us or about to overtake us. He taught me how much more relaxing it is to have a good driver and bad brakes than vice versa.

In the scenically unpredictable Andrantsay region of the Betsileo country every twist of the road revealed another blue-gold vista of untidy mountains, near or distant. Here the rice-farmers are challenged by very narrow valleys and very steep slopes, a much tougher challenge than the broad valleys and plains of Imerina, where drained marshes and swamps have created fertile areas comparatively easily cultivated. However, in Betsileo country God has fitted the back – and the brains – for the burden.

These people are renowned for their energy and the ingenuity of their terracing and irrigation works. (We had been puzzled by the lack of terracing in Imerina: the explanation is that so far the Merina have not needed to develop this art – but soon they may.) The terrain here discourages villages; we rarely saw more than two or three dwellings (Merina-style) together. Often these were perched on ledges in the cramped valleys, above or below terraced fields, some scarcely bigger than a hearth-rug. Yet this land – so awkward to deal with – is exceptionally fertile. After Independence, when various *vazaha* agricultural experts were invited to Madagascar, they recommended the Betsileo to grow potatoes, beans, carrots, sweet potatoes and cereals during the eight months of the year when their paddy-fields lie idle. We saw some signs of this advice having been taken but most fields were enjoying their winter rest. The extremely conservative Betsileo village elders wield more power than their counterparts in Imerina and object to any changes in land distribution or methods of food production. It does not of course follow that they are invariably wrong; the *razana* may have discovered centuries ago that the land hereabouts needs its rest. In some areas of Nepal, during the 1960s, rice-production dropped catastrophically as a direct result of taking foreign advice.

The Betsileo look almost as Polynesian as the Merina, whose passion for Western education they have always shared, sending the majority of children of both sexes to school; and those needed on the land sometimes learned to write and read from literate neighbours. During the nineteenth century Christian missionaries turned this region into their own sort of unedifying battleground and in the few little towns we passed through churches of both denominations faced each other defiantly. Statues of the BVM, protecting the entrance to and exit from each town, tell who won that engagement. While Tana was from the beginning the centre of Protestant missionary activity in Madagascar, Fianarantsoa (sensibly known as Fianar) soon became the Catholic centre. Most of the Betsileo seem not to have taken sides; they didn't care who educated them as long as someone did.

In 1962 the Betsileo annual per capita income was estimated at $US30. Yet the people were not impoverished, the area being more or less self-sufficient with a long tradition of the migration of its more academic youngsters. By now however the population increase has caused many more to migrate in search of paid employment; there is virtually none in Betsileo country, apart from a few rice-mills and the wood-working industry of Ambositra, where generations of craftsmen have created a tradition of magnificent marquetry work, carving and furniture manufacture.

Rosy & Co. decided to eat at Fandriana, known as 'the nursery of civil servants'. This small town has an unexpected number of imposing residences built by migrant Betsileo who prospered in the administration before retiring to their own region. We had invited our companions to share our picnic lunch, since Zanoa had provided enough for a platoon, but they looked at her meat-filled pastries and elegant sandwiches and dainty home-made biscuits with a suspicion that quickly turned to revulsion. None of that rubbish could compete with a foot-high mound of rice.

Beyond the cultivated land, Route Nationale No. 7 showed what French engineers could do in the years just before the First World War – assisted of course by many thousands of Malagasy involuntary workers. For miles we were corkscrewing up, crossing mini-ravines by bridges whose state of disrepair must be causing those engineers to spin in their sepulchres. The golden slopes were occasionally broken by smooth chunks of silvery rock or sparse eucalyptus plantations. Then we were over this massive barrier and amidst a seemingly endless disarray of darkly forested mountains: the result of colonial enterprise. The French Forestry Service experimented with hundreds of species before choosing the Mexican pine for long-term commercial timber purposes. This superb tree grows three times faster throughout the Malagasy Highlands than any conifer can grow in the northern hemisphere.

The French term for Central Madagascar – the *Hauts-Plateaux* – is even less appropriate in Betsileo country than in Imerina. For hours we saw no level ground and few habitations. The wildness of this region contributed to the easy Merina conquest of the Betsileo, whose scattered communities had little contact with each other. Thus they never achieved the sort of unity that came about quite naturally in the more open country to the north. When Andrianampoinimerina chose to expand southwards it took him less than a decade to secure the vast Betsileo territories. There was little fighting; most of the Betsileo chiefs amiably agreed to become Merina vassals and were allowed to go on ruling much as before. According to Betsileo folk-history, those chiefs came long ago from the Antemoro tribe of the south-east coast, the only

Malagasy tribe to show a marked Islamic-Arabic influence. They arrived late in Madagascar, at the end of the fifteenth century, possibly from the Somali area of south-east Ethiopia where a tribe called Temur went missing at about that time. But in the Malagasy melting-pot they soon lost both their Muslim faith and Arabic language, though they are mainly responsible for the seepage of Arabic loan-words into Malagasy.

As the sun set, flooding the sky with a surge of crimson, we turned onto an open stretch of road just below the crest of a high ridge. Away to the west, beyond a shadowed jumble of lower hills, an unbroken chain of mountains stood out against the lingering fiery afterglow. And from their smooth summits, silhouetted against that incandescent horizon, rose scores of widely spaced, isolated, eroded rocks – sharp, twisted, angular, slightly sinister yet wondrously beautiful. They seemed not to belong to their mountain bases but to be mysterious additions, fantastic pranks of the Creator Andriamanitra that might have vanished by tomorrow. I woke the sleeping Rachel, who blearily peered westward. 'No wonder they're animists!' she said – and slept again.

Soon it was frustratingly dark but I consoled myself with the thought that we would have to return by the same route. Happily I could not foresee that by then I would be in no condition, for a variety of reasons, to appreciate the landscape.

Rachel continued to sleep and Rosy was companionably silent, apart from reassuring shouts in response to alarmed yells. His mates on the load were often in danger of being dislodged by overhanging branches. Buses, taxis and private cars avoid this road at night but occasionally a truck came towards us, visible for thirty or forty minutes as it crawled up and down the black bulk of the mountains ahead, its lights waxing and waning according to the density of the forest. I realised that for all my addiction to solitary travelling I was enjoying the feeling of comradeship that enveloped our little caravan of intrepid traders (1980s-style). During the last two hours our weak headlights illuminated many weather-beaten French signs announcing some village ahead. But not even the tiniest hamlet ever appeared and these repeated announcements of non-existent places became a trifle eerie. Later we discovered the French mania for listing, and putting on maps, two or three minute dwellings – often some distance from the road – which they elevated to the status of 'village'.

No distant urban glow marked the Betsileo capital. Suddenly, at 9.50, we were in it: a town completely silent and almost completely in darkness, its few fifteen-watt street lights merely hampering one's night-vision. We stopped beside a cliff-like construction – next morning we identified it as the rear-end of a disused sports stadium – and Rosy explained that because of Fianar's notorious gradients the loaded truck could go no further. He had however promised Gervais to escort us to a friend of Zanoa's who was half-expecting us, though probably not at this late hour. Leaving his mates guarding the beer he led us off into the night, carrying both our rucksacks and every so often pausing to warn us about holes in the road. Ten breathless minutes later we were on level ground and Rosy plunged into a maze of rough laneways where our stumbling progress aroused a series of dogs who woofed half-heartedly. When he pushed open a wooden gate it came off its hinges and I fell over it. A turkey-cock gobbled – an invisible watchman challenged us – Rosy explained – I knocked on an invisible door and the watchman shouted. Long moments passed before the door opened and our hostess, wearing a *lamba* over her nightgown, welcomed us with a joy which cannot possibly have been genuine but seemed so. Before departing Rosy assured us that he would be back at 6 a.m. to escort us to the bus for Ranohira – the town nearest the Isalo lemur-reserve.

I shall refer to our hostess as Madame T., partly as an exercise in discretion but mainly because her surname has nineteen letters. She was a portly woman and very small – well below five feet – with a round honey-coloured face, round dark eyes, thick lips and straight greying hair worn in a bun. Her slightly comical stature and girth were counteracted by an unmistakable air of authority, perhaps explained by her being an eminent member of the legal profession – what we would call a High Court Judge. (Judges were the senior officials of the Merina Court and throughout this century there have been many women judges in Madagascar.) Madame T.'s husband had died young and as her three children were all studying in Tana she lived alone – unusually for a Malagasy – in a large detached house jerry-built some thirty-five years ago. The hall door led directly into a high-ceilinged, meagrely furnished living-room occupying the entire ground floor; on the left, as one entered, a wide marble staircase with wrought-iron banisters led to two upper floors. (It turned to wood beyond the first landing.)

When we had insisted that we needed no supper we were shown

to our spacious room, furnished with a double bed and a small table and chair. If there is such a thing as a five-watt bulb that room had it and the wall switch was in such a state of disarray that I approached it wearing a boot on my hand. In the nearby bathroom Madame T. showed us how to deal with the loo; after flushing, one had to spend some time manipulating a lever high up on an adjacent pipe. This operation eventually enabled the overhead tank to refill but there was an art in it: the lever had a temperament. As I coaxed it in the small hours I thought wistfully of our Antsirabe earth-closet.

At 5.30 I dragged a groaning Rachel out of her flea-bag; we had to be ready for Rosy by 6. Then we heard much confused shouting below our window – it was still pitch-dark – and moments later Madame T. knocked on our door. The Ranohira bus was leaving at 6, not 6.30 – we must hurry – there might not be another for days – Madame T. would accompany us to the bus station. The snag about rucksacks is that you cannot pack them both securely and quickly. I thrust my money-belt into Rachel's half-awake hands and told her to go ahead with the rest to secure our seats; I would follow with both rucksacks.

When I lurched downstairs under my double burden the smiling watchman was waiting; he shouldered my rucksack and from the edge of the garden we descended a cliff-face by a ladder-like stairway carved out of red earth. This led to a motor-road and just opposite was the open-air bus station. We were half-running towards the relevant wooden hut (each destination has its own hut) when Rachel, Madame T., Rosy, his mates and several other interested parties – friends, it seemed, of the watch-man – came strolling towards us. No 6 a.m. service was running to Ranohira as there were not enough passengers to fill a bus. Nor was there a 6.30 service. No bus would leave for Ranohira before 10 a.m. Rachel handed me our tickets; everybody except the *vazaha* was taking this situation for granted and we pretended to. Soon such pretence would be unnecessary; we were about to learn a lot.

Rosy and his mates then disappeared from our lives and Madame T. led us up the cliff with astounding agility. 'At least this means we've time for breakfast,' muttered Rachel as we reached the top – where the turkey-cock displayed his tail and made xenophobic noises.

Thus far we had had scant opportunity to become acquainted

with our hostess, but now we realised that she was a heart-warming eccentric. Beaming kindly, she hastened into the cubby-hole kitchen off the living-room and drew aside a blanket lying over an object in one corner, to reveal a coop full of hens and baby chicks. Retrieving six warm eggs, she placed them in a large bowl and handed it to Rachel. She spoke no English and her French was incomprehensible to us both. But when she laid a packet of tea (real, not herbal) on top of the eggs and pointed to the hall door we got at least half the message. On the way in we had noticed the watchman's tiny charcoal stove.

The watchman had gone to the *boulangerie* leaving an iron cauldron simmering outside the 'Wendy house' (bent branches overgrown with vines) in which he and the turkey-cock spent their nights. I lifted the lid and we gazed speculatively at scraps of brown vegetation floating in a few litres of water. 'If I blow on the charcoal the water will boil and we can cook the eggs,' said I, perspicaciously. Rachel protested that this would ruin the watch-man's tea but I was in a ruthless mood. To me breakfast is the most important meal so I oppressed the underdog by dropping the eggs in the water and blowing on the charcoal. Ten minutes later Rachel fished out the eggs with the watchman's spoon and I threw half the packet of tea into the cauldron – at which point Madame T. reappeared, as though on cue, bearing a large enamel basin, containing at least a pound of sugar, into which we poured our brew. This basin was given a place of honour on the long, handsomely carved dining-table and our hostess ladled the scald-ing, strong, sweet tea into enamel bowls, while urging us to eat all the eggs. When the watchman arrived with an armful of long crusty loaves she insisted that we must take two of them with us. Then she had to go – she was hearing her first court case at 8.30 – but she instructed a bewildered-looking young manservant, who had just appeared, to cherish us.

We spent the next two hours climbing up and down steep flights of steps exploring 'the town where good is learned' – which is what 'Fianarantsoa' means. In 1830 Queen Ranavalona decided to make Fianar, then a small hilltop village, into her second capital. The French also favoured it as an administrative centre and a strong missionary presence, combined with the Betsileo dedica-tion to learning, led to its becoming Madagascar's intellectual centre. Yet it still feels as much village as town. At the foot of the mountain paddy-fields separate different sections of the shoddy colonial commercial quarter (pretty dormant for the now being), and the poultry and pigs busying about the residential areas seem more relevant to the present than those pompous French administrative buildings which dominate the town's middle tier. Near the summit is an attractive tangle of ancient streets where the inhabitants' average IQ is reputed to be way above normal and the genius of Ambositra's wood-carvers is much in evidence. Churches abound – some handsome, none well-maintained – and one of the two small, battered-looking mosques (both built by the Asian trading community) is Ismaili. Most Fianar folk are a shade or two darker than their Imerina neighbours but equally agreeable. Rachel however developed an irrational prejudice against them after we had come upon a piteously mewing kitten tied by one (rubbed raw) leg to a stool outside a Zoma stall. She tried to buy it but the woman banana-seller protested that it was too thin. I hustled Rachel away before the implications of that judgement could sink in.

We had been requested to report back to our ticket hut at 9.30. So we did, to the surprise of the man who had made the request. He was a middle-aged, plumpish, well-dressed Betsileo, consistently courteous to us but sometimes snappy with his poorest customers. Six other would-be passengers were sitting on their luggage – bundles wrapped in blankets – on the dusty ground outside the hut. One family consisted of a grandmother, mother and two small daughters. The children continuously nibbled at sticky confections bought from a perambulating seller – a youth wearing a tray around his neck who insisted on giving us three pastries for the price of two because we were *vazaha*. That mother remains in my mind as the only Malagasy parent I saw being unkind to children. The younger girl, aged perhaps three, was afflicted by an open festering sore on one ankle and whenever she whimpered she was either shaken or struck – treatment of which Granny evidently approved, though otherwise she seemed to have many points of disagreement with her daughter and they quarrelled sporadically for hours. Obviously that family's *vintana* had been messed up; maybe they lived in a house facing the wrong way.

The other would-be passengers were powerfully built young Sakalava police officers going home on leave to Tulear. From them we learned that the Ranohira bus is the Tulear bus; for the same fare we could have gone all the way to Tulear on the west coast, our post-lemur destination. In practice Route Nationale No. 7 expires at Fianar and because of southern Madagascar's transport problems no bus owner will gamble on Ranohira–Tulear passengers replacing Fianar–Ranohira passengers: hence our having to pay full fare. When eventually we saw Ranohira we perfectly understood this reasoning; its inhabitants are not the sort who range far and wide.

By 10.30 our group had not grown and the ticket-officer announced that we would have to wait a little longer to fill four more seats. At 11.30 I asked my interpreter if he had really said *four* – or was it *forty*? Rachel raised her head from Michael Holroyd's *Lytton Strachey* – a suitably proportioned volume for Malagasy bus-travellers – and said it *might* have been fourteen . . . At 12.15 the ticket-officer, in response to a query from one of the Sakalava, said the Tulear bus would be departing at 4 p.m. but all passengers should report to the hut not later than 3.15.

We strolled back to the town, leaving our rucksacks in the hut, and decided to study up-market Fianar in the Hotel Moderne du Betsileo, opposite the railway station. There, had we recently won the Sweep, we could have bought a large bottle of Coca-cola for £4.80. The two customers in the bar were a young Frenchman and an elderly Gujerati, drinking coffee and vehemently denouncing import restrictions. Most of Madagascar's Asian businessmen speak fluent French. We looked for the loo; the signs leading to it were not visual but olfactory and it was – and had been for a long time – devoid of water but not of other things.

Next we investigated the railway station which was deserted apart from a dog – remotely related to a red setter – who sat scratching himself by the ticket office. Fianar's station serves only one town, the east coast port of Manakara. This line was built in 1927 when French colonists were planning to settle the fertile land around Fianar. Then someone discovered that Manakara port, being unprotected from the heavy Indian Ocean swell, is unable to take modern shipping. And so the Betsileo country was left to the Betsileo and the Fianar–Antsirabe–Tana railway link was never built.

The door to the platform was locked but through the large keyhole we could see a brand-new bright red pick-up van, with a green canvas cover, standing inexplicably on the track near a tree laden with scarlet blossom. Above the keyhole a prominent notice announced that tickets are on sale twice a week but only between

5.10 and 5.40 p.m. I was beginning to find the Malagasy obsession with *precise* timings morbidly fascinating. Why, for instance, had our ticket-officer asked us to return at 3.15? Rachel plausibly suggested that for most Malagasy time, in our sense of that term, does not exist. When such importations as bus and train services seem to require some hour to be specified, they simply mention a time at random.

We mooched across paddy-fields and climbed a scrubby hill by a looping cart-track, passing several nineteenth-century Betsileo villas. As we rested on a rock – it was very hot – and were gazing west over an alluring expanse of low irregular mountains, Rachel suddenly asked, 'Are you miz about taking buses? Do you wish we could trek to Tulear?' She was evidently suffering from a rush of guilt to the heart, feeling she had become a blight on my travelling life.

'Not at all,' I replied, truthfully. 'You can hardly call this "taking buses", in the generally accepted meaning of that phrase. Anyway we couldn't trek through the south – too many bandits and too little water.'

On the way down we admired a faintly Byzantine red-brick church beside an elaborate missionary compound – a school and hospital built around quadrangles. Then we dawdled back to the bus station via a very dormant colonial shopping street displaying the usual barren shelves. Fianar, as is to be expected of an intellectual capital, has a remarkable number of bookshops. But their stock is now reduced to sun-dimmed, fly-spotted tomes of 'missionary press' provenance – in both Malagasy and French – widely spaced in the windows to make a better show.

We found half a dozen additional passengers within the hut, most of them asleep. The ticket-officer was also asleep, sitting sprawled across his small shaky desk, but the *vazaha* voices caused him to jerk up, blink and smile. His smile quickly faded when we asked at what time – *exactly* – the bus would leave. (Madame T. had invited us to a meal at 4.0 if we were still around.) He silently conveyed that this is not the sort of question tactful people ask in Malagasy bus stations. The bus would leave when enough people wanted to go to Tulear. Given that obvious fact, it is tiresome to keep on asking '*When?*' How could any ticket-officer be expected to mind-read and calculate at what hour forty-eight Fianar people would want to go to Tulear? Meanwhile all human (Malagasy) life was there in the bus station to keep us amused.

Leaving Rachel and Lytton Strachey reunited, I went on a food-gathering expedition. As the 'departure when full' principle applies to most bus services, hundreds of Malagasy spend thousands of hours in bus stations – which have, therefore, something of the character of nomad settlements. At Fianar the large 'restaurant' shacks around three sides of a dusty quadrangle seemed mere relics of more prosperous days; the majority were offering only a meal of rice or take-away rice-buns. But savoury smells led me to an exception, where four men were enjoying rice garnished with something which required extraordinary feats of mastication. Coffee too was available here and while considering my next move I drank a cup standing by the counter. At my elbow a fat infant in a brief vest sat thoughtfully playing with his penis. His mother and a friend were de-lousing each other's heads, occasionally pausing to attend to a sizzling pan of frying offal or stoke the mud-stove. I decided against garnished rice and returned empty-handed to Rachel.

On the way I counted four ailing buses and 'taxi-brousse' receiving attention. (The latter soon became 'bashies' in Murphy-speak.) A pall of discouragement hung over the groups surrounding these vehicles; the Malagasy are a patient people but they do get tired towards sunset. And it is tough to have waited all day for a full load, only to find that your vehicle, when loaded, will not move. Most bashies are antique Renault 1000s with fifteen to twenty seats, or antique Peugeot 403 pick-ups in which seats scavenged from dead motor-cars have been screwed, more or less securely, to the floor-boards.

Rachel had startling news – '*Tourists* are going to Tulear! Two of them, on our bus!' She had been snooping in the hut, reading the passenger list, and seen 'Jamie' and 'Adrian'; our ticket-officer used only first names, possibly because most Malagasy surnames would not fit on his dockets.

'Don't worry,' I said, 'anyone trying to get from here to Tulear on a bus is *not* a tourist.' I was right. Adrian and Jamie (just down from Cambridge: a mathematician and a geographer) belonged to that new breed of rather serious-minded young – the post-hippie generation – who like rapidly to sus out three or four continents before the age of twenty-three, travelling rough but never bumming and usually taking a concerned interest in 'North–South' problems.

I was sitting at the ticket-officer's table, being given an unfruitful Malagasy lesson by a jobless Betsileo engineering graduate (Moscow University), when Adrian and Jamie discovered us – to their boundless astonishment. Jamie spoke fluent French, which in various ways as yet undreamed of was to simplify our lives over the next few weeks. (I mean no disrespect to Rachel's French, but the Malagasy are unaccustomed to French As She Is Spoke in Irish schools.)

It was now 3.45 and a long time since anyone had seen the ticket-officer. Jamie passed on a rumour that no bus was going to Tulear that day and I rejoiced, not wishing to travel in the dark. But then our friend reappeared and announced, with an unjustifiably complacent smirk, that we would be taking off in a bashie at 4.30. When he pointed to a nearby Peugeot pick-up the boys shuddered. To us it looked pretty fit, as bashies go, but Adrian grimly drew our attention to its four completely bald tyres.

By 4.45 we were all aboard. At 5.0 our canvas cover was securely lashed down; from a bashie you can see nothing, by day or by night. At 5.10 we left Fianar, in a daze of incredulity. The front seat beside the driver took three adults and a baby. The ten seats in the back took sixteen adults, five children and three babies.

At 5.40 we stopped by a roadside coffee-stall.

'I don't believe it!' muttered Jamie.

Adrian, the mathematician, began to calculate how long it would take to cover five hundred and eighty miles at twenty-five miles per hour if the bashie stopped for ten minutes every twelve and a half miles.

I untied the knot beside me, drew up the green tarpaulin and peered out. The driver and his male companions were sharing a bottle of colourless but not odourless liquid. The baby was being fed from a saucerful of what might have been mashed yam. Its nappy had been removed and by the light of the stall lantern I could see a small girl scraping its contents into the ditch with a length of firewood, preparatory to folding it neatly over for replacement.

A moment later we realised that our stop had a more serious purpose than baby-care. Another jam-packed bashie passed us, whereupon our driver (etc.) stuffed themselves back into the cab and followed it closely. Its health was so bad that the two bashies were to travel to Tulear in convoy so that ours could give first aid when (not if) necessary.

Soon a sturdy seven-year-old girl was asleep in my arms, her head resting on my left bosom. She had neatly braided hair which reeked of rancid coconut oil. The two-month-old baby beside me was frequently fed by its very young mother and as frequently puked over my rucksack, wedged half-under the seat. Moments after each spurt of vomit the infant wailed pathetically, causing its mother to look grief-stricken and make loving mooing noises while producing a breast from which it again sucked avidly – though with difficulty, because it had a cold in the head. 'Too much milk of human kindness,' diagnosed Adrian neatly, from behind us. Obviously the real problem was a stuffed nose, leading to too much air being sucked in. I tried to console the mother by explaining this: she looked about Rachel's age and was almost in tears of anxiety. But she spoke no French and my attempts to deliver a Dr Spock lecture in sign-language merely provoked gales of laughter among our fellow-passengers. Gradually most of the inexhaustible contents of those balloon-like breasts seemed to find their way, via the baby, into my rucksack. (Hence those missing Antsirabe pages; my diary was in the direct line of fire.)

Meanwhile a nine-month-old baby was sleeping soundly across Jamie's knees which, as the night wore on, became damper and damper, causing him to revise his views on fatherhood as a desirable future role.

I had cunningly secured a front seat, which allowed a few extra inches of leg-room. But soon I was repenting of this selfishness. Two tattered lengths of electric flex were hanging from the roof just in front of me – serving no discernible purpose – and whenever the bashie leaped over a particularly rugged bit of road these gave a display of miniature forked lightning and emitted showers of sparks. At last the milky young mother beside me lost her nerve and shrieked at the driver. A few minutes later a disembodied arm and hand emerged from the cab to wrap newspaper around the flexes and shove them into a convenient aperture. Adrian advised us how best to escape if a fire started; he reckoned not much brute force would be needed to dismantle the crudely welded tarpaulin-frame.

When our twin had its first puncture at 8.45 Adrian suggested a stroll. But there was no time; even in the dark the Malagasy change tyres or wheels with the speed that comes of much practice.

The engine complication that followed took longer to sort out. Someone needed to pee but we discovered that we were locked in and that the arcane knowledge required to release us was possessed exclusively by one of the men lying under our twin. Suddenly I got the giggles; the comic elements of Malagasy life have a cumulative effect. My mirth proved so contagious that soon our bashie shook with laughter, to the driver's uneasy astonishment.

Scavenged car seats are rarely without blemish and soon terrible things had been done to the boys' buttocks, less well equipped than ours to withstand metal protrusions. Around midnight Jamie's left buttock, especially, became a major cause for concern – his concern. By then the laughing was over and we had each become too obsessed with his or her own exquisite discomfort to give a damn about anybody else's.

From my diary I quote:

'All night a rising fog of fine grey dust through the floorboards – not as pretty as red dust. Makes us cough. Why doesn't it make the Malagasy cough? Also worries Jamie dreadfully as he thinks it may get into his rucksack (which it will) and spoil his clean shirt. Suspect him of dandyism. But he's heroic with that baby though complains much of 'ethnic pong'. With some reason. It's very distinctive. Interesting to analyse: filthy garments, rancid coconut oil, inferior petrol, infantile effluent, homemade alcohol (cane spirits?), dust, rotten fish (no doubt a present for Someone Special), bad breaths, fresh sweat – only stale socks missing as all feet bare. Night air so cold no ventilation possible. Superb frosty sky – a glory of vibrant stars. Lots of time to star-gaze during other bashie's breakdowns. One so severe needed help from big oil-truck coming from Tulear. Lucky it came when it did; little other traffic. Our driver quite good: only a few wild swervings when he seemed almost out of control. For long stretches he achieved about sixty bone-jarring miles an hour in defiance of horrendous corrugations. Elsewhere we crawled at fifteen or less over what felt like lunar surface. Stopped 1.45 a.m. to eat in mud shack in middle of nowhere. Everyone sits at long trestle table, lit by one candle stump, and gets a heaped plate of rice. Communal tin basin of fish-stew in centre. Everyone that is except the Murfs who've had fish-stew. Adrian gives me a fistful of his rice and I wander out to eat by starlight. Flat landscape. Soon after pass through Ihosy – only town en route. Stop twice not far

beyond for small children to be thrust into cab from edge of
pitch black roadside. Jamie wonders – "Is there a slave
market in Tulear?" I wonder how four adults, two children
and a baby fit in a cab made for two. At 3.30-ish we all walk a
mile or so across a river-bed – only empty bashies can cope
with that. Arrive Ranohira at 5.15. It took exactly twelve
hours to cover 260 miles. The mathematician by then past
doing sums but Rachel says we averaged about twenty-one
mph.'

The bashies did not linger and as their engine sounds faded we
walked slowly by starlight up Ranohira's main street, between
silent shuttered houses. Then a few men appeared, noiselessly
passing us: no footwear to warn of their approach. The starlight
emphasised their extraordinary height – extraordinary because
we had become used to the smallness of the Merina and Betsileo.
These seemed giants, striding out of the blackness. We were now
in Bara country; and the Bara tribe, traditionally warriors and
cattle-herders (and rustlers) are among the most African-looking
of all the Malagasy. Those men, we later learned, were going to
work on the new Fianar–Tulear road being constructed by a
French company.

Beyond the main street the road turns sharp right and the
houses become shacks. Here one could feel the immensity of the
flatness all around; this was a new land. And not only topographi-
cally: the spirit of the place was quite unlike the Highlands. I
wondered afterwards how this difference had come through so
strongly, within moments of our arrival. Had we travelled from
Fianar by day it might have been otherwise; our 'Mystery Tour',
like an air-flight, allowed no adjustments to be made en route.
Also, my completely sleepless night may have left me in that odd
state of hyper-sensitivity sometimes brought about by lack of food
and/or sleep.

On the edge of the town we sat facing east and breakfasted off
bread and chocolate while awaiting the dawn. Within moments it
came, memorably – first a mere draining away of the darkness and
stars being quenched, then a strange murky yellow glow like a
smoky bush-fire, then redness seeping into and finally conquering
the yellow. And above it was suddenly blue, a mild silvery blue
that soon would darken and harden.

Up and down the street doors now opened and from them, like

an answer to prayer, came women bearing tall Thermos flasks. These were placed on roadside tables, soon to be joined by maize-flour buns and little bowls of bony fish. Ranohira profits from a steady flow of daytime traffic (perhaps three vehicles an hour), this being the only east–west road in the whole vastness of southern Madagascar. We made euphorically for the nearest Thermos. A dignified Merina woman shook hands and served us large mugs of excellent coffee, then called her teenage daughter who hurried out with a cloth-covered basket of hot brown buns. Most of the coffee-ladies, we noticed, looked more Merina than anything else.

Our next need was the Bureau d'Eaux et Forêts officer; he would register our presence, take our fee, see us through the police post and show us the path to the Reserve. Our coffee-lady spoke no French but when shown our permits directed us to the Post Office, far down the wide straggly street. Not surprisingly, it was closed at 6.15 a.m. (Later we discovered that it rarely opens.) We again showed our permits, to a tall haughty-looking youth wrapped in an ankle-length orange and white blanket and wearing a jockey-cap of the same material. He shook his head, bemused, and hurried away from us. Then, up a narrow laneway beside the Post Office, Rachel spotted a yellow sign fifteen feet wide and six feet long saying – PARC NATIONAL DE L'ISALO. On closer inspection this board's significance was far from clear. It stood where the laneway faded out amidst a scattering of African-looking mud huts with thatched or tin roofs; and its bilingual small-print information was no longer legible. Irresolutely we surveyed the golden-brown landscape ahead, dotted with spindly top-heavy trees and banana-surrounded compounds. Then, from behind a tangle of thorny scrub, came another blanket-wrapped man – middle-aged, mahogany-coloured and moustached (unusual in Madagascar). He nodded knowingly at our permits and pointed to a group of three nearby huts.

The family were just getting up. Astonished children of all sizes came tumbling around us, rubbing sleep out of their eyes. I extended our permits to the eldest, a comely adolescent lass carrying a baby. She stared at it blankly, stared at us equally blankly – then suddenly began to laugh, louder and louder, leaning against the nearest mud wall and rhythmically slapping the baby's bare bottom. Her siblings and cousins joined in (at least we hoped some of them were cousins) and this storm of hilarity brought distant neighbours to their hut doors. It was highly infectious mirth; I sat on the verandah floor of the biggest hut and succumbed to it. Only Rachel – not of an age to relish being laughed at – remained po-faced.

Mamma appeared then, short and fat and blowzy, tying a handkerchief around her tight curls. She seized the permit, thrust it into her bosom, grabbed my left hand, tapped my watch, held up seven fingers and pointed to the closed door behind me. 'Bureau!' she said – her only utterance. Appearances notwithstanding, she was a very with-it lady. A moment later we heard her shouting at (presumably) her husband who was (we assumed) the Forêt Officer. He was chuckling when he came around the corner, securing his trousers with a length of brightly coloured cotton. He shook hands vigorously, his eyes twinkling at us as though we were long-lost friends. ('They're all crazy around here!' muttered Rachel ungraciously – but she had had less than three hours sleep.) Pappa was indeed the Forêt Officer, yet nothing could be done until the Post Master arrived at 7. Ours not to reason why. We laid our weary bodies full length on the verandah, using our rucksacks as pillows – to the squealing delight of the smaller children, now augmented by their contemporaries from far and wide.

As we had noticed in Tana, the Bureau d'Eaux et Forêts is uniquely efficient. At 6.55 the Post Master was beside us, breathless and beaming, his trousers ending six inches above his bare feet and his too-small woman's shirt-blouse not meeting his waistband so that an area of darkness was visible between the two. He greeted us in French – doffing his straw Homburg to reveal iron-grey curls – then ushered us into a bare, cobwebbed office where our footprints on the carpet of dust proved how rare a species the Isalo tourist has become. The Visitors' Book confirmed this; the signatures since 1972 filled less than a page. While the Forêt Officer slowly copied the details of our permits into a ledger, using my pen, the Post Master suggested that we pay on our return because he could not change my 5,000 FMG note. Isalo trekkers have to give a date of return and if they then fail to appear a search-party goes out – at least in theory. This precaution was instituted by the French because of the lack of paths and water.

The Post Master led us through the town – a mark of honour, we realised, as the populace (what there was of it around) saluted him deferentially. He had an odd gait, a shuffling trot that roused the dust. In a dismal deserted market-square behind the main street we stopped outside a fly-loud butcher's shop. For ten minutes our guide talked earnestly to a sullen young woman who must have just finished disembowelling a carcass: she was blood to the elbows. The conversation was all about the *vazaha* – but why discuss us in such depth with the butcher's wife? Then a small smudged notice on the door caught my eye; it revealed that this was the headquarters of the People's Executive Committee.

Next stop, police. Beside a long colonial bungalow in a barren sisal-hedged compound rose the ruins of a radio transmitter, rusty against the sky. A French idea, our guide explained superfluously. It symbolised modern Madagascar for me: a country that has involuntarily sampled Hi-Tek and decided it is not worth the effort. After the Post Master's third shout a tall, unsmiling Bara policeman came slouching along the verandah buttoning his tunic; he was still wearing pyjama-legs. He took our passports and permits gingerly, as though they might contain a letter-bomb, and gave them some thought. Then he disappeared. He had gone, said our guide, to look for writing-paper. What he found scarcely answered that description – a sheaf of filthy scraps that might recently have been wrapped around his breakfast. The Post Master sensibly abandoned us at this stage; his daughter was married to a policeman and lived in a nearby hut. When he returned some twenty minutes later the paperwork was nearly complete and the policeman looked strained and exhausted. He had been copying out verbatim the Irish Government's request in Gaelic that everyone everywhere should treat us nicely.

From the edge of Ranohira the low blue-grey Isalo escarpment looks deceptively commonplace: just another stretch of rock-mountain, about an hour's walk away. As the only cleft in the wall was plainly visible we urged our guide to come no further, but he insisted on leading us down a manioc-planted slope and across a mile of scrubby flatness where tall unknown trees marked the course of a winding stream. Near the base of the escarpment our path vanished in dense, coarse, shoulder-high grass. The Post Master hesitated, looking both apprehensive and embarrassed, so I insisted on his turning back. He was an elderly man and clearly not very fit.

Deep fissures soon deflected us from what had seemed the obvious route into the cleft. We wasted scarce energy by climbing too high on one of its golden-grassed walls, scrambling between grey crags. Already the heat was fierce and my sleepless night began to tell; I reflected that I too am getting elderly. When the sound of running water led us back to the path we paused to shed the bashie dust in a cold clear pool, secluded among bushes. A small shiny black snake slithered away from us over the mud and swarms of tiny black flies tormented us as we dressed.

Fifteen minutes later we were climbing the escarpment, hauling ourselves up with the aid of rocks and shrubs, curious to see what sort of terrain lemurs favour as a reserve but unaware that we were approaching a frontier. Much may have been written in French about Isalo, but I had found only passing references in English to this eroded limestone massif, some 4,000 feet above sea-level and uninhabitable – by humans. French geologists invented a word to describe it: *ruiniforme*. Occasionally English writers appropriate this by knocking off the 'e' but it is not in any of my dictionaries. Reaching the top of the escarpment, we appreciated the need for a new word. A moment before, we had been in a normal though exotic environment. Here we might have been on another planet.

Half-an-hour later Rachel suddenly stood still, looked around and said – with perhaps a faint edge of unease to her voice – 'This is a lost world.'

That evening I wrote in my diary:

'Over the escarpment we found a weird expanse of flat rock surrounded on three sides by – you can't possibly call them mountains. Or peaks. Or ridges. Or cliffs or hills. I've seen the work of erosion in many places but never anything like this. It is, literally, incredible. You don't believe it. You think you're hallucinating. And it gets more so. As we crossed the rock (fresh breeze: no longer too hot tho' 11 a.m.) our boots were loud on the bare slabs – smooth here, with low thorny tufts growing in the crevices and a sly olive-green weed that filled our socks with almost invisible agonising barbs. Off the rock onto a thin carpet of razor-sharp red grass. Under a scattering of green trees lay green-brown fruit, hard and bitter. Then we faced a contorted silver rock-wall, friable and full of holes. Curved 'handles' of rock were left along the crest. We stared at a row of sculpted 'busts' in the near distance: an Egyptian Pharaoh, a tangle-haired caveman, a neat-headed woman. The hallucinatory feeling strengthened. How can wind and water have done all this? And the lichen colours! Sweeping splodges of yellow and red and green – some monster's palette. Our ghost of a path ended here, at a narrow gap in the rock-wall. Below lay a flat square of land, some four miles by four: grey gravel with separate tall clumps of orange grass glowing like fires between misshapen scrawny green trees. And on all sides ridges covered with inconceivable distortions of rock. The hundred foot descent was eased by shallow holes conveniently placed in the sloping cliff – man-made? But inconvenient to break a leg here: thought I might do better without an unbalancing rucksack and rolled it down. We looked for a path but could find none. Saw many smallish termite hills and thick ground-spider webs. Slim three to six inch lizards scuttled hither and thither. Very few birds. A silence like nowhere else. Everything harsh, dry, grotesque – most things painful to touch. Only the sky looks familiar. A puzzling number of tall burnt trees – still standing, main branches intact, but completely blackened – macabre skeletons. Yet no trace of recent ground fires. Are these victims of pasture-burning long ago, or of lightning? Probably the latter; scores of Malagasy are killed annually by lightning. This region can't ever have been grazed. People don't even come here to gather fuel – deadwood lies all around. We camped at 3.30 where there were enough loose stones to build cairns for the pegs; impossible to find any patch of ground to take them. So a shaky tent. Sleeping under the stars not on: too many giant scorpions, and various species of ants, and flies that go bite in the night; not to mention the ground-spiders – the Malagasy say they dart out of their burrows and attack without provocation. This seems unlikely but am not disposed to increase the sum of zoological knowledge by personal experimentation.'

When I look into my memory, I find our Isalo days on a shelf entirely apart from any other mental souvenir of travel. On that first evening Rachel was asleep by 4.15 (a bad case of post-bashie exhaustion) and for two hours I walked alone through the strangeness – in a wide circle, lest I might lose the tent. The unique sense of isolation was inexplicable, with Ranohira and Route Nationale No. 7 only a few miles away. We are after all accustomed to far more remote regions, many days' walk from the nearest town or motor-road. But in the Isalo Massif, though it may sound crazy to admit it, the isolation feels temporal as well as spatial. On levels other than the visual, this is an hallucinatory place. Something very odd happens to *time*. An eerie out-of-the-present sensation overwhelmed me in spasms; but whether the movement was backwards or forwards (or both) I never could decide. Beyond any doubt certain areas of this massif – so specially sacred to the Malagasy – have a richness of unremembered history; the atmosphere is saturated with more mysteries than erosion can conjure up. Such flawless solitude usually brings me tranquillity; but not, somehow, in Isalo. It is subtly sinister, although – if this can be imagined – enjoyably so.

We remarked next day on the illusion of immensity, despite the comparative smallness of this landscape's scale. There are, by the standards of the world's great mountain ranges, no vast expanses, no profound chasms, no awesome peaks. Perhaps this illusion has to do with being alone in a place now virtually abandoned by man.

In one day's walk we found solitary symmetrical rock humps a quarter of a mile long – rocks sharp and smooth – rocks compacted and aerated – rocks in tidily arranged, multicoloured layers – rocks hollow and perfectly circular like small barrels – rocks underfoot in long pitted sheets – rocks overhead parodying huts and castles and skyscrapers – and acres of wavy rock on a gorge floor, like a stormy sea immobilised forever. Occasionally, too, we came upon a rectangular stack of very thin rock slabs, each stack some eight feet high, six feet wide and twelve feet long, partly overgrown by bizarre vegetation. These ancient tombs were the only visible traces of mankind and at first glance they seemed just another geological extravagance. Nobody now knows whose ancestors lie within.

We saw only two flowers, both peculiar to the massif. One had long waxy pinkish-orange petals on three spindly foot-high stems growing from a cactus of the same size and construction as a globe artichoke; the hard shiny outer leaves, curling away from the heart, were changing colour to match the flower. The second blossom belonged to a pale grey cactus, swede-turnip-sized, which felt hollow when tapped. At first I mistook it for a miniature baobab, yet another of those strange Malagasy mutations. It had a disorganised sprouting of thick stems one of which bore a solitary yellow flower no bigger than a primrose.

Early on our second morning the whisper of distant water led us

through a maze of free-standing cliffs – all grooves and cornices –
to the edge of a sheer-sided, winding canyon miles long and 300
feet deep. Ribbons of short *green* grass accompanied a clear stream
along the canyon floor. Aeons ago, the massive plateau directly
across from us had cracked slightly to form a side-canyon, its
precipitous slopes densely forested. Here and there amidst that
lush growth we glimpsed the sparkle of a waterfall. 'That *could* be
lemur territory,' I said – and before Rachel had time to reply I saw
a flash of white between two trees high on the cliff directly opposite
our own.

Exulting, we flung off our rucksacks and settled down with our
binoculars, legs dangling over the abyss. Soon we could see five
lemurs: but for me there remains an incomparable magic about
that first glimpse of white. All were sitting upright on the branches
of small trees growing from the precipice; and all were facing east,
to catch the first warmth of the sun which moments before had
reached their cliff top. The Malagasy believe these sifaka lemurs
to be sun-worshippers, because of this morning ritual, and for
centuries to kill them was *fady*. But alas! the *razana* rescinded this
taboo more than a generation ago when a rapidly increasing
human population began to cause seasonal food shortages.

Our ecstatic study of the sifaka continued all day, facilitated by
their thick, silky, pure white fur (apart from a red-brown 'cap').
They needed no protective colouring before man came to Madagascar. While feeding, resting or grooming they keep their very
long furry tails curled between their legs. But when they leap –
covering enormous distances with arms outstretched towards
their branch-goal, as in a gesture of welcome – those tails plume
out like horizontal parachutes.

During the noon hours the sifaka disappeared into their forest
and were still. We then set up a nudist colony on our cliff top; you
can safely do that in Isalo, as on a desert island, and for some odd
reason I felt much more at ease with this place when stark naked –
apart from footwear. Our return to nature was not however very
practical as that site provided an unprecedented level of camping
discomfort. The only shade around was a meagre bush under
which lived a city of savage ants. Merely to brush against any of
the abundant adjacent vegetation, whatever its form, drew blood.
To walk by the edge of the canyon invited a broken ankle or
severed vein amidst a loose rubble of knife-sharp rock-fragments.
The whole area was a masochist's paradise. There was not even

one tolerable seat, erosion having produced an eruption of small jagged points on every available boulder. And the many carnivorous insects – undesirable as bedmates – prevented us from sitting on our flea-bags. The least penitential resting place was a sloping slab that looked as though it might at any moment slide forward into the canyon. It was placed symmetrically between two fantastic rock formations: oblong, hollowed, shaped exactly like children's coffins with the lids off. The longer I looked at these, the more possible it seemed that this had once been their function. Without a shred of scientific knowledge or evidence, I was beginning to suspect the presence of man in the Isalo Massif long before the first settlers arrived from Polynesia – or wherever. The Malagasy have an oral tradition that the Vazimba people were indigenous to Madagascar, a belief scorned by *vazaha* experts because the earliest archaeological evidence of human settlement dates from the ninth century AD. But maybe the Malagasy know best.

Soon after three o'clock branches began to move in Lemurville: slight movements up and down the forested precipice. 'This is very suspenseful,' murmured Rachel, as we studied those small stirrings amidst the dense greenery. It seemed that tea-time might involve no more than sitting around invisibly (from our point of view) chewing berries. But soon the whole group – six including a baby firmly attached to mother's chest – moved out into the main canyon where their forest overflowed onto the lower part of the yellow-grey wall. We rushed along our fissured cliff top, disregarding the various injuries inflicted on us en route by the environment, and about a mile upstream found an ideal vantage point – an outcrop of rock – from which to observe the sifakas' main area of operations until their sunset bedtime.

There could be no question of erecting our tent on this site but we used it as an anti-insect double sleeping-bag, arranging the mosquito-netting windows over our faces to allow for star-gazing and ventilation. The least unsuitable 'bed' – a rock-slab clear of vegetation – sloped radically and had immovable limestone protuberances. We talked more than we slept, as the golden patterns of the constellations glided across a wide black sky. Around midnight some nearby creature – whether bird or beast I know not – called hoarsely, plaintively and persistently for about an hour. Examining each other's bodies by the light of dawn, we saw that the night's 'rest' had been a bruising experience.

Soon three of our Antandroy sifaka – found only in southern

Madagascar – were again visible, just below their cliff top, awaiting the first warmth. I focused on them with affection; in that arid world of warped stone and hostile plants, of utter silence and immobility, those cheerful lively little creatures, in their lush inaccessible oasis, by now seemed close friends. Rachel was perhaps a trifle disappointed that the gorge always separated us, but I craved no greater intimacy. It was good that they slept and played and fed and sun-worshipped beyond the reach of man, as their ancestors had done for countless millennia before man existed.

Back in Ranohira, approaching the 'Bureau' to report our safe return, we were fascinated to see a young man standing on a table in front of the Parc National sign, meticulously repainting it. Already the Malagasy small print had been made legible and he was starting on the French side. Was this a direct result of our arrival? Had we revitalised Ranohira's Bureau d'Eaux et Forêts, giving new hope and pride to all concerned? But despite this apparent resurgence of faith in its future, we left the Bureau half an hour later with heavy hearts. It is hard to believe that Madagascar's conservation laws will be enforced in time to save the sifaka. Unlike some other lemur species – notably the popular ring-tailed lemur – sifaka do not survive in captivity. If the Malagasy cannot be induced to cross them off the menu, they will inevitably join the many other unique creatures, furred and feathered, who have comparatively recently become extinct in Madagascar.

To find onward transport from Ranohira you wait at the roadside for an unspecified period – an hour, a day, two days . . . No passing bus or bashie will have room for extra passengers, but so what? No Malagasy driver will scruple to increase the sufferings of his already tortured cargo.

At 2.30 p.m. we settled down on a carpet of small sharp stones close to a coffee-table and opposite the Catholic church – large, tin-roofed, newly white-washed, its neat tower and slim tin spire rising above the poinsettia and young pines planted by the resident Italian priest. As we wrote our diaries a dozen chubby toddlers sat cross-legged in front of us, solemnly staring. Then one of the coffee-ladies took pity on us and provided a seat of paper sugar-sacks in the shade of her cactus-hedge.

Twenty minutes later Roland from Amiens leant out of his new red Land Cruiser and invited us to stay at the nearby road construction base-camp. In a day or two, depending on the arrival of a spare part, a camp truck would take us to Tulear on its weekly mission to fetch food and fuel-oil.

The base-camp was a scattered hamlet of bungalows each with a mini-garden, plus a thatched bar open to the breeze on three sides, a communal dining-room-cum-kitchen-hut, and a three-roomed guest-hut with a six-foot-high refrigerator which did not work. The colony's living conditions were austere but adequate; unlike American exiles, they had not attempted to re-create their homeland in the middle of nowhere.

During the next day and a half we were cherished by that odd little enclave of *vazaha* whose long exposure to the Malagasy way of life had left them with no alternative but to adapt to it – or become nervous wrecks. Presumably the building of 220 miles of road through semi-desert is, in the normal course of events, routine stuff for a major construction company. But when the course of events is abnormal it becomes virtually impossible. For the past two years, we were told, the Malagasy government had not paid their agreed share of the costs and there was some doubt about the Ranohira–Tulear stretch being completed. The 60-mile Ihosy–Ranohira stretch was almost finished; for three years 500 men had been working on it. The Malagasy machine operators (mainly Betsileo) were paid 45,000 FMG a month, the labourers (mainly Bara) 20,000 FMG. These were excellent wages, though with the rate of exchange at 650 FMG to the pound sterling they did not seem so to us at first hearing. Roland was gloomy because two days previously the government had announced its intention of buying from the USA 12,700 tonnes of rice, and 1,400 tonnes of cooking-oil, at a total cost of 2.1 million FMG – in his view a needless expenditure, entirely owing to the mismanagement of agriculture over the past decade. How much better if all those FMGs could have been devoted to road-building! And yet, he mused, is there much point in building roads when there is no evidence that anybody will maintain them when the builders have gone home?

Despite his Ranohira frustration, Roland – the director of operations, within a year of retirement – seemed to have no serious adjustment problems. He had grown up in Tamatave, the son and grandson of French settlers, and he loved Madagascar with a quiet, touching intensity. His bungalow was like a well-cared-for natural history museum, crammed with magnificent specimens of butterflies, beetles, birds, snakes, sea-shells, semi-precious stones, dried flowers and leaves, polished samples of rare trees and bits of Aepyornis egg-shells. (The Aepyornis was Marco Polo's 'Roc'.) For him this last job, after a working lifetime spent in French colonial Africa, was a good excuse to be where he most wanted to be. His wife, however, felt otherwise. She had implacably retreated to Amiens after a year in Ranohira. It was not, we agreed, the sort of place where a middle-aged gregarious housewife could be expected to thrive. No other respectable Frenchwoman lived within 200 kilometres (we longed to hear about the unrespectable ones), letters to and from France took from four to six weeks and the only telephone link was with Ihosy: a town Madame Roland felt no urge to be linked with. Also, she was afraid to drive around on her own. Bandits abound in southern Madagascar. And there is no petrol station on the 112-mile stretch from Ihosy to Sakaraha.

Most of the *vazaha* workers had recently been recalled; because of the cash shortage there was no longer enough for them to do. Apart from Roland, only three Frenchmen remained on site: all unmarried and in their thirties with semi-resident local mistresses. The chief mechanic was a German-Bolivian whose English-speaking Brazilian wife had an effusive half-grown Siamese cat named Missee and a self-confessed dependence on valium. Only Roland took any interest in things Malagasy and he, as the Malagasy-speaker, dealt so indulgently with the superlatively inefficient Bara domestic staff that each meal-time became an impromptu farce. 'You can't be angry with them,' he explained, 'because they try so hard to please.'

One of the semi-resident young women, Annemarie, spoke some English and taught at Ranohira's primary (and only) school. Her great-grandfather had been the Merina Governor of Ihosy under the Monarchy; in 1891, during a Bara raid on the small Merina garrison, he died for Queen if not for country. His son later served in the French administration under Colonel Louis Lyautey. Lyautey, appointed to 'pacify' southern Madagascar, attempted to obey orders from Paris by replacing Merina administrators with local *mpanjaka* (tribal chiefs). But soon the French Central Audit Office in Tana was making unreasonable demands, looking for things like 'clear statements of forms of expenditure in the Bara country'. Having witnessed a few Bara *mpanjaka* trying to comply with these requests, Lyautey informed Governor-General

Galliéni, and Paris, that Madagascar could not be administered without the Merina.

Annemarie, though born two years after Independence, was an ardent Francophile, rather naively dreaming of married bliss in France with her construction engineer. Having observed the couple together, we doubted if this dream would come true. In another exotic place, her beloved would almost certainly want another exotic mistress. She explained that her family would approve of her marrying an 'educated' Frenchman but would oppose any *mésalliance* with either an uneducated Frenchman or a non-Merina. Although I did not like to ask, I think we may take it that they would equally disapprove of an 'uneducated' (peasant: *Andeva*) Merina. But how would they decide between an 'educated' (though dark and crinkly-haired) Bara and an *Andeva*? Probably they would go for the latter, reasoning that you can educate a peasant but you cannot de-black a Bara. Colour-prejudice is not exclusive to us whites, though it has been remarked that the arrival of Europeans in Imerina at the beginning of the nineteenth century seems to have accentuated Merina class- and colour-consciousness.

Modern Malagasy marriage taboos can be confusing for the *vazaha*. Often class barriers seem higher than tribal barriers, yet among the Merina and the Betsileo it has always been taboo to marry anyone with the faintest trace of negro blood. When making such genetic judgements hair-type is taken more seriously than skin-colour; long, straight, silky black hair is a hallmark of Polynesian ancestry that cannot be disputed or feigned. The merest hint of crinkliness is assumed to betray slave blood – rather illogically, given the Malagasy's probable history en route to Madagascar.

The fact that the Malagasy Republic now feels like a united nation must be attributed to one of its citizens' most attractive characteristics: forbearance. I first fully appreciated the unifying power of Malagasy culture in Ranohira, where the tribal mix is so evident: Merina and Betsileo peasants crossed with Bara, Sakala-va, Mahafaly and Antandroy, to mention but a few of the possibilities. Such unity seems even more remarkable when one remembers how recently certain tribes – the Bara, for instance – lost their independence.

During King Radama's reign (1810–28) the Bara tolerated the Merina occupation of their capital, Ihosy – which we had passed through in hours too small to tell us anything about it. Yet these warriors never considered themselves to have been conquered and as the Merina expanded south the Bara maintained their own expansion to the west, founding a new capital – Ankazoabo – in 1838. At intervals they resisted further Merina encroachments and in 1873 thousands of troops were sent from Imerina to suppress a major 'rebellion'. The renowned commander of this force was Ravoninahitriniarivo, later Queen Ravalona's Foreign Minister. He wore a velvet glove, paying lavishly for all supplies and releasing prisoners instead of enslaving them. The Bara submitted to him within weeks, but despite such temporary victories the Merina found it impossible to keep a firm grip on Bara territory. It was effectively conquered only by the much more ruthless French, in 1900.

After our close encounters with Isalo's rare insects I was in a pitiable state that night, either dementedly scratching or applying ineffectual ointment to a mass of inflamed welts and running sores. At 2.30 a.m. I decided to try a cooling shower but there was no water. Rachel too scratched almost incessantly, yet never woke.

Next (Sunday) morning we found Ranohira's two churches quarter-full. Both were urgently in need of repair and without interior decorations, apart from a garish Italian Stations of the Cross. Schoolchildren made up fifty per cent of the congregations and from the porches we enjoyed their enthusiastic hymn-singing, our presence within having proved too much of a distraction. Everyone was spruced up for the Sabbath but the relationship between colour, class and creed was striking: Protestants fairish and mildly prosperous, Catholics darkish and obviously poorer.

No one would voluntarily linger in Ranohira yet I was glad Fate had arranged this glimpse of small-town life in southern Madagascar. The contrast with what we had seen of small-town life in the poorest region of Imerina was instructive. Compared to Ranohira, Manalalondo, though virtually inaccessible to motor-traffic, seems like Paris: the reverse of what one would expect, Ranohira being on a National Highway. Certain features are of course shared. Neither area has electricity or a medical service (no health care is available in Ranohira, and very little anywhere else between Fianar and Tulear). Yet life expectancy in Imerina is fifty-six years, as against forty-two in southern Madagascar. The Merina have a high traditional standard of public hygiene – their villages are conspicuously clean and tidy – and a more hard-working population on more fertile land means a better diet.

However, we saw no extreme poverty in Madagascar. The Ranohira people were reasonably well dressed and seemed adequately fed and housed. Their dreary domestic architecture was obviously French-inspired – or uninspired – but the town must have looked less dismal when regularly white-washed, as in colonial times. (Several disused official buildings proved that the place has lost some status since Independence.) The only attractive houses, built a little way beyond the town on dusty plots growing sugar-cane and banana plants, were Betsileo- or Merina-owned. Thatched and golden-walled, some had a kitchen-replica of the dwelling nearby – small, but not so small as the four-foot-high hen-houses, also replicas of the family home, which stood by many gable-ends. As Rachel remarked, the dwelling, the kitchen and the hen-house, all identical in design and materials, created a Three Bears effect.

Ranohira has no market, the population being only two thousand and the surrounding area virtually uninhabited. We investigated its shops in depth, searching with wild optimism for portable food. The two main stores, having no room for customers to enter, displayed their goods in tin basins by the roadside: a little rice, maize-grain, sugar and salt. The cloth-merchants sat in cubby-holes lined with cotton bales. Two other shops were so small and dark you could easily miss them and it would not matter if you did. They stocked only the ubiquitous and dubious tinned zebu, a few rusty tins of Nestles milk, a few bars of mouldy chocolate and a few packets of nauseating biscuits. Ranohira's three hotels are pretty dormant for the now being. One was previously owned by a French couple responsible for the town's conversational and distinguished-looking cats, all bearing signs of Siamese forebears.

After church, some worshippers stopped on their way home to buy a fistful of small fresh fish or large prawns, being sold by the coffee-ladies. These delicacies arrive on vehicles passing through from Tulear. Less virtuous types had been celebrating the Sabbath by spending their road-construction wages on home-distilled spirits. We passed three young men wavering down the main street at 10 a.m. and Rachel charitably concluded that for them this must be the end of Saturday rather than the beginning of Sunday. Later we asked Roland how the majority spend their high wages – on more zebu, he said, for their families' herds.

At the end of a long walk across the pastures that form Ranohira's agricultural hinterland – vast expanses of coarse red-brown grass – we returned dehydrated to the town. The local water is to be avoided, even after the treble treatment of boiling, filtering and pilling, and we were feeling guilty about our depletion of the camp's precious supply of Coca-cola and Antsirabe fizzy orange. So we made desperate efforts to be self-sufficient and were directed to one of the defunct hotels. Five minutes of battering on the locked door roused a grave, poised young Merina woman wearing a nightgown under her *lamba*. She sold us her remaining stock: two bottles of Coca-cola and a bottle of *limonady*, costing £2.50. These came from a non-functioning refrigerator, once gas-powered. The *limonady* was so sickly that we had to try not to taste while swallowing it. I felt sorry for that young woman; one sensed that she was enduring a considerable degree of unaccustomed hardship. Such people are hardest hit by Madagascar's economic collapse. The land-owning peasants can get by; the small hotelier or craftsman or merchant or bashie-owner suffers a cruel decline in living-standards when there is almost no flow of cash or goods.

We left Ranohira at 7 a.m. under a strangely beautiful sky; no blue, all white and dove-grey in wavy layers – a gentle dreamy canopy over the wide harshness of the Bara country. At dawn Ranohira had had its first rain – a five-minute sprinkle – in several months.

Our truck averaged twenty-seven mph over the hundred and sixty miles to Tulear. But that figure is misleading. For the first sixty-eight miles, to Sakaraha, the speedometer needle rarely went above twelve mph. Then the road became broken tarmac, the needle soared and we were glad to be tightly wedged in the cab as the empty oil-tanker swerved at speed around yawning craters – or on occasions (still worse) did not swerve in time. The driver was a Betsileo, his mate a dusky Vezo from a village near Tulear, where we paused for him to deliver to his wife a sack of charcoal bought cheaply en route. Both men were uncommonly large: the Betsileo very fat, the Vezo very long. Life in that cab was sweaty.

It would be easier to enjoy Madagascar's terrain if one were an ecological innocent. Just beyond Ranohira another aspect of the Isalo is revealed as Route Nationale No. 7 – here gruesomely weather-mangled – winds through the edge of the massif. Isolated silver crags, tinged red, yellow and pink, rise gauntly from a flat plain, golden-brown and sparsely grassed. Unsteady-looking stacks of rock-cubes, a hundred feet high, have brown whiskers of leafless scrub. And here too are many sculptures; the driver pointed out a wind-carved figure known as 'The Queen' who is so greatly revered that many travellers place money in a crevice near her 'feet'. Between these scores of limestone outcrops a few zebu graze. Only a few, nowadays, because on this grossly abused soil nourishing grass is being fast replaced by the inedible bunch-grass of which we had seen so much within the massif. This freakish *aristidia* flourishes where no other grass will grow, propagating itself by underground fibres instead of seeds and never sending up succulent young shoots to tempt zebu. As it needs no organic nutrients of any kind it thrives on cracked bedrock, or on savannah where over-burning and over-grazing have reduced the soil to sterile dust. Aesthetically it is pleasing yet my heart ached when, beyond the massif, we crossed an immense undulating plain on which *aristidia* has almost completely taken over from what the zebu need. Solitary palms, standing far apart, broke the monotony of this plain. Some were lanky medemias, others smaller and wider – wind-torn, looking like so many tattered fans. Many medemias had been snapped in two by those cyclonic winds which devastate Madagascar during the rainy season. Many telegraph poles had also been snapped. The French used to replace damaged poles after each cyclone; the Malagasy do not. Hence the limitations of Ranohira's telephone service.

Suddenly we were overlooking an inhabited green oasis where dense foliage marked the course of a narrow river. The truck splashed and lurched through the foot-deep water – bridges are an unknown luxury hereabouts – then stopped to refresh its engine. A tall leafless tree, laden with russet bobbles, overhung a group of huts crudely assembled from wooden stakes, sheets of iron and strips of raffia matting; they had neither doors nor windows. 'Nobody here is afraid of bandits,' I remarked to Rachel. 'They probably *are* the bandits!' she retorted. Three women sat outside one shack, wrapped to the ears in gaily coloured blankets; for them this was a chilly morning. Black pigs, white geese and scrawny brown hens swarmed happily amidst the glossy riverside growth. An ibis and several cattle egrets flew past. A long-haired chocolate-coloured cat dozed on the edge of a table beside manioc-flour buns; there was no coffee. An old blanketed man squatted on the beige earth slowly stirring a large black pot on a small charcoal fire. A toddler in a short pink skirt cuddled a tiny white puppy; both had bloated bellies. 'They've given each other worms,' noted Rachel gloomily. Nobody took any notice of the *vazaha*: we were just another manifestation of the road-building team. When the driver had washed down a plate of mashed manioc with a swig of cane-spirits we rattled on, allowing the mantle of silence to fall again on that microscopic community.

Our map would not tell us whether that was a real river or merely a watercourse. In this area there are many brief emergences above ground of what is, apparently, quite a plentiful underground water supply. Our stream in the Isalo entrance canyon was one such; long before reaching Ranohira it had seeped back into the earth.

Soon we were among low hills clothed with the remains of the deciduous forest that once covered western Madagascar from Tulear to the northern tip of the island. One-fifth survives, but for how much longer? Even today, twenty-five per cent of Madagascar's surface is deliberately burnt each year. This is what Rachel Rabesandratana, lecturer in botany at Tulear University, has described as 'Our suicide by fire'. Yet there is still hope, in western Madagascar, if the annual firing of grasslands can somehow be controlled. The deciduous woodland, unlike the east coast rainforest, is an efficient self-regenerator if given a chance. But how to convince the Malagasy of the need – *their* need – for fire-control? By temperament they are disinclined to look more than twenty-four hours ahead, on any issue. Nobody has stated the problem more succinctly than Dr Alison Jolly, one of Madagascar's most valuable *vazaha* friends. In *A World Like Our Own* she wrote:

'It is a question of balance. If there are the right number of cattle, they find rich hay in the western savannahs and feel no need to invade the forests. In the dry season they live on the 'green bite' (the new grass shoots that spring up when fires pass). Some fire, and some green shoots, are clearly necessary in a balanced cattle economy. [But] this fragile equilibrium can be destroyed by human population increase, by increase in the cattle herds, and by some forms of increase in the market economy. As usual, all the factors relate to one another. More people want more cattle and more cash. Cash crops in this region means shifting cultivation of peanuts and therefore cutting the forest for fields, or else irrigated cotton on black alluvial soil in the streambeds. In turn the cotton fields involve keeping the cattle out of what was once rich pasture and forcing the displaced herds to put still greater pressure on the drier grass and woodland . . . The loss of woodland in the long term affects the water-supply and drainage, so cattle and people may find themselves in a tightening trap as a consequence of their own attempts at expansion.'

As we were descending a forested hill – our road visible for miles, ascending the next hill – a dark wave came flowing over the crest ahead. We stared in wonder at this herd of zebu, apparently hundreds strong. When they were about two miles away the truck stopped, obeying a local rule of the road, and we took out our binoculars. Zebu were still pouring over the crest, not at the easy amble of Irish cattle but trotting purposefully, aware of being on a long journey. Here Route Nationale No. 7 is accompanied on each side by a zebu-track wider than the road and now this triple highway was flooded with a river of splendid beasts – many only half-grown – their hoofbeats like muted thunder, their horns tossing, mouths frothing, tails swishing. They were not at all put out by the stationary truck and as they surged past we realised that they numbered thousands rather than hundreds. We saw too that they were divided into eight separate herds, each with its own herdsmen who worked hard to prevent any accidental mingling. So many animals travelling together might seem impractical but there is safety in numbers. In this territory cattle-rustling remains, as it has always been, Big Business: the region's only large-scale enterprise. These beasts, representing the total wealth of several Mahafaly villages, were escorted by about forty young men – dusky-skinned and handsome, finely proportioned though not very tall, wearing ragged shorts and traditional blankets. Each carried a long sharp spear that glinted in the sun: my first sight of spears in use, as it were – not mere romantic relics of bygone times. A few also carried ancient shotguns that might be envied by a War Museum. And one carried a battered-looking rolled-up umbrella, whether as a third weapon or as a sunshade I know not. Their intent expressions were those of men on a difficult and dangerous mission, yet big smiles flashed in response to our shouted greetings. As we moved forward I watched through the rear-mirror and saw the herd turning off onto a track leading south. It saddened me to think that those zebu and their owners, representing an unbroken link with Madagascar's pre-European past, should also be the greatest threat to Madagascar's post-European future.

Sakaraha seems important on the map, for lack of competition, but is no more than a large, dispirited-looking village. Yet it has two resident *vazaha*, an American missionary couple whom we later met in Tulear on their monthly shopping expedition. In their mid-twenties, with a nine-month-old baby, Ruth and David lived in a fortified mud hut, sans telephone service, postal delivery, electricity or any reliable water-supply. One bucket of nappy-washing water had to last three days. Ruth did all the cooking and baking on a tin charcoal stove. In lieu of radio batteries (available only on the Black Market, eschewed by missionaries), David had devised a solar panel – and it worked. The police had lent them a gun each for protection against bandits, their immediate predecessor having been speared in the neck and lungs in the course of a robbery. They had been forbidden to open their door after dark, whatever the appeals to their Christian charity. While pregnant, Ruth had been advised by her local friends to take extra care as some *ombiasa*, far out in the bush, still like to get hold of unborn babies; the sun-dried heart and eyes of the unborn are added to their necklaces as particularly powerful charms. This sounds like an extract from one of the more luridly heathen-bashing chapters of the Reverend Matthews or the Reverend Ellis. Yet when I recalled the faces of a few of those Mahafaly herdsmen it seemed not entirely impossible that in certain areas such customs survive.

Ruth and David, and two other American Lutheran missionary couples working elsewhere, had ambitions to set up village Health Centres, concentrating on preventive medicine. They had made a start in Sakaraha and the government was 'observing' their activities but not yet helping. David's work often took him away for four or five days, on solo bullock-cart journeys to remote villages. For these trips he dressed in threadbare garments as your modern bandit finds smart clothing an irresistible temptation. Neither the local Lutheran pastor nor any other Malagasy would accompany him into bandit territory and when his return was delayed by a day or two, as occasionally happened, Ruth prepared herself for the worst. 'But,' she said, 'you become used to the waiting, as part of life.' And she meant that. She and David were untainted by any awareness of their own heroism – which is not, I think, too strong a word. They had of course been bred to the job, born and brought up in southern Madagascar as the children of missionaries. Ruth could just remember the days when Tulear's shops were well stocked with every sort of French import, not unreasonably priced. It is hard to imagine an American-bred couple of their generation, however full of missionary zeal, adapting so uncomplainingly to life in the Sakaraha region – or being so sympathetic to the Malagasy temperament and traditions.

Ruth and David confirmed our Betsileo driver's information about the few wretched villages between Sakaraha and Tulear. Over the past several years thousands have fled to the city, from these and many other villages, to escape the bandits' regular night-raids. Men armed only with spears cannot hope to defend their cattle and homes against the new type of bandit, who has somehow recently acquired guns. In Tana we heard many rumours that either the CIA or the South African government (or both) were supplying the guns in question, by way of helping to de-stabilise President Ratsiraka's too-Socialist régime; and stranger things have happened under the influence of Cold War emotions. Whatever the cause of this situation the security forces are finding it hard to control and much of southern Madagascar has reverted to its previous status of 'unpacified' territory, with petty thieving as a new and alien complication. Previously this was 'not done' by the best bandits; like the old-fashioned Mafia, they had their own perverse code of honour. They were cattle-rustlers and proud of it; they did not enter a man's home and sneak away with his non-bovine possessions. (But was this only because such possessions were then almost worthless?) Now they behave like boring common criminals; a week before our meeting, David had had his tape-recorder stolen from the living-room one afternoon, while he and Ruth were tending the baby in an adjacent bedroom.

Beyond Sakaraha we passed two small trucks untidily loaded with cotton and saw it being picked in the ill-tended remains of a colonial plantation. The cotton trade explains why once upon a time Route Nationale No. 7 was well maintained between the port of Tulear and Sakaraha. Descending to the coast through hilly spiny desert, we noticed how much poorer and less healthy the peasants looked than their highland cousins. Yet their gaily decorated tombs – some adorned with many zebu horns arranged on tall 'totem-poles' – were larger and more elaborate than any seen in Imerina. Most were freshly painted and looked from a distance like solid new bungalows, in astonishing contrast to the flimsy shelters which house the living. When a strange shape appeared on the horizon, a high rectangle miles long and flawlessly flat, I had become so bemused by these tombs that I fancied for a moment this must be yet another – honouring perhaps some mighty king. It is in fact Tulear's only landmark, prosaically known as 'Table Mountain'. And now, between the grey hills ahead, we could also see glinting slivers of blue – the Mozambique Channel. Rachel cheered; she hoped soon to be snorkling over coral reefs.

7

Days and Nights with Fotsy and Merk

Snorkling was scheduled to happen at Moro-Moro, eighteen miles north of Tulear. At the bus station our Betsileo friend shouted an enquiry about onward transport and someone pointed to a ramshackle bus-truck, crammed with humanity beneath green tarpaulin. Less than five minutes after arriving at Tulear we were on the way to Moro-Moro. 'This can't be true!' said Rachel. Moreover, though our remarkable vehicle took ninety minutes to cover those eighteen miles it did not stop once.

Sixty-two other adults were on board; we did not try to count the children. The conductor's insistence on our going up front led to a marathon of apologetic climbing over everybody, inflicting minor injuries on their offspring and belongings – these being often indistinguishable, half-stuffed under the seats. Squeezed into a corner, embracing our rucksacks, we could see little of the landscape. Soon we had to close our eyes against the dust, but even then it was obvious that most of our fellow-passengers were filthy. Their natural skin colours varied yet within half an hour we were all a uniform grey-brown. Nobody talked. To do so meant inhaling ounces of Madagascar. When we stopped at Moro-Moro everyone looked understandably apprehensive and we did more unavoidable damage on the way out. The conductor could have helped by taking our rucksacks through the side but he clearly enjoyed the *vazaha*'s embarrassment. He was not a typical Malagasy.

In Antsirabe an ancient Frenchman had advised us to go to Moro-Moro for snorkling and sharkless swimming. He knew the owner of the hotel, which our favourite guidebook describes with enthusiasm:

'Village Vezo "Moro-Moro", Main Road No. 9 Manombo-Morombe. Manager: Mr Jacques Ducaud. 10 comfortable

bungalows at the side of the lagoon equipped with complete
sanitary amenities, twin beds, possibilities of having two
superposed extra beds. Electricity 220 volts. Fish, shell-fish,
barbecue. Bar – Swimming-pool – Diving-school – Submarine exploration with autonomous diving suit – Hire of
canoe – Visit of the reef, etc. Charming site, very good
welcome. Club atmosphere.'

This does not sound, perceptive readers may think, quite *me* –
though curiosity about the nature of superposed beds and autonomous diving suits might possibly have outweighed the horrors of
barbecue and club atmosphere. Our Antsirabe friend had however assured us that Moro-Moro is now tourist-free; and indeed
Monsieur Ducaud viewed our approach with unconcealed amazement. He then thought it only fair to warn us, before we booked in,
that snorkling would be impossible. (Alas! poor Rachel!) He
pointed to the horizon, where a fringe of white marked the reef,
and bade us listen. When you can see that surf, and hear the
distant roar of the Indian Ocean, you can neither snorkle nor fish.

M. Ducaud's hotel, planned by himself, is a civilised 'tourist
development'. He began by buying a grove of immense pines
which sway and sigh in the wind from the sea like sentient beings.
In their shade, on soft golden sand, he built ten one-bedroom huts,
widely separated, and a long high-ceilinged open-plan chalet as
dining-room and lounge-bar. Only local materials were used:
wood, cactus, palm, bamboo. The chalet has no sea-facing wall so
one eats within a bone's throw of the wavelets when the tide is in.
Even if Moro-Moro Hotel were packed, with superposed beds all
over the place, it could hold no more than forty people for whom
there would be an eight-mile beach. 'Five humans per mile,' as
Rachel calculated.

In 1973 it seemed that Madagascar might benefit slightly from
the world tourist boom but instead its limited tourist trade
collapsed. M. Ducaud's empty huts worried Rachel but he
assured us that the position was not as dire as it then seemed;
enough guests still trickle through to keep the shark from the door.
Four German botanists were expected the following week – most
vazaha visitors are scientists – and ex-colonists still resident in
Tulear appreciate the restaurant. Rich Indians come too: nowadays almost the only Malagasy citizens who can afford a holiday.

One felt that this trickle satisfied M. Ducaud. He looked happy reclining under his pines, listening to Beethoven quartets as the crimson sun slid into the ink-blue sea. Like Roland he was a third-generation colonist, but one who had spent all his life in Madagascar and most of it near Tulear. He said, 'This is my country, my *only* country . . .' – the plaintive claim of so many ex-colonists. 'Natives' were not the only victims of colonialism. A recent fifteen-day visit to Paris, his first in ten years, was 'fourteen days too many'. He considered himself lucky to be able to live so cheaply amidst such beauty. Fuel for the electricity generator (needed to power Beethoven quartets) was his main expense. Fish and vegetables for himself and his platoon of servants ('How could I dismiss them? They *need* their wages!') cost little. His bar-service revealed a trusting nature. The chalet was usually empty, yet he showed us a notebook on the wall, and how to open the refrigerator behind the bar, and asked us to jot down each drink we took. Even a Malagasy tourist boom would not, I suspect, make him a millionaire.

On our first afternoon the sky was completely overcast and the sea not too warm. Floating far out, I gazed back at the golden emptiness of our crescent beach, overhung by weird vegetation, and reflected that there can be few other 'sea-side resorts' where, at the end of July, two people could monopolise so much. Meanwhile Rachel was trying to snorkle over the off-shore coral reefs. But the heavy swell made even this too hazardous; open coral-wounds can be troublesome in tropical countries.

Moro-Moro introduced us to the fantastic botanical excesses of southern Madagascar. I use 'fantastic' deliberately. The long strip of vegetation that here stretches beside the coast, a few hundred yards inland, seems pure fantasy – something out of a sadistic, unfunny cartoon film. No serviceable similes come to mind. What grows in the Malagasy desert is like nothing else on earth – animal, vegetable or mineral. This forest (an inappropriate word, though commonly used) is colourless, dusty, desiccated, with powdery dirty-yellow sand underfoot. In winter it is a drab tangle of greenish-grey. There is no beauty here and the fascination of the place is undeniably morbid. Vicious plants, armed with burrs, spines, thorns, hooks and spikes, reach out destructively from every side – and from above and below, drooping out of the sky, hidden in the sand, coiling, springing, bending, dripping. The gross bottle-trees, like miniature baobabs, are the most normal-looking things around, their distended trunks tapering towards the top and producing a tuft of short branches bearing in winter great dangling fruits like tennis balls covered in brown velvet. Dominating all else are the didierea, not even remotely related to the cactus though any lay person would assume them to be at least second cousins. They grow to thirty feet, always at a slight angle to the ground, always bending south. Each slim, separate pillar of a clump is covered in steel-strong six-inch spikes, needle-sharp. Then there is the monstrous harpoon-burr, each growing far apart on an otherwise bare, thin branch – the only plant I have ever seen to which one involuntarily applies the adjective 'evil'. It is in fact a mass of harpoons topping long wiry stems, all growing from one hideously shaped heart. The wound it inflicts takes three days to begin to heal. And there is also the insanely contorted latex tree, which flourishes no cutting weapon. Instead it drips a white sap on passers-by, causing skin-ulcers and sometimes total blindness.

For light relief at Moro-Moro we bird-watched, much more successfully than in the Highlands, despite the aridity. During one sunrise hour I spotted twelve 'unknowns'.

We visited a few Vezo settlements up and down the coast, walking to them along Route Nationale No. 9 – ankle-deep in dust – and returning along the coral- and shell-strewn beach. The Vezo are best known for the eroticism of their tomb decorations. Some consider them a branch of the Bara tribe but to us they seemed a few shades darker and several shades shyer. They are Madagascar's main fishing tribe and their settlements give the impression that they belong, in spirit, to the sea. Down the coast towards Tulear they live in tiny corrugated-iron hovels: intolerably hot, one would have thought, during summer. Up the coast towards Ankilimalinika their scattered huts are cactus-thatched, built of drift-wood and set in dreary patches of manioc or maize. High sand-dunes, sprouting a straggle of grotesque trees, shelter them from the south-easterly trade winds. Here we saw our first herds of Malagasy goats, unwisely imported to encourage rug-making; they may yet prove Madagascar's last ecological straw.

The gale was inhibiting fishing activities but we watched two single outrigger canoes, with small square sails, venturing out to attempt, unsuccessfully, to lift lobster-pots. These vessels have remained unchanged since the migrations from Polynesia, though they are smaller than the double-outriggers used by the ocean-crossing *razana*. Vezo fleets fish the length of the west coast, as far

north as Nosy-bé. Entire families take off for months in twenty-
five-foot canoes and camp on shore, making tents from their sails,
while drying and smoking their catch for the inland markets. It
would be a mistake to deduce great poverty from their dwellings.
They are rightly esteemed for their fishing skills and their trade is
profitable. They may go ragged and barefoot but the majority
have splendidly developed bodies, sound teeth, clear eyes and a
general air of physical well-being that any affluent city-dweller
might envy.

During our last walk we collected a more precious souvenir
(and easier to carry) than anything tangible. At sunset we were
wandering across flat grassland where the wide jagged crowns of
nearby pines seemed black beneath a green-tinged sky. Then we
turned towards the invisible shore and saw, on higher land, an
intricate frieze stretching for miles against an apricot glow. Now
they were beautiful, those didierea, giant aloe, sword cactus,
euphoria, latex trees and writhing leafless vines, merged into a
single eerie pattern in the fading light. But then it seemed the light
was strengthening – and a half-moon sailed free of the woodlands
to the east, while still the afterglow lingered in the west, apricot
turning to copper. Moments later Venus too became visible, as I
have never seen her before – not merely outshining her companions but distinctly an orb, pale gold and brilliant, defying the
moon. This was a magical confluence of light, an excitement of
loveliness that heightened as we reached the shoreline, to walk
home by a luminous sea through a silver-black mesh of tree-
shadows.

In such places one becomes very aware of the quiet soul of
Madagascar. For all the talk of bandits, it was impossible ever to
feel threatened. We did not doubt the bandits' present pervasive-
ness in the south, but atmospheres have their balances and in
Madagascar the benign far outweighs the malign. The bandits
have not yet made their psychic mark; let us hope the *razana*
ensure they never do.

That evening will be my most abiding memory of Moro-Moro.
Rachel's perhaps will be the three lemurs – ring-tailed siblings,
born in the hotel – who co-existed peacefully with a smug fat cat
and two grey-muzzled labradors. In the chalet this lemur trio
played tag among the rafters or hide-and-seek between the hessian walls. At frequent intervals they paused to urine-mark their
territory (i.e. the whole hotel), causing our host to mutter

insincere apologies. As we diary-wrote they sat on our table, helping themselves from the sugar-bowl and 'stealing' our drinks. But at meal-times they were banished. Before bringing our plates the grinning waiter waved a catapult at them – the sort used by herdsmen to control zebu – and they bounded outside to sit in the nearest pine tree looking hard-done-by. A fourth lemur lived in the trees, on excellent terms with everyone but unwilling to enter any building: he had been born free.

Tulear stands eighteen feet above sea level; as a port it is pretty dormant for the now being. Since Independence, Indians have come to dominate what remains of its commercial life. It has about forty-eight thousand inhabitants and is the capital of a region covering a hundred thousand square miles, with a population of a million and a quarter humans and countless million zebu. It did not exist as a town before 1895 and there are not a few who feel it should have stayed that way. During most of the year it is crucified by the sun (we were lucky, the south-easterly was still blowing) and the climate evidently atrophied the inventiveness of the French architect who created it. (His name escapes me which does not matter too much; it would be unlikely to ring many bells.) The gridiron effect is alleviated only by a graceful *kily* tree – the tamarind, sacred in Madagascar – growing at each intersection. The dreary look-alike administrative buildings, now being inexorably dismantled by the climate, seem ludicrously pompous. A few would-be with-it hotels mark what passes for a sea-front. Behind them stretches an expanse of grey sand-cum-mud (this is the beach) which serves as the town latrine. Nearby is the port, where the rusting hulk of a merchant ship is anchored beside a disintegrating pier. But the people are a delight: friendly, smiling, courteous, helpful. In Madagascar the Malagasy redeem every situation.

There are superficial resemblances between Tulear and some small coastal town in south India – heat, dust, flies, piss'n'shit smells, roadside foodstalls, palm trees tall against a very blue sky, rickshaws, bullock-carts, dark skins, run-down colonial houses and gardens, shanty-settlements on dog-infested wasteland (these are the refugees from banditry). But there are far fewer people, much less motor-traffic, much less merchandise in the shops and market, much less malnutrition; and there is no enthralling architecture. Of the six Malagasy towns on our route (there are only two others of any size) Tulear seemed the least capable of ever developing a character of its own. It is a blatant colonial imposition on occupied territory, pointless in relation to its surroundings.

Anglo–Malagasy relations first blossomed in the Tulear region, centuries before the LMS pioneers – or any other European – had set foot in Imerina. During the seventeenth century British East India Company ships regularly took on supplies along Madagascar's west coast, mainly from the Bay of St Augustin, twenty-two miles south of Tulear. In 1636 the Courteen Association, a short-lived rival of the East India Company, had ambitions to establish a colony there under the seventeen-year-old Prince Rupert of Bavaria. His sensible mother, Queen Elizabeth of Bohemia, who by that date had more than her share of worries, opposed the idea. She observed cannily, 'I thought if Madagascar were a place either worth the taking or profitable to be kept, that the Portugalis by this time would have had it, and having so long time possesst, most right to it.' (A revealing glimpse of the expansionist ethics of the time; it occurred to no one that the Malagasy had 'possesst' it longest of all.) That first scheme fell through for lack of funds but by 1644 it had been revived and a colony of 120 English men and women settled on the coast under an unsavoury character called John Smart. He tried to live up to his name in his dealings with the Malagasy, who had received the settlers amiably, and Anglo–Malagasy relations soon deteriorated. A year later twelve survivors left for home; the rest of the colony had either been killed or died of starvation. (Easily done, in these parts.) One of the survivors, Powle Waldegrave, wrote: 'I could not but endeavour to dissuade others from undergoing the miseries that will follow the persons of such as adventure themselves for Madagascar ... from which place God divert the residence and adventures of all good men.'

A happier experience was described by George Buchan, one of the passengers on an East Indiaman wrecked on Tulear's reef by the south-easterly in August 1792. Forty were drowned, the other 240 made their way to the court of the King of Bara, near Tulear harbour, and were generously entertained and protected for seven months, until rescue came – by which time ninety had died of malaria and heat-stroke though all the ten women survived. Vezo fishermen brought up the ship's treasure and gave it to the king, whose legal property (as salvage) it now was. At once he returned it to the ship's officers, who later expressed gratitude for 'such disinterested attention as would have done honour to the most civilised Christian'. In due course the East India Company acknowledged the king's help with a suitable gift. George Buchan's account of this adventure records:

'The king, though held in habitual reverence and, so far as we saw, promptly obeyed, cannot be considered wholly despotic; for in the event of any undue severity, his subjects will leave him and migrate to another state . . . The practice which seems to exist of making all weighty questions matter of public deliberation, must have a powerful effect in upholding independence and elevation of mind. I remember being quite struck with the fluency of speech and oratory which we sometimes heard . . . I think I may call them, among themselves, a social and happy people . . . They enjoy apparently much domestic harmony. Polygamy is allowed but is far from being generally practised. Their kindness to their slaves is quite remarkable . . . Their general turn of mind appears that of lively quickness, accompanied by a thirst for knowledge. The king seemed to be about 25 years of age; not tall, and rather slimly made, but well-proportioned. His complexion was remarkably white, approaching copper colour. When occasion required it, he appeared with a good deal of what might be called in their way magnificence, but he did not seem fond of the royal state, and generally went about with very few people.'

Even after seven months as the king's guest, Buchan makes no attempt to transcribe his host's name. But this Tulear King of Bara was presumably a Masikoro chief who at that date would have been a tributary of the powerful Sakalava King of Menabe. It is interesting that Buchan remarks on the king's fair colour, though he also reports that most of his subjects were dark-skinned Vezo fishermen. This was before the first Merina effort to conquer the south. But the comments of Buchan, and of other early travellers who observed life around the Malagasy coast, reveal that the chiefs and nobles of many tribes were lighter-skinned than their subjects, if not as purely Polynesian as the Merina. The observation about 'migrating to another state' indicates an unusually developed sense of what we would now call 'nationhood'.

At the same period, it would have been unthinkable for an African tribesman who disapproved of his chief to push off to another territory just like that. But the Malagasy, sharing a common language and culture, felt free to migrate to any part of their island, at least in theory. In practice, temporary political/military conflicts, and climatic extremes, must have limited their movements. Yet in spirit they were already *Malagasy*.

By the end of the eighteenth century the use of English names, and some knowledge of spoken English, had become quite common up and down the west coast, but particularly in the Tulear area. The King of Bara's wife was Queen Charlotte.

Now the main *vazaha* influence is American, chiefly through the Lutheran Church Mission. But we also saw several long, wide, vulgar American automobiles being driven at high speed and looking as out of place as a strip-tease artiste in a monastery cloister. Our missionary friends explained apologetically that these belong to an oil-seeking team that for years has been unsuccessfully busy in southern Madagascar. We had passed their headquarters outside the town and recognised it as 'a little bit of America'.

Both Roland and M. Ducaud had been discouraging about our chance of getting to Fort-Dauphin, on the south-east coast, by road – mainly because there is no road, which sounds logical enough. People fly from coast to coast, at vast expense. Air Mad is a paragon of efficiency, compared to any form of Malagasy land transport, and it was murmured that a free flight might be arranged for a travel-writer. But flying defeats the main object of travel-writers, which is to see where they're at. So we continued to enquire about transport across what Nigel Heseltine has described as 'a large area of sclerophytic bush dominated by endemic *Euphorbiaceae*' – which indeed is just what it looks like.

Ruth and David reassured us; their base was at Fort-Dauphin so they knew the route well. True, there was no road. Yet a brave mission vehicle occasionally did the trip and sometimes they used the weekly truck-bus service. David escorted us to the appropriate bus station and organised tickets (£15.50 each) guaranteeing our eventual arrival at Fort-Dauphin, though no arrival date was specified. Departure time was 5 a.m. next morning. Later, in our doss-house, we were told that the Indian tycoon who operates this service pays protection money to bandit leaders in three villages en route. I felt sceptical; such an arrangement assumes a degree of sophisticated organisation rarely found in Malagasy government departments, never mind among tribal bandits. But perhaps the bandits are smarter than the bureaucrats.

In daylight this bus station was a half-hour walk from our doss-house; in darkness it was a good deal further. At 4 a.m. the moon had just set, there was no street lighting, we had no torch batteries and Tulear's deserted streets – long, wide, straight – seemed shorn of all their carefully noted landmarks. Soon Rachel was limping badly; at Moro-Moro she had cut her foot on a giant razor-clam embedded in sea-grass. (As our guidebook so frankly points out, 'There are many pearls on Madagascar's see-shores'.) When a solitary woman appeared ahead we momentarily terrified her by looming out of the night – two sinister rucksack-misshapen figures – but she forgivingly went a mile out of her way to guide us. At the bus station there was not a trace of a truck-bus. 'Told you so!' said Rachel, who had seen no need to rise before dawn.

Several bashies were preparing by lantern-light for short journeys to such places as Ankilimivany and Ambohimahavelona. We were told that our vehicle is loaded elsewhere and there seemed to be a warning note in our informant's voice. Smiling coffee-ladies stood behind lamp-lit tables and we breakfasted well on enamel bowls of strong black coffee and long French loaves bought hot from a nearby bakery.

At 5.40 our Mercedes arrived: a singular vehicle, ingeniously adapted for a singular task. We came to respect it profoundly. Although cruelly uncomfortable, it was mechanically sound. You cannot take chances when only one vehicle regularly crosses a hundred thousand virtually uninhabited square miles of 'sclerophytic bush'. As this weekly service represents the entire coast-to-coast public transport system, for both goods and passengers, it was no surprise to find Adrian and Jamie already aboard.

Our home for the next few days merits a pen-portrait. Luggage was roped to the roof under a green tarpaulin, tightly secured by night but rolled up by day to allow an excellent view between the widely-spaced wooden side-slats. Entry was by a strong permanently attached iron ladder at the back, leading up to the roof. The arched hessian ceiling, on wood and iron struts, gave a covered-wagon effect – as though we were about to open up The West. The main cargo was many – *very* many – sacks of Portland cement. These had been loaded first, being tightly packed, one-deep, over the entire floor space. Then the front two-thirds was equipped with old metal bus-seats, expertly wedged between the sacks, three on each side with a narrow aisle where small sacks of grass provided for an extra passenger in each row. The seats were backless, apart from an iron bar at shoulder-blade level. An average of nine passengers (excluding children) occupied each row of seven seats. Up front, facing the rest, sat ten passengers whose knees were permanently jammed against those opposite. In this death-row only the two at the ends had anything to hold onto during times of acute disequilibrium – which were not infrequent. But it was the mass of humanity occupying the seatless one-third space at the back who had it roughest. There the cement sacks were four deep, with a top layer of other sacks containing a hard knobbly unidentifiable substance (or objects), covered by raffia matting. The back side-slats had no gaps, which at least meant the five hens and three ducks could not easily escape, and the general situation recalled Doré's depiction of devils forcing the damned into a crowded pit exhaling sulphureous fumes. (Only our fumes were diesel.) I am no stranger to Third World motor-transport but this ride was something else again. My diary tells all:

'We moved off at 6.45, towards an opening fan of pink-gold effulgence above Table Mountain. Our first thirty miles, on Route Nationale No. 7, took us to Andranovary where a track turns south. The map (Paris-printed in 1964) describes this track as Route Nationale No. 10 but I maintain it can never have been more than a gleam in the eye of some French engineer. Jamie, however, argues that a lot can happen to a Malagasy road in twenty years.

'Andranovary is a sad small town: it would seem a village anywhere else. Had we known we were to stop there for an hour and a quarter we could have explored. But Fotsy, our driver, made a point of giving no such information; he is one of Nature's bully-boys who didn't improve (or not much) on acquaintance. Aged perhaps thirty-ish (Malagasy ages are hard to guess), he evidently belongs to one of the south-east coastal tribes who have Arab blood. (Antanosy? Antesaka? Antefasy? Antemoro? – I'll never get that lot sorted out.) His crinkly hair looks good with a dark copper skin and he has a fine straight nose and a thick moustache, neatly cultivated. Tallish, well-built, well-dressed: a handsome fellow and aware of the fact. We soon realised that he enjoyed having us all – however many we were – at his mercy for 390 unique miles. His too-prominent eyes flashed angrily whenever anyone was slow to obey orders – and a lot of orders were given at Andranovary. Leaving Tulear, we'd marvelled at the numbers on board. But that was for starters. A queue awaited us at the junction and Fotsy walked around the truck, peering through the slats, pointing to unfilled inches and yelling orders as more and more grinning men and chuckling women came through the back. Such a journey would be intolerable with any other travelling-companions; Malagasy good humour and good manners seem indestructible. Then we had to wait for late-comers – and for several sacks that arrived on a zebu-cart in the fullness of time.

'Judging by colour, about half the passengers were of highland extraction. I suppose only the élite have occasion, or can afford, to travel Inter-City. Among the unfortunates facing us from death-row were two adolescent girls, their brother aged nine or ten and a toddler sister. Four very lovely faces, the colour of dark honey. The boy, especially, sitting immobile on a sister's lap, had an extraordinary beauty. An oval face of ethereal innocence, framed in short slightly curly hair, with a high domed forehead and wide tranquil eyes. A Coptic saint in a classical Amhara painting. When the going got really rough I anaesthetised myself by gazing at that face. It enabled me to forget that I was numb from the waist down and in agony from the waist up.

'We all had to sit immobile. Rachel was wedged between Adrian and a skinny Merina daddy with short-cropped hair, clad only in what appeared to be a long-sleeved nightgown and nursing a bare-bottomed infant. Between him and me, on the grass sack, sat a timid, weedy (luckily for us both) young man wearing a natty linen baseball cap; sun-glasses hung from an elegant brass chain around his neck. On my right side was an amiable but regrettably stout elderly man (Betsileo with one slave great-grandmother?) whose most cherished possession seemed to be an object made of zebu-hide, resembling a giant brief-case. This treasure, "superposed" on the cement sacks at our feet, totally inhibited my leg movements. Beyond this gentleman, a hefty Bara youth with tragically long legs and an engaging smile was squeezed against the slats. He read for hours on end, as did several of the passengers, from dog-eared paperbacks of missionary origin. We were privileged, having a seat each. In front of us four substantial young women shared three seats and beside them rose a juvenile pyramid: a little girl holding a toddler holding a baby. For all the sweetness of the Malagasy child-nature, that situation got a bit fraught at times.

'Beyond Andranovary green bushes speckled a flatness of brown grassland, merging into sparse forest. Then, dramatically, there was a new world ahead. Far below, filling the distance for hundreds of hot grey miles, lay the lands of the Mahafaly and the Antandroy – conquered only on paper, unexploited because there is nothing to exploit. Sharply one felt the strangeness and separateness of this territory, where only the tribes who belong – and their zebu – can survive.

'We seemed to be groping along the edge of that wooded escarpment, seeking a way down. Then our track of unstable earth, rocky and vividly red, began a steep descent in a series of tight bends – the only conventional test of Fotsy's skill and he passed with distinction. (Thereafter he needed stunt-driver skills.) As Adrian commented, no Indian merchant would entrust a bad driver with an irreplaceable "Merk".

'Lunch-break happened at 11.30 in Tongobory, a friendly village of straw shacks and mud huts in an oasis of fine leafy trees – including banyans. Nearby the broad Onilahy, one of Madagascar's biggest rivers, wound towards the Bay of St Augustin below a long scrubby mountain. Obviously our Merk's arrival was the event of the week for Tongobory. Laughing women and children crowded around the truck selling whole grilled fish, baked manioc, boiled corn-on-the-cob and my favourite local delicacy – maize-buns boiled in oil. I was among the many passengers too faint-hearted to struggle out. Already I had a guilt-complex (later to become a severe neurosis) about my nailed hiking-boots. These must have seemed like lethal weapons to our fellow-passengers as I scrambled to and fro over their defenceless bodies. They often had no alternative but to tread on each other, always with profuse apologies as they stepped lightly from shoulder to buttock to thigh to forearm. Had I stepped on anyone bones would have crunched. But I enjoyed my freedom of movement when Mr Brief-case and Mr Long-legs went out.

'Seeing Mr Brief-case crawling back across the knobbly sacks at the rear, I stood up and moved – half crouching – towards the aisle (the juvenile pyramid was still out) in a rather hopeless attempt to ease his seatward progress. Unfortunately one of the substantial quartet was simultaneously returning to the row in front of us, bearing on her head a large round basket of newly purchased manioc. Tripping over the timid young man, she fell heavily on me crushing my ribs against the nearest iron seat-back. Mr Brief-case also stumbled and to his intense embarrassment found himself with an arm around my neck and his hat (marvellously like Paddington's) over one ear. You have there a typical vignette of life aboard Merk during halts.

'We moved on at 12.50, Rachel carefully noting the time so that she could do her end-of-journey "average mph" calculation. For some reason I now had a smallish sack of assorted footstuffs on my lap. It seemed to belong to Mr Long-legs, who himself was hugging a much larger sack, and it meant that soon I was being strangled by the straps of my binoculars and shoulder-bag. The timid youth had been demoted to the Inferno at the rear and beside me sat a stout party carrying something bulky under her *lamba*. This object pinioned my left arm; for hours I couldn't even look at my watch. And the padlock on the zebu-hide brief-case was pressing into my right shin. Earlier the heat had been bearable but now the sun shone directly onto our side. Suddenly I realised that the chocolate in my shoulder-bag had melted. Fearing for this precious note-book, I got stroppy. To free my left arm, I forced the stout party towards the Merina daddy. Then I frantically licked the chocolate off note-book, maps, camera, pens, mug, torch. This provoked such widespread merriment that we felt the mini-calamity had been worth while; people needed cheering up by that stage.

'Our wedged state was a safeguard as Merk lurched and lumbered, like some crippled prehistoric monster, along what seemed to be a dried-up river bed but was still – I suppose – Route Nationale No. 10. For much of the way we were going below a normal walking speed; twice a spear-carrying tribesman effortlessly overtook us – the only humans we saw all afternoon. Merk stalled repeatedly on the way out of rocky gullies and Fotsy rose rapidly in our estimation. Patiently he would back and twist and coax while Merk roared and shuddered and displaced hundred-weights of desert, before yet again sticking fast. For Fotsy however this is a twice-weekly (there and back) routine and eventual defeat is Merk's lot. I said as much, causing Jamie (again a martyr to his buttocks – both this time) to express the view that there must be a limit, which might at any moment be reached, to the endurance of even the most superior Mercedes truck. "In Germany," he pointed out, "designers don't plan for *roads*" – his lip curled – "like this."

'I was the only *vazaha* to draw solace from the landscape. Hour after hour of "endemic *Euphorbiaceae* and *Dideriaecea*" seemed, inexplicably, to depress the others. Broadly speaking – very broadly: hundreds of miles broad – this was the vegetation we'd met in Moro-Moro. But much of it was on a bigger scale and with giant baobabs added, some specimens visible for miles across the flatness. The density varied, from a threadbare blanket of low scrub and cacti to impenetrable forests of didierea and aloe and all the rest – often swathed in leafless vines.

'Tea-break happened at 4.30 in Ejeda, which seems an urban sprawl on the map but is almost invisible. Adrian said it sounded like an Irish swear-word – true enough if pronounced phonetically. But alas! nothing in Malagasy is phonetic. Here Jamie, out on a buttock-soothing stroll, discovered that we would be spending the night at Ampanihy where Fotsy keeps a mistress. By the time we got there I reckoned he'd earned her.

'Beyond Ejeda Route Nationale No. 10 pulls itself together and Merk sped along, covering the next thirty-one miles in two and three-quarter hours. A tribesman would have had to run to keep up with us. My below-the-waist cramps had long since been replaced by a blessed numbness; I didn't even register the interesting fact that the padlock was rubbing the skin off my shin. By moonlight – the *whitest* I've ever seen – that landscape was a botanical lunatic asylum. I stared in dazed wonder at all those looming black shapes which somehow looked as though they might at any moment attack us. And then they did. We'd left the track to skirt some impassable gully and as Merk forced a way through the vegetation those nearest the slats were assaulted by viciously lashing barbed whips. Poor Mr Long-legs yelped with alarm and ducked down behind his sack. Someone shouted a plea to have the tarpaulin lowered but Fotsy had more pressing concerns. Once he misjudged and Merk was held fast between a baobab and something else. As we backed there was a rending sound overhead and I congratulated myself on having had the foresight to keep my rucksack within – for which privilege Fotsy had unsuccessfully tried to charge me an extra 8,000 FMG (about £12!).

'Ampanihy had of course gone to bed when we arrived at 8.15. But the moonlight illuminated what looked like a major cathedral; the desert does odd things to one's sense of proportion. As we came to rest in the enormous dusty market-place I felt I needed a drink quite badly and went on my first Malagasy alcohol-hunt. Local hooch was my quarry; one couldn't hope for beer in Ampanihy. Desperately I quested through a maze of low-roofed eating-house shacks around the market-place. Most were closed. The rest, lit by tiny oil-lamps, were innocent of hard liquor. "Just as well," said Adrian. "Have you ever smelt it?"

'Jamie is travelling without a flea-bag – silly boy! – so we enquired about lodgings: any doss-house, however "ethnic". There was none; odd when Ampanihy is a regular stopping-place, but Madagascar is like that. The travelling Malagasy are too sensible to waste money on lodgings. Many of our fellow-passengers were settling to sleep in the truck. Others were sleeping under it, a few were camping beneath trees. As there were only three of those we booked one – a tamarind in the centre of the market-place – before eating. The advantage of being under a tree, instead of just lying around anywhere, is that you can wedge your possessions between your sleeping self and the trunk.

'Jamie had found a cramped eating-shack run by a young Merina woman, friendly and gracious, who spoke excellent French (according to Jamie; we couldn't judge). The others ate rice and zebu stew with very hot chilli sauce. I wasn't hungry. By then I knew Madagascar had become the fifth country in which my ribs have been broken. I'd been trying to ignore the evidence; pain usually goes away if not encouraged by being brooded on. But not always. In our ill-lit "restaurant" I began to feel slightly faint and was glad of the shadows. Drinking endless cups of sweet herbal tea, I consoled myself with the thought that cracked ribs mend quickly – though our present life-style isn't very therapeutic. On the way back to our tree we passed the substantial quartet and their offspring, sitting around one of several camp-fires now enlivening the market-place. They were roasting manioc.

'I slept fairly well on the soft sand; perhaps the sacred tamarind helped. Luckily there were no insects; we had lent Jamie our tent to use as a sleeping-bag. I might have slept even better but for the group of half-drunk young men who had gathered round Merk as we painfully disembarked. (I wasn't the only cramp-victim; that disembarcation scene recalled an ambulance being emptied after a minor rail-crash.) The young men's behaviour was a little unsettling and in my sleep part of me remained alert. Ampanihy (population about 3,000) is the Mahafaly capital and among the French had a reputation for xenophobia. This "Spiny South" has always been an *ombiasa* stronghold and anti-*vazaha* feelings can still erupt unpredictably in defence of the old *razana* traditions unadulterated by Christianity.

'Once I woke when the moon was high and saw three UFOs gliding low overhead – soundless ebony shapes some four feet across. A dream, perhaps? Then I remembered that Ampanihy means "the place of many bats" – many *Pteropus refus*, Madagascar's giant fruit-bat with fox-red fur and often a five-foot wingspan.

'Fotsy had announced that we would depart punctually at 6 a.m. This seemed unlikely, given the nature of his social engagement at Ampanihy, but just in case I roused my companions, with some difficulty, at 5.30. We struck camp by the last of the moonlight and at the first shack to open ate cold rice-buns while a quiet lemon-pale dawn seeped up from the east. The yawning younger generation pointed out reproachfully that none of our fellow-passengers was yet stirring. I know when I'm not loved so I wandered off to the conspicuous disused well in the centre of the market-place and peered into its accumulation of scum, very far below. In Moro-Moro we'd been told of its extraordinary history, to illustrate the difficulties of "developing" the Spiny South – which doesn't in the least want to be developed.

'Ampanihy's last district commissioner was a colonial "goody" who had spent a lifetime serving the Malagasy in the least salubrious corners of their island. When he took over Independence was near and he longed to provide Ampanihy with an enduring and practical memorial to the colonial era. A permanent supply of pure water was the obvious parting gift; the town had only a rudimentary well, dry as often as not. He supervised its enlargement, had it lined with dressed stone and designed a covered fountain. When his Tana superiors objected to the cost of an American petrol-powered pump, he contributed some of his own savings to the project. Two specially trained young Mahafaly mechanics were put in charge, the pump did all that was expected of it and the town enjoyed an endless flow of clear, cold, pure water. Then one morning the automatic cut-off failed, either because of damage done on the transatlantic voyage or because the machinery had been abused through ignorance. The mechanics descended the steel ladder to investigate and were overcome by carbon monoxide fumes. Cruelly, it was the district commissioner, walking to work, who found their bodies and yelled for help before himself descending the ladder – from which he was rescued, unconscious, moments later. He paid for the funerals (one Protestant, one Catholic, both expensive). When the necessary repairs had been carried out, and the well drained and cleaned, the fountain again went into action. But by that time the local *ombiasa* had made it *fady* to use the well; its water-spirit, outraged by sacreligious *vazaha* meddling, had drowned the Christian mechanics to punish their lack of respect for the *razana*. No Mahafaly man or woman has ever since approached that well. Quarter of a century later the Ampanihy folk are still going to collect opaque water from the pitiable trickle of the local river; or, when that disappears, to scanty water-holes far away in the bush. The machinery and fountain superstructure have long since vanished. Only the massive stone-lined well remains, deep and dark and shunned.

'I leant on its cut-stone rim (a very un-Malagasy construction, solid and precise) and watched Ampanihy's weekly market getting its act together: not a speedy process. Slowly too things were happening around Merk as people shuffled off their somnolent coil and drifted away towards secluded corners. (Unlike many races who lack "sanitary equipments", the Malagasy are shy performers.) Of Fotsy however there was as yet no sign.

'One bashie appeared and a newly slain zebu was carried to the tin-roofed concrete meat-market close to the well – the only other colonial amenity in sight and not a very good idea without nearby water. Traditional meat-selling, under a shady tree by the river, would be healthier. Small, blood-spattered boys hacked at the warm flesh with blunt choppers and customers gathered quickly. So did the flies. But soon several dogs had reported for duty as public hygiene officers.

'A dozen covered zebu-wagons made up the rest of the market traffic. When the zebu had been unyoked and given cactus breakfasts the carts were parked in a neat row at the far end of the square. Most of their cargoes could easily have been carried on one human head. Rachel and I strolled between little groups of women and children squatting on the sand selling or bartering eggs, hens, marble-sized tomatoes, purple onions not much bigger, manioc, maize-grain, dried beans and peas, dried fish of various sorts and small bunches of green leaves that seem to be on sale throughout Madagascar as a salad vegetable or flavouring. The only fruit available was de-thorned prickly pears – the Barbary fig, sweet, juicy, pippy. We bought five for the equivalent of a penny from an ancient wrinkled woman with a wonderful smile – the sort of smile that stays with you all day. Rachel wondered why people pay for this fruit which grows wild everywhere like blackberries in Ireland. The answer is that the slighest contact with the plant produces violent pain and itching; one pays not for the fruit but for the risks involved in collecting it. Roland warned us that the wind-borne minute hairs of the ripe fruit often get into people's eyes and the irritation drives some unfortunates to true hysteria. Occasionally those hairs cause permanent blindness. Yet it seems this new strain is harmless compared to the old Mexican prickly pear, known in Madagascar as *raketa* – of which more anon.

'We met a young woman carrying a sewing-machine on her head and a long bale of cotton material in her hands – the ultimate in self-confidence! Then we noticed a gaunt elderly woman staring at us with a startled sort of hope. We realised why when we saw the wares at her feet: a small pile of the famous (comparatively) Ampanihy mohair rugs – white or brown, with mysteriously sophisticated traditional tribal patterns. She looked as though she'd sold nothing for years and we hurried past wishing we could afford to cheer her up.

'I'd like to be able to spend a few weeks in Ampanihy, and thereabouts. Instead of the highlanders' poised charm, the Mahafaly have their own sort of untamed dignity. They seem strong and fierce; I'd hate to quarrel with one. But there is much kindliness too in those fine dark faces. Our first unfavourable impression – the inebriated young men – was cancelled out by those three hours in the market. And we found the boys felt the same.

'Our fellow-passengers, unlike the *vazaha*, had not been enthralled by their unscheduled exposure to Ampanihy Zoma and Fotsy had a disgruntled cargo when we departed at 8.50. But quietly disgruntled: there is a marked lack of aggression in the Malagasy make-up. We jolted past dingy, almost empty Indian shops, and stone hovels, and dejected two-storey colonial villas, once white-washed, and another assertive church. The Catholic church has two towers, the Protestant church one. But the Protestants – despite this architectural handicap, at one time taken very seriously – are said to have most influence among the Mahafaly especially since Independence.

'Soon people were admitting that the delay had been worth while. With many fewer sacks and five fewer passengers, the rear Inferno had been transformed to Executive Class. We envied those remaining there, now able to move their limbs quite freely and release their hens and ducks which Rachel fed with prickly-pear skins. Our own agony was not much reduced. But at least it was possible to look at one's watch and scratch one's dust-irritated nose. And Mr Long-legs had shed his sacks and Mr Brief-case had been persuaded to turn the padlock away from my shin.

'Between Ampanihy and Tranoroa (twenty-five miles) humanity abounded. We must have seen ten or twelve people. A glint of metal would catch the eye, moving above thickets of grey thorny scrub. Then perhaps the spear-owner would emerge to cross some open expanse of stone-littered

red earth. A handsome, lithe, muscular figure, clad only in brief cotton shorts – the modern equivalent of the loin-cloth – and ignoring Merk's clumsy, noisy, dust-stirring travail as though such crude intrusions were beneath his contempt. Elsewhere in Madagascar, as in most countries, cattle-herding is a task for boys armed with sticks and slings. In the lands of the Mahafaly and the Antandroy it is man's work – warrior's work.

'The few women – in loose cotton gowns – were balancing on their heads ugly tin jerry-cans or plastic buckets: shapely earthen pitchers are no more. An occasional roadside settlement consisted of a dozen or so flimsy huts of woven straw with tousled thatches. Their size varied; all were small, some were minute. A son cannot own anything equal to – never mind better than – his father's. So three grown-up generations means grandson being restricted to a large dog-kennel. (*Vazaha* experts complain that this *fady* prevents a forward-looking young man – not that there are many of those around – from getting the most out of his land or herd.) But accommodation for the living is unimportant to these southern tribes. Tombs are what count and these are stunningly elaborate and gaudy. Some are surrounded by spacious walled 'gardens' in which hundreds of up-turned zebu horns (from the beasts killed for the funeral feast) replace flowers. The concrete or stone 'garden' walls are also brilliantly painted and look insanely incongruous, amidst a wilderness of scrub, near hamlets of the *most* primitive dwellings I've ever seen. Neither these tombs nor their decorations show any highly developed aesthetic sense, but they make it believable that in this area 80% of the average family's income is spent on the dead.

'Tombs apart, the day's only colour came, infrequently, from a ten-foot weirdie – its monstrous leaves brown and drooping, its immense, pointed, flame-red flower like a lighted candle in a tarnished candelabra. The roadside baobabs were clearly dated and numbered – by whom? These are a precious water-source *in extremis*: we saw a man drawing fluid from one through a bamboo pipe. Being very shallowly rooted they are easily felled in times of drought and famine; when stripped of bark they provide the zebu with both liquid and solid nourishment. (To the outsider it may look like permanent drought here, yet it's disastrous when the annual two inches of rain doesn't fall.)

'As Merk heaved free of yet another gully, I wondered why camels have never been introduced to this area. Not enough trading and travelling? Or everyone always too zebu-obsessed? I wondered too why there are so many ducks and geese, as well as hens, around the hamlets; it's no life for a web-foot in these parts.

'We accomplished the twenty-five miles to Tranoroa in two hours and forty minutes – "Pretty nifty!" as Adrian said. But then we stopped for an hour and fifty minutes, to the further annoyance of the passengers. This straggle of stone and matting shacks had nothing to spare; a Merkful of hungry travellers brought forth no food-sellers. I too got a bit restive; my ribs kept me in my seat and the action on Tranoroa's main street consisted only of two donkey-carts – the first donkeys seen in Madagascar – pulling tar-barrels of water. (Just as they did in Lismore during my childhood.) Rachel and Adrian went food-hunting – both give the impression of being forever on the brink of starvation – but found only technicoloured boiled sweets which they devoured with revolting enthusiasm. Jamie had Mally-belly and, being long and thin to begin with, looked like one of El Greco's more troubled apostles. Rachel explored further and met a tame lemur. Rumour attributed a Tranoroa mistress to Fosty but I discounted that. He reappeared looking rested, his moustache and hair newly combed, and had obviously been recovering from his Ampanihy exertions.

'Soon we had again left Route Nationale No. 10 to its own chaotic devices and were weaving through bush/forest along Fotsy's own special route, designed to make life easier for Merk. Then our ceiling of sacking began to disintegrate, showering us with detritus. I told myself that the only dangerous creature in Madagascar, a poisonous hand-sized spider, is almost certainly not an indoor animal. "This is the beginning of the end," decided Jamie. "I knew it couldn't hold together."

'Over that seventy-three-mile stretch we averaged fourteen mph – coincidentally, my average cycling-speed. I remarked on what a civilised rate this is, allowing one to appreciate the details of the landscape. But my companions, having long since had the landscape, disagreed. We didn't stop once, apart from those stops occasioned by Merk's method of negotiating various geological obstructions. Luckily the dry heat and the shortage of drinking-water obviated bladder-problems. This region seems virtually un-inhabited, though wayside tombs prove the existence of hamlets hidden away in the bush. Yet our map – a novelty much in demand among the Malagasy – gives the impress-ion that southern Madagascar is more densely populated than Holland. There is scarcely room on the sheet for all the villages it marks – places with names like Ampanimiongana, Antsakaoamitondrotsy, Ambohidnrandriand and Ambato-mandmbahatso.

'By 5.30 we were within an hour of our destination for the night: Tsihombe, a metropolis (according to the map) which is only seventeen miles, as the Aepyornis didn't fly, from the southernmost tip of Madagascar. Perhaps the ocean's near-ness had something to do with that sunset – from horizon to zenith a sheet of orange-red light – no clouds, no break or variation – just a vast brief flare of colour above a flat uncoloured wilderness. In silhouette two distant baobabs and a nearby giant candelabra cactus. Then suddenly all around us a forest of didierea – the tallest we've seen – and for moments nothing existed but that arc of light, darkening to crimson, and those black criss-crossing multitudes of sky-probing, thorn-studded stems. Jamie, putting away his camera, said, "The Spiny South does offer some rewards!"

'The full moon had risen when we arrived at Tsihombe where an oddly turbulent crowd mobbed the passengers as they stiffly descended into the central market-square. When the *vazaha* emerged the crowd became almost delirious, jostling us, laughing at us and shouting questions in chal-lenging rather than friendly tones. A peculiar atmosphere, not reassuring by moonlight; we couldn't see faces clearly enough to judge what emotions lay beneath all the hubbub. Unlike our Ampanihy reception committee, no one seemed drunk. And no one was trying to sell anything, or tout customers for hotels since none exists. Many were welcom-ing relatives or friends (evidently long-lost) but that didn't explain the hectic feeling in the air. Possibly it had some-thing to do with the full moon. Or perhaps life in Tsihombe is so boring that Merk's arrival simply drives everyone wild with excitement. In Ampanihy Jamie had been told that if we slept out in Tsihombe we would certainly be robbed and possibly murdered. I deprecate such alarmist warnings and had been dismissive; now I decided I'd really rather *not* camp out within reach of this lot.

'Jamie – the fluent French speaker – searched for lodgings while Adrian guarded the boys' luggage and Rachel and I stood in the middle of the market-place being viewed like something from outer space – which I suppose we are, psychologically, in Tsihombe. Jamie did well; the local Indian trade rep for Merk's owner invited us to be his guests. By the almost artificially brilliant Malagasy moonlight we were led through a maze of backyards to a large bare room, mud-walled and -floored but neatly swept, with two comfortable double beds, freshly sheeted, and a squat-over loo in a corrugated-iron shed across the yard.

'In an astonishing restaurant – small, clean, efficient: it had clearly known better days – an elderly Merina lady provided our best meal (almost *haute cuisine*) since leaving Antsirabe. Two slightly drunk Indians sat on a wicker couch in the tiny "bar", drinking their own smuggled bourbon. They longed to "help" us by changing money at black-market rates. We politely declined their kind offer. Madagascar's currency regulations are extremely strict and, unlike most Malagasy regulations, are rigorously enforced.

'Tsihombe looked more beautiful than it is as we walked back to our room through silent laneways where angular black shadows lay solid-seeming on gleaming pale sand. At nine o'clock all those rowdy citizens were abed and I felt vaguely ashamed of my earlier unease. But this routine of arriving after nightfall in an unknown town – usually in an unknown tribal territory – doesn't make for easy social intercourse with the unintelligible inhabitants. We passed Merk on the way, full of sleeping passengers. Fotsy had ordered us to reassemble at 9 a.m. so I warned the others I'd be missing – exploring – when they awoke. There were conflicting rumours about this late departure. Some said Fotsy keeps his favourite mistress in Tsihombe, others said his wife and family live here.

'Tsihombe by dawnlight – a ramshackle little town, built on golden sand, with an unexpectedly ex-colonial air. For almost half a century, until 1946, it was an important French military post: which explains that hint of *haute cuisine*. I drank good coffee at a food-stall run by a bent old woman – her dark skin loose and crumpled like a garment, her smiling eyes still young. On the sand nearby three small girls sat around a tiny woodfire eating golden boiled-in-oil buns and sharing a saucepan of coffee – drinking from it in turn. They were filthy and cheerful, with broad dark brown faces, curly but not crinkly hair, wide sparkling eyes and sturdy little bodies. Like most of their tribe, they looked vigorously healthy. The Antandroy have a high-protein diet – as well they might, possessing at least three zebu per person.

'The town slopes down to the left bank of the Manambovo; a major river, but now its wide sandy bed holds only a few pools of stagnant water. Zebu were drinking, women were filling tins with half-gourds – a slow operation. But what's the hurry? I could hear their laughter as I crossed the long strong French bridge high above them, the only surviving bit of Route Nationale No. 10. That laughter reminded me of an Alison Jolly quote from a UN Report on Agricultural Development in South-East Madagascar – "We find it extremely difficult to introduce economic improvements because the Antandroy seem to be happy."

'Beyond the bridge I turned onto a narrow red cart-track with foot-deep ruts, yet in much better shape than Route Nationale No. 10. (Later my map informed me that this is the motor-road to Itomampy on the coast – I could believe it.) Tsihombe marks the margin of the desert and under a sky of broken pearly cloud the air felt slightly humid – silky with moisture after the rasping dryness further north. There had been a heavy dew and tentative inches of wiry green grass gave an illusion of fertility to wide flat cactus-hedged fields – the soil poor and stony and at this season uncultivated. In five miles I saw five new birds; it seemed strange that none was singing to greet the crimson sun, climbing fast above tamarind-fringed Tsihombe, beyond the river's ochre cliffs.

'I revelled in the silence and solitude; I needed to be alone with Madagascar. Yet I wasn't really alone: the *razana* were everywhere. This whole area of green scrubland parodies an

affluent suburb, with meticulously maintained tombs standing like fine houses in spacious grounds. I looked furtively
around before approaching each extraordinary construction
– no two alike. (Who knows what the local *fady/vazaha/razana*
situation may be?) Most tombs look new – until the array of
zebu horns, grey and cracked, reveals their age. Many have
massive double doors, and small windows, and vivid paintings on all four sides depicting the activities of the residents
in this life – herding, reaping, fishing, marketing, fighting
with spears or guns. The Mahafaly specialise in wood
carvings, some of great beauty. If a man served in the French
army or colonial police, his wooden statuette, often perched
on an intricately carved pole, wears the appropriate uniform
and headgear. (In this undefined border territory between
the Mahafaly and Antandroy lands, both tomb traditions
are represented.) The majority of paintings and carvings
express that happiness which defeated the UN experts. They
are high-spirited, comical – the creations of people who
believe the Hereafter can also be fun. The Christian crosses
that surmount some tombs have a perfunctory look; they
seem mere nods in the direction of a more sombre theology.

'On the way back I joined two young women head-loaded
with prickly-pear fruit for the Sunday market. Eight men
followed, some carrying spears, some sticks – or so it seemed.
On the bridge each stick became a spear when the owner
produced a spear-head from under his *lamba* and fixed it in
place. The women found my ornithological activities quite
side-splitting; one of them was so overcome by mirth she had
to remove her load and sit on the embankment to recover.
The men were less happy about such inexplicable behaviour
and looked relieved when a policeman overtook us during
one bird-watching pause. This scowling young man in torn
shorts and a stained uniform jacket – swinging a heavy
truncheon – was not a *vazaha*-lover. He surveyed me with a
mix of insolence and suspicion and seemed about to confis-
cate my binoculars when the women, between bursts of
laughter, explained their purpose. Judging by their tones
and gestures, they were diagnosing me as a harmless lunatic.
The policeman however was not so easily deterred and two
of the men seemed to be egging him on. Then suddenly one
woman stopped laughing and pitched into all the men. If

there is a Malagasy equivalent of "male chauvinist pig" I would guess she used it. In theory Malagasy women must be subservient to their husbands, in practice they are a robustly liberated lot. The policeman fled. The other cowed males fell back, and silently followed us at a little distance. (As Rachel said when I told her the story, "Their shouts were worse than their spears.") Meanwhile the bird in question – thrush-sized, crested, black with red wings – was no longer available. I saw the policeman later in the market, lounging under the *kily*, still scowling. I'm glad he didn't detect me photographing the tombs. That walk aggravated my rib condition; I could no longer cope with a rucksack and had to unstiffen my upper lip and admit I was a casualty of Merk-travel.

'Tsihombe's main market is on Friday and the Sunday display was even sparser than Ampanihy's, though the small crowd seemed more animated. Yet I found this town's atmosphere less congenial. The people look a mixed lot and not all the fairer-skinned are Merina. Over two generations a strong European military presence makes itself felt – and, subsequently, seen.

'The rival sets of church bells rang out simultaneously, soon followed by zestful hymn-singing. We found the large Protestant church in a dangerous state of disrepair and only quarter-full. The equally large Catholic church had been recently painted – pale pink and white, like a birthday cake – and was three-quarters full, its congregation listening attentively, when we arrived, to a young Spanish priest new from Europe but eloquently preaching in Malagasy. Some efforts – certainly foredoomed – are now being made to straighten out Malagasy Catholicism. There were never as many priests as churches, so village catechists greatly influenced the adaptation of Catholicism to suit local tastes. As the Malagasy are great music-lovers, hymn-singing soon came to be, for most Christians, what church services are all about. Madagascar's Roman Catholics could indeed be described as pioneer liturgical reformers. At a time when the liturgy of the Mass was rigidly standardised all over the world they abandoned Latin, no doubt because of competition with Malagasy-language Protestant services; and gradually the Mass was transformed beyond recognition, each rural parish developing its own version.

'We departed quite punctually (10.40) and did the forty-two miles to Ambovombe in two hours on a track that might accurately be described as "motorable". Over one stretch we could see it for miles on a dark green ridge: straight, narrow and red, like a surgeon's incision. This was a more conventional landscape – still lots of botanical weirdies, but also eucalyptus plantations, fields of manioc and potatoes, two small flocks of brown sheep (how *hot* they must get!) and many more humans, dead and alive.

'Ambovombe is bigger than Tsihombe: but still small and at siesta-time on the Sabbath not lively. Fotsy parked in the miniature bus station, then curtly informed us that he and Merk were going no further. It would be easy, he said, to find transport for the last seventy miles to Fort-Dauphin. Bemused, but resigned by now to pretty well any fate, we collected our kit and said good-bye to Merk – I felt almost tearful on leaving this home from home. We were surveying the few unpromising vehicles on view, wondering how long our vigil would be, when Fotsy reappeared and handed each of us a 1,000 FMG note. He had sold us Fort-Dauphin tickets, he explained, so he owed us money. We were too pleasantly shocked to thank him coherently. It would have occurred to none of us – long since made punch-drunk by the vicissitudes of Route Nationale No. 10 – to demand a refund.

'By then my priority was a drink; the upper lip needed stiffening. In Tsihombe I had foreseen this rib crisis-point and bought a half-litre of hooch (unlabelled, colourless but cloudy) from an Indian shop that stocked little else. Unscrewing the top, I tried not to smell the fumes and took a swig. "Strewth!" said Jamie, holding his nose. Rachel viewed me with that austere distaste peculiar to fourteen-year-olds who feel a parent is letting the side down. "Why don't you bring pain-killers from home?" she asked irritably. "You know you're always breaking your ribs!" I took another swig, and was aware of a dual effect; my stomach was heaving but my upper lip already felt stiffer. There is no describing the dreadfulness of this hooch. It surpasses by light-years the most repellent alcohol I have ever met elsewhere. Beside it, the raki that blinded me for twenty-four hours in Nepal was like Jameson's Fifteen-Year-Old. But it worked. "Let's look for tickets!" said I, all brisk and cheerful, turning towards a wooden hut little bigger than a sentry-box.

'Our arrival had attracted an ebullient crowd of delightful children – curious, friendly, amused: no begging – plus a sprinkling of amiable adolescents and one charming ancient crone. These all followed us to the ticket office, where a sober young man sat silently behind a tiny table being harangued, between hiccups, by a very drunk young man. A third young man, unmistakably one short of the shilling, sat on a bench by the wall, laughing quietly at nothing in particular and clutching a two-kilo chunk of fresh raw beef. Two young women (wives?) were peering apprehensively through the small unglazed window, only their heads visible. As Jamie bought tickets for the next vehicle going to Fort-Dauphin (at some unspecified time), Mr One-Short tried to sell us his beef. A slight speech defect didn't deter him from expatiating at length on the excellence of zebu-meat. He had a happy smile and was altogether a most endearing character. "Two thousand?" he suggested. And then, "Fifteen hundred?" And then, pursuing us out of the hut, "One thousand?" The crowd awaiting our reappearance laughed at him, but not unkindly; we had the impression he was regarded with some affection, as a "card".

'The younger generation went in search of lunch, leaving me guarding the rucksacks. I had another swig and beamed benevolently at the excited throng of *vazaha*-fans. Mr One-Short tried again, taking advantage of a woman on her own. He dangled the chunk so close to my face that I could see white grubs hatching out in its crevices. "Five hundred?" he wheedled. I shook my head. "Three hundred?" – here a dozen giggling children each held up three fingers. But again I shook my head; and then one of the young women intervened, perhaps fearing the Sunday joint was about to be given away. Sadly Mr One-Short tucked the chunk under his left arm, shook my hand with a bloody paw and wandered off.

'The others rejoined me looking queasy. They had attempted rice and turkey-stew at the only functioning food-stall but even Adrian and Rachel couldn't stay the course. We moved to the shade of the ticket-hut, where several Fort-Dauphin passengers were waiting. Rachel went on another food-hunt. Jamie mooched about with his camera at the ready; occasionally a spasm distorted his face – no doubt turkey-stew being recollected in agitation. Adrian sat beside me, reading a Graham Greene paperback. The children got bored and dispersed. On my other side an elderly man, looking unusually depressed for a Malagasy, sat on a wicker coop from which protruded the heads of many ducks, hens and cocks. Jamie drifted back and expressed an uncharacteristically sadistic wish to see him being pecked on the bottom. Rachel returned to report no fruit, no buns, no chocolate. In despair she had bought what looked like two bamboo chair-legs – thick hard lengths of sugar-cane. She was already gnawing at one with the pathetic frenzy of a famine-victim and assured me they eventually yielded sweet juice. This proved inaccessible to my elderly fangs so I took out a razor-sharp camping-knife and began to hack. A moment later I was looking at the gleaming white bone of the lower joint of my left thumb. The inch-long cut had severed the tendon and blood spouted with gay abandon. I began to giggle; there's something in the Malagasy air that makes almost everything seem funny – especially after several swigs of hooch. Adrian raised his head from Graham Greene and stared at my thumb with horrified fascination. "You can see the *bone*!" I chortled. "But for God's sake" – said Adrian – "you can't just sit there *laughing* at it!" And he shifted his position slightly to get beyond blood-range. Jamie and Rachel were drawn back by my hilarity. "The woman's mad!" said Jamie. "*Yuck*!" said Rachel. "It's a nice clean cut," I pointed out, licking off the blood so that they too could see the bone. But they weren't really interested so I got out our First Aid box and applied a tight bandage which soon looked like a small chunk of raw beef.

'Then we noticed several of our ex-Merk fellow-passengers beckoning us: we were to join the Fort-Dauphin vehicle at the edge of the town. But near the edge it passed us – a remnant of a mini-bus, already crammed – on its way to the bus-station. As we turned back I felt sorry for the depressed elderly man with the poultry on his head, and still sorrier for myself. Face to face with this vehicle even we, battle-hardened as we are, concluded there *must* be another going to Fort-Dauphin; the addition of four *vazaha* and five Malagasy seemed against the laws of physics. But the conductor politely ushered us aboard, asking people to give seats to the *vazaha*. We realised too late that we'd have done better without seats; most were collapsing and my lot was an outside one-third, with a broken metal arm pressed firmly against my broken ribs. This arm's extraordinary angle made me feel like (among other things) a baby tied into a car-seat. A man was sitting on Rachel and me: half of him on her left shoulder, the other half on my right shoulder, his feet on the knees of someone behind us. Another man was sitting on the nearest window ledge, his torso outside the bus, his hands gripping the roof, his feet in the lap of the man on Rachel's right. At the back passengers lay on each other, piled to the roof. Luckier folk stood jammed all down the aisle. Adrian and Jamie were lost to view. Rachel fears no reader will believe my accounts of Malagasy vehicles, but we do have two English-speaking witnesses.

'At 2.30 we moved off – then thought better of it and backed into the shade of a tamarind for twenty-five minutes while the engine received attention and there was a debate about fitting two late-comers into the driver's cab which already held four passengers. From somewhere Adrian's voice reported that one of the new arrivals was a ravishingly beautiful Chinese girl, dressed to kill, whom the driver was understandably reluctant to leave behind. "Dressed to kill" seemed an unfortunate choice of phrase for a prospective sixth passenger in a driver's cab designed for two. Then we really were off – the Chinese girl probably on the driver's knee, could we but see – and the next three hours made Merk-travel seem sybaritic. I alternately licked my relentlessly oozing blood and sipped hooch. As the tarred surface of this road is in its death-throes, the noisome liquid tended to dribble down my shirt-front – eventually causing the invisible Jamie to shout, "Is your damn bottle leaking?"

'We'll be seeing Ambovombe again, en route from Fort-Dauphin to Tana. Route Nationale No. 13 (what does that hold for us?) runs west from Fort-Dauphin to Ambovombe, then turns north to join our old friend Route Nationale No. 7 at Ihosy. I'm glad we'll be returning, let us hope in less discomfort – though there is no rational basis for this hope –

along the Ambovombe–Fort-Dauphin stretch. We didn't see much of it yesterday.

'We stopped outside an isolated *hotely* at the foot of a pass over the Anosyennes range, which separates the Spiny South from the lushness of the east coast. Here, within five miles, there is a change of climate and vegetation akin to – but even more dramatic than – that caused by the Humboldt Current on the Ecuadorean–Peruvian border. We all got out, most of the able-bodied through the glassless windows. The *hotely* was selling baked manioc and fresh fish, being fried to order on an open charcoal fire behind the hut. Steep forested mountains rose directly above us; some smooth-crested, some wearing grotesque limestone crowns. We watched a bus-roof drama as we ate our manioc. An escaped duck was waddling across the luggage, playing hard to catch, quacking distractedly and drawing much comment from her companions within the coop. The two imprisoned cocks were crowing defiantly and being answered by the *hotely* cock, standing on a pile of zebu horns and bones, flapping his wings and boasting of his freedom. Five passengers left us here, including the young man who'd been mainly outside. There didn't seem to be anywhere to go but maybe they just couldn't take any more. Although this did nothing to lessen our physical torment, we were now able to see something.

'Slowly we ascended that pass, equally slowly we descended. This was our first alarming Malagasy mountain-road: very narrow, with a skiddy surface and drops from the verge into lethal depths. Over the watershed, 'normal' grass replaced weirdies on the steep slopes. On one side of these mountains the average rainfall is 200 m. a year, on the other side it is 2,500 m. Down at sea-level all was damp extravagant fertility; rows of generously spreading leafy trees, small paddy-fields, ditches and ponds of stagnant water – we could hear the mosquitoes even above the engine noise.

'At a cluster of palm-thatched shacks, huddled among mango-trees, a young Tulear woman and her beaming small daughter got off after fond farewells – we had endured much together. The pair were rapturously greeted by everyone in sight (three women) and I last saw the little girl bounding like a kangeroo towards one of the shacks. Throughout we'd marvelled at the patience and fortitude of the junior passengers. Not one of them – and there were very many – added to the sufferings of their seniors. Even the babies were virtuous beyond belief, only whimpering genteelly for food at reasonable intervals. In many countries docile children make me uneasy; I suspect them of being underfed or unduly repressed – or both. But here the average child is so full of fun and energy that their stoicism as travellers must be owing to the happy temperament and innate good manners of the Malagasy.

'Now the moon was floating silver in a royal-blue sky, above a black fretwork of tree-tops, while behind us great masses of cloud, still gold-tinted, shifted swiftly over the mountains. At the next brief stop we were offered a strange fruit called a "wood-orange" which resembles the real thing but is virtually inedible. Soon after, the moon gleamed on an Antanosy tomb: a boat carved in stone for the voyage of the dead.

'Suddenly, away to the left, we glimpsed a wide sheen that could only be the sea. Then a bulky row of unmistakably colonial buildings stood out on the sky-line. Moments later we stopped in what seemed to be a small subdued shanty-town – revealed this morning as the throbbing heart of Fort-Dauphin's commercial life.

'We crawled out, numbed mentally as well as physically. Fort-Dauphin had become fixed in our collective mind as a sort of Holy Grail, a place you go towards without believing you'll ever get there. To have arrived felt almost dismaying. It was 6.15 p.m. The 390-mile journey had taken three days and two nights, travelling at an average speed – Rachel tells me – of twelve miles per hour.'

8

'Sites of Dreams'

In 1642, the Société Française de l'Orient was granted a monopoly charter by Cardinal Richelieu, and at once Sieur Pronis set sail with a small force of soldiers and a few traders to establish a French colony in Madagascar. This was just two years before John Smart and his doomed companions arrived on the other side of the island to establish a British colony. Pronis had made a wiser geographical choice. True, malaria and the Antanosy soon got rid of most of those pioneers, who settled some twenty miles north of Fort-Dauphin, at Saint-Luce. But the south-east coast is less inimical to Europeans than the thorny waterless lands of the Mahafaly; when the surviving French moved to the narrow and quite easily defended peninsula of Fort-Dauphin their colony held out for thirty years.

Thus Fort-Dauphin became the legal toe-hold which 250 years later enabled France to climb all over the island and conquer the summit, Tana. (But by the 1890s Fort-Dauphin was only important legally; as a port it was no help to the invading French troops.) By our standards Pronis was simply being silly when he raised the *fleur-de-lys* near the southern tip of an island still unexplored by Europeans and laid claim to the entire island on behalf of His Most Christian Majesty King Louis XIII. Yet two and a half centuries later his action helped to change the course of Malagasy history. During those centuries the mutual understanding between Europe's rulers, and their common faith in the white man's civilising mission, had survived countless wars and revolutions at home and abroad. It is inconceivable that a 1985 'Declaration of Annexation', such as that made by France in 1665, would be accepted in 2235 as an important part of a legal argument for the take-over of a sovereign state by an invading power.

The French settlement grew around the fort built in 1643 and named after the child who had become king seven months earlier –

though the colonists had not yet heard the news. Poor communications were always to be, and still are, among Fort-Dauphin's main problems. Other seventeenth-century snags were diseases – particularly malaria – acute food shortages and the settlers' Antanosy neighbours who after all did own the place. Their chief, Andriandramaka, had spent three boyhood years in Goa, as protégé of a Portuguese missionary, and spoke fluent Portuguese. He was a baptised though non-practising Christian and well disposed towards all Europeans. Quite a few Antanosy had Portuguese blood, infused over the generations by shipwrecked sailors, and at first many were more co-operative and friendly than might have been expected. But Pronis antagonised all the local people, much as John Smart had done, by deceptions and betrayals. He was another of those unsavoury types often attracted to such commercial-colonial adventures and his treacherous capture of seventy-three Malagasy, for export as slaves to Mauritius, had disastrous consequences for the future of the little colony. This idea had been suggested to him by the Dutch governor of Mauritius, then critically short of labour. It had such an effect on the Antanosy that for generations most of them fled into the mountains at the sight of any approaching vessel.

The colonists had looked forward to an ample supply of 'black' labour and were much taken aback to find the Malagasy neither black nor at all disposed to labour – even for themselves (beyond the minimum necessary for survival) never mind for the *vazaha*. What the Antanosy really enjoyed was lying in the shade observing French agricultural methods with detached interest. And they adopted towards the settlers – innocently, meaning no offence – those attitudes of kindly condescension considered appropriate to the slave class. It was plain to them that these soldiers and traders, unhappily tilling the soil as an alternative to starvation, were the slaves Pronis had sensibly brought with him.

The young colony was also handicapped by its own sectarianism. A minority, including Pronis, were Huguenots; the rest were nominally Roman Catholics, though their behaviour rarely suggested any form of Christian upbringing. Pronis had soon chosen one of the chief's nieces as his mistress and some time later the chief demanded that he should marry the young woman. This he did, to the fury of his Catholic compatriots; they denounced the marriage as invalid and wasteful of public money. The latter accusation, at least, was justified. After the wedding, Pronis found himself responsible for maintaining droves of in-laws, in accordance with the custom of the country – which explains the chief's insistence on a marriage. Andriandramaka was not, as some of the French had naively assumed, a stickler for propriety in these matters.

The settlers mutinied in 1646, putting Pronis in irons for six months. Then a Company ship brought a consignment of new settlers and the Captain released Pronis after he had promised the mutineers an amnesty. The promise was instantly broken; twelve of them were exiled to the then uninhabited island of Bourbon (now Réunion).

Meanwhile trade was being hampered both by the internal dissensions of the colonists and by the eating habits of the Malagasy. Wax and hides were the most lucrative exports – prosaic goods, compared to the rare spices, and precious stones and metals, once expected of Madagascar. But the Malagasy fancied wax with their honey (a taste I share) and cooked their baked meats wrapped in hides which they also ate. So Fort-Dauphin never really took off as a trading-post. Things might have been different had the Company regularly despatched from France cargoes likely to tempt the Malagasy not to eat all their exportable commodities. But Paris soon lost interest in this squabblesome little colony which seemed unlikely ever to come to anything, and during one five-year period no Company ship (and very few others) çalled to Fort-Dauphin. This neglect led to a drastic deterioration in Franco–Malagasy relations; to feed themselves the French were forced to go into the cattle-raiding business.

Treachery was not of course confined to the Europeans. One of the later governors was a military commander and religious fanatic – Champmargou – and Lazarist priests unwisely encouraged his zeal. Strenuous attempts were made to convert an important Antanosy chief, Andrianmanangue, who had nothing against Christianity but resolutely refused to accept Christian marriage rules. He was devoted to his many wives and very properly felt permanently responsible for them all; the idea of keeping only one, and rejecting the rest, seemed to him downright immoral. He said so to one of the missionaries, who promptly tore the chief's sacred *oly* (talisman) from his neck and flung it in the fire. At their next luncheon party with the chief, three missionaries were poisoned. When only one reacted as planned, the other two were clubbed to death. The inevitable French punative expedition was ambushed by six thousand Malagasy and saved only by the arrival of the most extraordinary Frenchman then on the island. La Case had become a local prince by marrying the daughter of the King of Amboule and when this young woman inherited the kingdom she asked her husband to take over as ruler. He did so most successfully, soon endearing himself to his subjects and – what was even more remarkable – to his fellow-rulers. Without his repeated interventions as a mediator, the wretched Fort-Dauphin colony could not possibly have survived for thirty years.

Often the early missionaries over-reacted, yet many did heroic work under tougher conditions than any experienced by their nineteenth-century successors. They were inspired and supported by St Vincent de Paul, who had unrealistic visions of Madagascar as a fruitful vineyard for Christian labourers, and they found the Antanosy as avid for education in the 1640s as the Merina were to be in the 1820s. The chiefs begged for schools – for girls as well as boys – and when the French withdrew in 1674, after enduring hardships unsurpassed in European colonial history, twenty keen scholars had to be abandoned in their boarding-schools.

This first sordid chapter in Fort-Dauphin's story had a predictably tragic ending. On 27 August 1674 half the colonists were massacred and a fortnight later the survivors sailed away, having spiked the cannon within the fort. In three decades thousands of Frenchmen, including forty-five missionaries, had been killed by disease or the Malagasy. And the only tangible result was that fort which 310 years later we were deterred from examining by two surly young sentries armed with bayonets.

Yet there was one enduring gain: a book by a senior Company official who spent six years at Fort-Dauphin from December 1648, when he arrived to try to sort out the Pronis mess. The Chevalier Etienne de Flacourt belonged to an extinct breed; by now the frontiers of knowledge have been extended beyond the reach of any one mind. He was a scientist, a linguist, a humanist, an intellectual man of action – a final flowering of the Renaissance. He explored much of southern and eastern Madagascar, indefatigably taking notes on customs, language-variations, beliefs, historical folk-memories, medical lore, artistic traditions – and on the flora and fauna and geology and climate. For 150 years his *Histoire de la Grande Isle de Madagascar* remained the only reliable source of information about the Great Red Island and today scholars still find it useful.

The second chapter in Fort-Dauphin's colonial story was no less sordid but much briefer. This time, however, the settlers' leader caused an ecological upheaval throughout the whole of southern Madagascar.

Count Dolisie de Maudave was a French naval officer, a correspondent of Voltaire's and one of the earliest and most fervent preachers of 'la mission civilisatrice'. In 1768 he arrived at Fort-Dauphin full of high-falutin notions about running a colony without infringing on the chiefs' authority. But the brutal realities of local life soon got the better of his ideals and he became an energetic slave-trader, thus provoking the chiefs to massacre most of the colonists. Within two and a half years the French had again sailed away.

This time, however, they left a meaningful legacy: the Mexican prickly-pear cactus, introduced from Réunion's Botanical Garden by de Maudave 'to embellish the sea-ward face of the fort and by this means make it impenetrable'. With uncanny rapidity this cactus (*raketa* to the Malagasy) took over the southern desert, replacing local vegetation wherever red clay prevailed. It raised the water-level so that springs and wells rarely ran dry. It proved invaluable as fencing-material, as zebu-fodder, as food for the Antandroy and many of the Mahafaly. A French military officer and botanist, Decary, calculated that in the early years of this century, in his Tsihombe district, fifteen tons of prickly-pear fruit were eaten daily throughout the dry season. The Barbary fig had become the staple diet for tens of thousands of Antandroy. Also, its leaves were the main source of water during drought, and juices were extracted, by pounding, from the trunk.

When required to do so, the *raketa* formed solid walls twelve feet high and – because of its mighty spines – utterly impenetrable. It defeated Merina attempts to conquer the south and made the French 'pacification' much more difficult. The Antandroy often blocked paths – already securely *raketa*-walled – with ten-foot *raketa* barricades a hundred yards long. While the French troops tried to clear a way through, enduring agonising injuries in the process, they were constantly exposed to spear-assaults from invisible warriors whom they could not pursue. Decary observed that these experiences proved the truth of a local proverb – 'The Antandroy and the *raketa* are relatives'.

Then, as quicky as that relationship had been established in the 1770s, it was destroyed in the 1920s. To control the southern desert it was necessary to control the *raketa* and in 1925 the French introduced the cochineal beetle to Tulear. This Mexican insect, source of the crimson dye, is the *raketa*'s natural enemy which limits the cactus in their common homeland – where the beetle too has natural enemies. Without these, it spread so rapidly that by the late 1920s travellers were reporting being blinded and half-suffocated by swarming males. Everywhere the *raketa* died. As a direct result, tens of thousands of Antandroy and their zebu also died during the drought of 1931, and again in 1936, 1943 and 1956. Few people were aware of these calamities – even in Tana, never mind Paris and the world beyond. Then there were no TV camera-crews at the ready to jet to disaster areas and show us all what goes on. However, a few years before Independence French agronomists introduced beetle-resistant strains of spineless prickly pear, for use chiefly as zebu-fodder. As this is not self-seeding – each bush has to be planted by hand – it will never spread widely enough to raise the water-level and be a defence against famine and drought. Nor, of course, will it ever serve as a defence against armed invaders.

Fort-Dauphin is the only town to have been founded as a result of the several seventeenth-century efforts (Portuguese, French, English) to establish colonies on Madagascar. It is therefore the island's oldest town; Tamatave and Majunga, now much more important ports, were not founded until the early and mid eighteenth century, respectively. Yet Fort-Dauphin's geographical isolation, accentuated by a bay too shallow for modern ships and the idiosyncrasies of the Malagasy road-system, makes it seem strangely forgotten. It does not belong to the Spiny South beyond the mountains, nor does it feel very integrated with its own hinterland of the Antanosy. Transport up the coast to Manakara and the rail-link with Fianar, on Route Nationale No. 12, is hampered by the need to use ferry-boats across fifteen river-mouths. This road, by which we had hoped to return north, is now closed to motor-traffic and has been deleted from the newest maps; most of the ferries are not operating for lack of spare parts. ('The pieces are missing' – a phrase with which we were soon to become familiar.)

It is hard to believe that Fort-Dauphin has some sixteen thousand inhabitants. On the evening of our arrival it felt like another small town, as a kind young man led us around the bay by moonlight. ('What are we going to do when there's no moon?' wondered Rachel. But by the waning of that moon we were well adjusted to nocturnal arrivals in unlit towns.)

The cool evening air was invigorating and after three days immobility the freedom to walk made my rib condition seem trivial. There is much to be said for arriving in Malagasy towns by moonlight. They are not, in general, beautiful places. But their settings often are and here the moonlight emphasised forested encircling mountains, miles of smooth beach and a calm radiant sea. Meanwhile, derelict colonial offices, functional tourist amenities and tin-roofed shacks lurked unseen in the romantic shadows. When I suggested a moonlight swim our guide revealed that other things lurk unseen: the beach is grievously oil-polluted. As he spoke we rounded a corner and saw three giant oil-storage tanks from which pipes like bloated serpents ran across the sand – conspicuous even by moonlight. As usual, few citizens were visible; after sunset the Malagasy seem pathologically allergic to the open air.

The imposing three-storey Hotel de France is Indian-owned and in practice (though not in price) is no more than an overgrown doss-house. It was jerry-built in the early 1950s when Fort-Dauphin seemed to have been suddenly swept into the mainstream of Madagascar's industrial life. Uranium had been discovered not far away and as French experts and technicians converged on the town it made sense to invest in a sea-shore hotel with an arcaded façade and a shrub-filled patio – the sort of place to which the new arrivals would want to bring wives and children (or mistresses). But fortunately an abundance of uranium was soon after found in France's Massif Central. When the French Atomic Energy Authority hastily withdrew all subsidies from the Fort-Dauphin project the locals were stricken but the *razana* must have smiled in their tombs. Had the project proceeded, many demoralised mining families might by now have been suffering the consequences – and wondering how they could have so enraged the *razana* that an epidemic of lung-cancer seemed an appropriate punishment.

We had the hotel to ourselves that first night. Entering the patio – stumbling over broken paving – we climbed two flights of concrete steps to a wide balcony. Several big rooms opened off it, their double-doors ozone-warped, their locks defective, their bile-green walls damp- and dirt-splotched. Our rooms each had two single iron beds with lumpy and smelly straw mattresses; but the sheets were clean. Electric light – much dimmer than a Malagasy full moon – was spasmodically available for a few hours after sunset. A corner cubicle contained one ragged dingy towel and a discoloured wash-basin from which the water splashed away through a hole in the sloping floor. At intervals this hole released what seemed like waves of poisoned gas; we did not need to be told that Fort-Dauphin suffers from a sewage-crisis of awesome duration and magnitude. There was one loo per balcony; no illumination was required to find it. However, the wild-life in our room (no extra charge) made up for a lot. Most of these creatures were unidentifiable; but while bringing my diary up to date I was distracted by a ferocious and long-drawn-out cockroach fight, worthy of a Norse saga. Size-wise it was a most uneven contest: one protagonist resembled a large mouse, the other a small mouse. Roland's museum at Ranohira contained preserved specimens but I never expected to have the good fortune to witness them in action. Eventually David won and chased Goliath – limping perceptibly – under my 'desk', a roughly made cupboard which was the room's only furniture.

On our first day we spent some time looking for the town centre before realising that Fort-Dauphin does not have one. Surely, you think, there will be some semblance of a main street round the next corner. But, delightfully, there never is. The few short streets that look as though they might be the beginnings of a town – lined with run-down Indian shops – never come to anything. Fort-Dauphin is in fact a village sprawling all over a very beautiful peninsula, plus several large government buildings, two enormous Christian churches, two enormous Christian colleges and a neurotically guarded military post surrounding the original fort. Sandy laneways serve as roads and the sea seems to be everywhere. The mountains, rising almost sheer from the bay, look higher than they are; St Louis, the highest peak, is only 1,500 feet. Most dwellings are cheerful little shacks surrounded by untidy little gardens and built in long rows on miles of sand-dunes. Anti-gale stones weigh down the thatched or tin roofs and strange things grow in the gardens. The natives are friendly.

Here, as in Antsirabe, many of the older generation frankly admit they wish the French had stayed. While their children accept Fort-Dauphin as it now is, they recall how beautiful it once was. It is the old, sad story. Inevitably, a European settlement will only look good if European standards are maintained. Had Fort-Dauphin been built by the Malagasy for their own purposes, using their own materials according to their own designs, it would I have no doubt be even more beautiful, because more in harmony with its surroundings, than the colonial town of thirty years ago.

While queuing one day at the Post Office (those letters never got to Ireland), I met an English-speaking Merina from Tana. A middle-aged woman, she had studied nutrition in the USA and was now doing a survey ('Probably futile', she admitted) of southern diet deficiencies. 'I'm just another expert,' she said gloomily. 'And for twenty-five years Madagascar has had teams of foreign experts from dozens of countries and organisations doing "surveys" – and then disappearing. You could build a dam with their reports. But they only change things in one way, by selling their fleets of jeeps and Landrovers before they leave – usually at a good profit.' I had already noticed a few of these vehicles, decorated with the emblem of one of the more notoriously corrupt international agencies.

My companion sighed when I quoted the UN complaint that it is difficult to help those who do not want to be helped. 'True – we Malagasy hate work. The few officials who take their jobs seriously get high-blood-pressure and ulcers because they are not used to pressure – it's not part of our tradition – to us the work-ethic is a meaningless concept. So the few who do work are regarded as eccentrics and their colleagues leave it all to them.'

By this stage we were drinking coffee at a stall in the covered market-place: and we had exchanged names. 'Here in the south,' said Rebecca, 'so much more could be grown with irrigation! But nobody's interested in new schemes. They don't think about the next drought and famine – they can't think ahead. And then we have our taboos. The country is over-run with poultry but it's *fady* for pregnant women and small children to eat eggs. Mothers beg vitamin pills for their one-year-olds but it's *fady* to feed them with carrots or beans or bananas till they're two. Zebu give almost no milk but it's *fady* to cross-breed to provide dairy produce. The size of the hump is all-important – the *razana* would never forgive them if they bred cattle with a smaller hump – and suppose the hump *disappeared . . .!*'

Rebecca's main objective was to enlist the aid of the more liberal *ombiasa* in a campaign against those *fady* which frustrate health-education and the practice of preventive medicine. This, she argued, could be done without undermining essential religious beliefs or seeming disrespectful towards the *razana*. Many taboos have already been eroded by twentieth-century requirements or developments. Rebecca gave as an example the postal system which, however ineffectual and little used, has weakened the *fady* against telling one's name and address. Also, the common-sense element within basic Western education has to some extent made its mark on most regions. Fifty years ago the Antandroy believed it necessary to burn a house in which someone had died, a *fady* that probably started as a health-precaution. Then one day a dying twelve-year-old boy asked to be moved outside, so that his parents might be spared the trouble and expense of rebuilding. His request was interpreted by the *ombiasa* as a message from the *razana*, rescinding this *fady*, and gradually the news spread that there was no longer any need to rebuild after a death.

'The *ombiasa* are not all bad men,' said Rebecca, looking at me rather accusingly as though I had condemned them. 'The French and the missionaries always treated them as enemies, greedy crooks terrorising the villagers for their own gain. But it's more complicated. There are all sorts of *ombiasa*, good, bad and indifferent. And of course there are the men who practise black magic, as you would call it, but they are another sort. The good *ombiasa* have always tried to protect their people from exploitation, so the *vazaha* said they were bad. The fanatical ones did a lot of harm, urging the warriors on to fight when they had no hope of winning against European weapons. But even they weren't the sort of cynical megalomaniacs the missionaries liked to write about. It's not possible to have cynical manipulators growing up in these tribal communities in the middle of nowhere, never having been in contact with the outside world. Even the bad *ombiasa* weren't just playing on the superstitious villagers. They shared and still share most of those superstitions – they are sincere, they are part of the communities, not parasites on them. But the Malagasy have flexible minds – we are not fanatical by temperament. We are adaptable. So it should be possible to co-operate more with the *ombiasa* in my sort of work. A big problem' – continued Rebecca – 'is bad relations between the southern tribes and the people from Tana. Too many Malagasy officials have treated the tribes with contempt and tried to bully them, even more than the French did.

Or at best they know nothing about conditions here. The 1971 trouble started because the government kept the high tax on cattle after half the herds had died in a drought. Local leaders tried to co-ordinate the uprising but of course that didn't work. In some towns tribesmen raided the gendarmerie barracks for arms and took over the buildings. In a few places they killed all the gendarmerie. When troops and police were sent out from here some gendarmerie shot up whole villages in revenge, though the army behaved well. But there are many memories still – much resentment. And the corruption – the Antandroy hate it. Now President Ratsiraka is dismissing hundreds of corrupt minor officials but there are lots left. You have seen what the roads are like – and when local leaders complain they are told by government officials they must pay for road improvements with so many litres of bush-alcohol. And some demand the use of village girls – and so on. All that makes it hard for outsiders like me to be accepted. But southern hospitality is wonderful when you are trusted. Maybe it's easier being a woman! They try here to give me armed escorts but I know I'm safer going alone.'

Then Rebecca had to leave me, to drive her own jeep on a non-road to some village north of Ambovombe. She was, I suspected, a very long cactus-thorn in the flesh of quite a few bureaucrats.

Fort-Dauphin's Malagasy name – Taolankarana – means, according to our guidebook, 'sites of dreams'. But for me, much as I liked the little non-town, 'sites of nightmares' would be nearer the mark. These came under four headings: medical, legal, financial and climatic. (The last was of course a shared nightmare.)

Our first task on our first morning was to find something to hold me together and expedite rib-knitting. The collapsing hospital had nothing: no bandages, no plasters, no doctors and (apparently) no patients. Eventually however we tracked down a roll of wide French sticking-plaster, in the Pharmacie du Tropique. This was not just what the doctor would have ordered at home; but when Rachel had bound me tightly I felt able to tackle the next, legal, nightmare.

According to the Malagasy Embassy in Paris, renewing our visas would be no problem in Tana: a mere matter of form, plus another vast sum of money. The snag was that we were very far from Tana when those visas expired and en route we had heard chilling rumours of visa-less *vazaha* being deported at twelve hours notice. The problem was familiar; in many countries immigration departments work on the assumption that travellers remain always within easy reach of the capital city. In Peru we had been arrested, and deported, under almost identical circumstances. I am therefore hyper-sensitive on this subject and had decided to touch the hearts of the Fort-Dauphin gendarmerie with a sob-story about broken ribs having delayed our return to Tana. My bandaged left hand would strengthen this alibi. (The sorts of pain produced by broken ribs and a severed tendon are so different that in an odd way they seemed to be cancelling each other out.)

My sob-story was never needed. We wandered from office to office, across miles of sand-dunes, trying to persuade someone to take an interest in our status as illegal immigrants. Unfortunately none of those concerned spoke a language that Rachel recognised as French. (Even Jamie might have had problems.) With increasing desperation we presented our expired visas to gendarmerie officers, to a woman clerk at police headquarters, to an important-looking jet-black gentleman in the Post Office, to the *Chef* of this and that Bureau and Department. They all shook hands, welcomed us warmly, invited us to sit down, took our proffered passports and wondered where Ireland was. When I pointed to the date of expiry on our visas they peered and laughed and said Paris was in France.

We made a third visit to police headquarters, still hoping to chance upon an adequate French-speaker. The whole place was empty – a substantial colonial building atop a sand-dune, surrounded by shacks and poultry and patches of manioc. As we penetrated to its inner offices, in search of some sleeping policeman, I noticed a yellowed bilingual notice nailed to the back of a door. It listed Malagasy visa requirements and revealed that the local gendarmerie were empowered to issue visas. True, it was exactly twenty years out of date and Christian Marxists might like to do things differently. But it looked useful as a starting point for action.

We returned to the entrance and sat on the doorstep. In the fulness of time a fat wheezing elderly officer appeared from one of the shacks; he had obviously just woken up and yawned at us in astonishment. I took him by the arm, led him to the notice and pointed to our visas. He laughed nervously, shook his head and vanished.

Again we sat on the doorstep. Twenty minutes later Wheezy was back with the woman clerk and two more officers whom we'd met earlier in the day. All four studied our visas, read the notice and were thrown into a state of confusion painful to witness. In a small front office they argued among themselves with impassioned eloquence at extraordinary length. Then they told us to go away and return at 5 p.m.

That visa-quest used up three to four hours on each of four consecutive days. It involved long waits in offices that turned out to be the wrong ones, and abortive journeys to police headquarters (usually nobody was present at the prearranged hour), and much queuing for a special sort of stamp no longer available in Fort-Dauphin, and a long search for a passport photographer who charged £4 for each of six prints. (Our 'spares' had fallen foul of my melted chocolate.) An aura of make-believe surrounded the whole enterprise. Clearly none of the officials concerned took visas seriously, though they were prepared to go through any number of puzzling bureaucratic hoops to satisfy the *vazaha*'s incomprehensible lust for getting papers in order. Luckily our acclimatisation to Madagascar was by then complete. The main psychological adjustment required of Western travellers has to do with one's attitude to *time*. When that has been brought into line with the Malagasy attitude, life is fun. But a failure soon to achieve this adjustment can expose the traveller to very real hazards, like ulceration and dementia. Had we attempted to fit our visa-quest into busy sight-seeing days we would soon have needed sedation. But for us it became a pivotal part of the Fort-Dauphin experience – and it had many rewarding moments, as when a wandering turkey-hen perched on the edge of a police officer's desk and shat accurately onto an open ledger.

In the end, not to our surprise, we left Fort-Dauphin still visa-less. During the last round of negotiations we were instructed to write a letter each (in French) to the relevant government Minister. Those letters, and our photographs, and the Permit-to-Emigrate forms we had filled in in quintuplicate (in lieu of visa-application forms) would, we were assured, be forwarded to Tana where we could collect our renewed visas on arrival.

We were returning from one gendarmerie session when a pair of attractive adolescent girls approached us, giggling shyly and urging each other to do the talking. Finally one of them greeted us in French with the information that their father was our friend – a bewildering declaration until we discovered him to be one of the police officers dealing with the visa crisis. We were invited to meet Mamma and led up and down several densely inhabited dunes. Often our companions shouted to acquaintances, drawing attention to their *vazaha* guests. This whole area was remarkably litter-free – and stink-free, unlike the Hotel de France. Primitive but well-cared-for 'sanitary equipments' are far preferable to defective mod cons.

The tin-roofed, two-roomed wooden shack was raised above the ground on short stilts. Mamma appeared on the narrow balcony, smiling and waving a welcome in response to her daughters' excited summons. She was very tall, very fat, immensely gracious – almost a regal figure in a billowing magenta gown, calf-length and sleeveless, that looked quite splendid against her glowing brown skin. She invited us to sit on a single bed just inside the door, apologising for the lack of chairs; given ten children to educate, there was no spare cash for furniture. Her explanation was matter-of-fact, offered with no trace of either embarrassment or self-pity. Some children had been, others were being and the rest would be educated at the Lutheran Mission College, a fee-paying school. This was a very Malagasy order of priorities: few possessions, but the best possible education for five sons and five daughters. The frames of both glazed windows and the inner walls were painted apple-green; the only visible luxury was a transistor radio, hanging uselessly on a wall because of the battery shortage. Presumably most of the children slept on the floor; the bed we sat on, and a double bed in the inner room, were supplemented by stacks of bedding neatly folded and piled almost to the ceiling.

Mamma was a seamstress, which explained why all the visible children (six) were so well dressed. She told us, when asked, that she worked seven days a week. (Can it be that Malagasy women are less work-shy than their mates?) We found it hard to believe that she was forty-nine; she looked about thirty-five, her thick tight curls un-greyed, her broad plump face unwrinkled. She had lost four babies in infancy – dysentery, we gathered. The living ranged in age from twenty-five to three. On hearing that Rachel was the only fruit of my womb, Mamma registered appalled sympathy. As we talked the younger children were playing in the cactus-hedged 'garden', a huge sloping sand-pit. The whole family looked happy and healthy and radiated mutual affection.

Opponents of birth-control would have found them first-rate propaganda ammunition. But as we walked away down the dunes, past many similar groups of young Malagasy, I thought twenty years ahead and wished the Tana government would do something *now* to reduce the birth rate. Madagascar still has time – just – to keep its population at a level suited to its size and resources.

Paying for our visa photographs brought my third Fort-Dauphin nightmare to crisis point. We had left our surplus traveller's cheques in Antsirabe, taking only what seemed like ample cash for the southern journey, and I had miscalculated so badly that now we were indigent gentlewomen. The solution might appear simple: telephone Antsirabe and ask our friends to transfer cash to a Fort-Dauphin bank. But in Madagascar one has to survive without reliable modern communications, which is partly why I fell so hopelessly in love with that country. We were as cut off from the highlands as Pronis was in 1647 and our situation would have been serious but for the boys' comparative wealth. Having listened attentively to their financial discussions I knew they could afford to lend us our fares to Antsirabe, where we planned to go our separate ways. Never before have I had to borrow from fellow-travellers (and in any circumstances I am allergic to borrowing) so I needed an extra swig of uninhibiting hooch before going to the boys' room. That was on the evening of our third rainy day and they, poor things, were sitting shivering on their beds, wrapped in blankets, their sodden clothes hanging all over the place and their floor two inches deep in rainwater. They had, as it happened, been discussing the Murphys' obviously indigent state and were about to offer us a loan.

One thinks of islands in the Indian Ocean as places of perpetual sunshine where calm blue seas lap palm-fringed beaches and tropical blossoms scent the languorous air. But one is quite mistaken. Fort-Dauphin's weather, during our first three days, can only be compared to mid-winter on the Aran Islands. Even within that sheltered bay the ocean frothed and pounded, sending towering breakers roaring landwards to crash and spume on the cliffs below the fort. A gale drove sheets of cold rain across the peninsula, lifting roofs off shacks and almost lifting us off our high balcony as we struggled, drenched to the skin after some marathon visa expedition, to turn our key in the rusty lock. By night the noise of the storm kept even me awake; by day the dark low racing clouds made it hard to read in our room. After three days of this the younger generation all had streaming colds; I escaped infection, possibly because of a considerable intake of pain-killing hooch. We did not then have a dry garment between us and group-morale was lowish. However, Rachel and I at least had a dry room; the boys' seaward window was broken and their ceiling leaked badly. In Fort-Dauphin during mid-winter three-day gales habitually alternate with several days of sunshine.

On the morning of our fourth day all was stillness and brightness as I set out for the bus station at 6 a.m., leaving Rachel snuffling in bed. It was my turn to bashie-hunt; each day one of us made enquiries every few hours. Fort-Dauphin has no formal bus station but the little traffic that enters and leaves usually stops and starts near the market-place. There is no regular Fort-Dauphin–Fianar service comparable to the weekly Tulear–Fort-Dauphin Merk. Nor is there any central ticket-office, or any person or persons with authoritative fore-knowledge of vehicle movements. In the market-place one simply wanders around, asking questions on the off-chance that someone might have news. Rumours of course abound. A mini-bus might be leaving on Friday morning, a bashie might be leaving on Saturday afternoon, or maybe at midnight on Sunday, or it could be at dawn on Monday. Vehicles depart when enough people want to go somewhere and that might be twice a week or once a month. Hence our constant enquiries. Getting away from Fort-Dauphin is even harder than getting to it and none of us could afford to be too long delayed. The boys wanted to explore the north of the island, we wanted to explore the east.

From my cliff-top track the dawn was tumultuous: great banks of plum-coloured cloud poised above a long strip of lemon-yellow, then a change to hectic pink and molten gold – while below the sea still heaved uneasily, made sullen by churning sand.

In the market-place I was greeted on all sides. We had become familiar figures and were subjected to much leg-pulling about our hopes of getting to Fianar in the foreseeable future – an ambition which seemed to be regarded, with some reason, as unrealistic. (Among the Malagasy such teasing is not always as straightforward as it seems; in an odd way it can be a test of the *vazaha*. Responses to it in the same vein of humour are much appreciated, but a failure to see the joke may be taken badly.) If anything was going to Fianar that day nobody knew about it. After half-an-hour and several cups of coffee I ambled off, feeling rather relieved. My ribs were mending nicely but seemed not quite ready for an unknown number of days on Route Nationale No. 13 – which, we had been reliably informed, is twin brother to Route Nationale No. 10.

Group-morale was up that sunny morning and we planned to join the boys on Lebanon beach after running the last lap of our visa marathon. Returning from police headquarters we passed the sandstone bulk of the Italian-run Catholic College – rather like a handsome military barracks, with nine hundred pupils. Suddenly an outburst of hallooing and yelling came from a bungalow garden: nothing to do with us, obviously, yet we looked around as one does. Two gesticulating figures were literally jumping up and down with excitement – and, unmistakably, they were beckoning *us*. Rachel recognised them first – 'Our Aeroflot friends!' And so they were: the elderly Italian father, the young Malagasy mother, the three endearing boys. The parents rushed to embrace us and their joy at this reunion did even more for our morale than the sunshine. They escorted us into a neat little living-room, furnished from Italy, and produced coffee and banana-cake and explained that Mario's nephew was a priest-teacher at the College. Would we join them next day on an expedition to a leper colony? We would: the appointment was made for 9 a.m.

Lebanon beach is everything a good beach should be: crescent-shaped, sheltered from the oil-polluted east by a wooded promontory, its deep water shark-free, its golden sand innocent of those crustacean hazards which, according to our guidebook, make 'bear-feet' inadvisable on almost every other Malagasy beach. It is cedar rather than palm-fringed and behind rise grassy undulations on which the 'Centre Touristique' is inoffensive – 'Six comfortable bungalows with complete sanitary amenities, riddance, terrace'. 'Riddance' baffled us, but no doubt it is a useful extra amenity. The sun was not too hot for tan-acquiring, the breeze was not strong enough to blow sand around, our fellow-swimmers were not too numerous and mostly attractive young Malagasy – high-spirited children and teenagers, doing acrobatics on the sand and stunts in the water. There was however one snag: several sleek young Indian males on noisy, smelly motor-bikes. Rachel recognised one of them; twice he had pursued her to the market-place and tried to chat her up – behaviour unimaginable on the part of a Malagasy youth.

Those Indians were, objectively, no more or less tiresome than any other macho motor-bike freaks. But as they snarled around the grassy dunes, swerving between the cedars and yelling challenges, it was possible to sympathise with the intense though subdued Malagasy dislike of their 'Indian' compatriots. (In fact more than half of these settlers came originally from what is now Pakistan.) With the Malagasy unable to obtain petrol for essential journeys, or spare parts for ancient vehicles, one could not help resenting those insolent youths on their trendy machines. Given the state of the non-roads for hundreds of miles around, such machines could serve only one purpose: to flaunt an affluence based on the exploitation of the Malagasy.

For generations Madagascar's retail trade has been largely controlled either by Chinese merchants (in Tana and along the east coast) or by Indians, many of whom have been settled on the island since the beginning of the nineteenth century. (Their sort of imperialism is more durable than the European variety.) Both groups also act as money-lenders, yet their reputations are very different. The Chinese are said to be tough and shrewd but fair and honest; the Indians are accused of slyness and ruthless dishonesty. There must be many exceptions in both communities, but this is how most Malagasy see their minorities. The Indians rarely intermarry with the Malagasy, the Chinese often do. Numerically Indians form a tiny, aloof fraction of the population but their financial power is enormous – and growing. President Ratsiraka's austerity campaign has made it much more obvious, creating as it does ideal conditions for Black-Marketeering. The Indians have proved by far the most efficient operators of this system and when criticised they point out that but for their resourcefulness Madagascar would be even more destitute and chaotic – which to an extent is true. They fly to Réunion and organise the illegal import of everything from motor-tyres to toilet soap, on all of which their average profit is forty per cent. Their Black Market charge for one new Landrover tyre in 1983 was £300. Having accumulated substantial capital over the generations, Indian merchants were best placed to 'use' the austerity era. The smaller Malagasy merchants, without any capital, could not begin to compete and many have recently been forced out of business. Mario's wife, Rabado, is sister to a Fort-Dauphin general stores merchant who in 1982 had to shut up shop. Indian 'cornering' also infuriates the Malagasy. Tinned milk – the only sort available in this country of umpteen million cattle – disappeared in Fort-Dauphin for a year, then reappeared in every Indian shop at more than double the old price. It is not surprising that the Indians are now being blamed for all shortages. In early 1983 sugar was unobtainable in Fort-Dauphin for three months. Then news filtered through that an uncontrollable surplus existed at Majunga, one of Madagascar's main cane-growing areas. Mountains of sugar were lying outside the refinery stores, exposed to rats, birds and weather: and at once the Indians were blamed for conspiring to create an artificial shortage. In that case however lack of transport was the problem. There were no vehicles in Majunga sound enough to get the sugar from one end of the island to the other – an explanation which did not even slightly strain my credulity. We had remarked on the odd colour of Fort-Dauphin's sugar-supply: neither white nor brown. Pessimists said it came off the exposed mountain and was stained by rat-piss.

During our banana-cake session Mario had likened the role of Indian businessmen in Madagascar (or East Africa) to the traditional role of Jews in many societies. Indian traders have a capacity for hard work and long-term planning, a well-organised mutual support system, an inborn ability to induce profits to breed more profits, a nose for new opportunities and a flexible conscience about how to use them. All those traits, said Mario, are alien to the Malagasy character. As he spoke I thought of my coffee-lady friend at the covered market near our hotel, a youngish woman with five helpful children and a rheumaticky grandfather. Every morning I went to her stall with our big Thermos and bought half a dozen crispy fried pastries. And every morning she added a gift cup of coffee to the Thermos and a gift seventh pastry to the pile – with a loving though incomprehensible phrase and a squeeze of the hand. She is unlikely ever to save enough money to buy a little shop.

We were not the only *vazaha* on the beach; at the base of the promontory cliff five missionaries were picnicking. When I swam to that side of the bay, using a sedate breaststroke suited to my condition, I recognised Ruth and David, just flown in from Tulear. The Norwegian-American Lutheran Missionary Society (from Minnesota) has had its base in Fort-Dauphin since 1888 and Ruth's baby is the fourth Madagascar-born generation. Will he carry the torch into the twenty-first century? Few pupils remain at the Fort-Dauphin school, once thronged with the children of missionaries – when these were thick on the ground throughout southern Madagascar – and with young Malagasy Lutherans. In Independent Madagascar missionaries are not actively opposed, but neither are they encouraged. And perhaps after a century's heroic effort even these single-minded people are beginning to realise that among the Bara, the Mahafaly and the Antandroy, Christianity – in any recognisable form – is for the birds. Yet a Lutheran pull-out would be a tragedy for those tribes; no one else at present in view is likely to put so much disinterested work into the establishment of rural health-centres.

At sunset it was again my turn to bashie-hunt, again unsuccessfully. Returning by the main coast road, my passport was demanded – for the first and last time in Madagascar – by an aggressive young policeman carrying a lantern. (It was very dark, the moon not yet risen.) Our having spent so much time at police headquarters made his attitude all the more irritating. His inordinate stupidity strengthened my impression that the gendarmerie do not represent the finest flower of Malagasy manhood and helped to explain Fort-Dauphin's 'security paranoia' stories.

It seems the local security forces are obsessionally afraid of a South African invasion, with some odd results. A few months previously a party of primary school children had been taken by their teacher to camp near the summit of St Louis, overlooking the town. Before retiring, they used camp-fire torches to signal to their friends at home – a pre-arranged game. On descending next morning they were surrounded by the army and accused of having signalled to an enemy submarine: 'Time to invade – town abed!' They and their teacher were then imprisoned, for half a day, while the school authorities, supported by the leaders of both churches, argued with the CO – who must have known that his men had behaved like lunatics but was reluctant to admit it.

Still odder was the story of one of Fort-Dauphin's remaining colonists (there are quite a few) who found a box of ship's flares at the back of a cupboard and decided to try one out. It worked perfectly, landed in the middle of the market-place and caused not only total panic in Fort-Dauphin but nationwide alarm. The Tana press reported it as a probable bomb-attack from either Japan or the USA (why not South Africa?) and Madagascar's television network (which covers the whole island but is ninety per cent invisible) flew a cameraman to Fort-Dauphin to film the damage.

These stories disturbed me. They reveal how credulous and unsophisticated are the majority of Malagasy – and how excitable, beneath their calm, easy-going exterior. That combination leaves a country open to the most devastating mischief-making by Foreign Powers who wish to influence its destiny.

Mario's sense of time has survived marriage to a Malagasy; by 9.05 we were en route for the leper colony in a twenty-three-year-old Landrover, already as full as a bashie when we joined the merry throng in the open back. All Rabado's younger relatives seemed to have come along for the ride and four women sat in front with (or on) Mario, laughing uproariously at each other's jokes and tickling each other in the ribs – a freedom which I envied them. The family tendency to run to fat perhaps explains Mario's eccentric driving. Route Nationale No. 12 (now deleted from the maps but still used as far as the first ferry) was equally eccentric; I tried to hold my own ribs together as we bounced for fifteen miles through a riot of lush vegetation, past two wide lakes and several hamlets of palm-thatched bamboo huts from which children spilled by the score to stare at the passing vehicle.

At the unmarked turn-off to the colony there is a sense of moving into an emotionally or psychologically 'restricted zone'. Numerous *fady* are still associated with leprosy though the knowledge that it is curable, and not infectious on sight, is spreading among the east coast tribes – its main victims in Madagascar. It has never been widespread on the island but is persistent throughout the rain-forest.

The track wound through a gold and green world – sun flooding between pines, palms, eucalyptus, lychee, and a variety of medicinal shrubs whose Malagasy names I was told but did not take in. To the west, very close, rose a roughly crested ridge of the Anosyennes range: sheer, densely forested, inaccessible, a refuge for plants and insects and tiny mammals found nowhere else on our planet.

At the wooden reception-hut a seventy-seven-year-old French priest greeted us; he has spent forty-seven years in Madagascar, most of them here, caring for lepers. One felt he had opted out of Time: he might have been one of the original Lazarist missionaries despatched to Fort-Dauphin by St Vincent de Paul. Not so however the youngest of this colony's eight Sisters of Mercy, a twenty-five-year-old Fillipino who guided Rachel and me. She told us that among the Antanosy villagers marriage is virtually unknown and a woman may have seven children by seven different fathers. 'The men tend to drift off when a woman becomes pregnant,' she explained cheerfully. 'But the children are always *much loved* – and maybe God thinks *love* the most important thing? *We* can't know!'

The other seven nuns are elderly Frenchwomen for whom it may not be easy to find replacements; and if these missionaries were not caring for the lepers nobody would be. The Lazarist order has been locally involved since the 1670s; the first Malagasy nun was a Sister of Mercy who ran the girls' boarding school at Fort-Dauphin, having begun her association with the *vazaha* as mistress to one of the French colonists. Her lover's early death so affected her that she became first a Christian and then a nun.

The colony's 'estate' covers broken land: 'split-level', as Rachel said. We walked down to a little reed-fringed lake where the less crippled patients fish from home-made dug-outs, and then cook their catches for themselves in their own individual thatched-hut kitchens. On other levels they grow vegetables and fruits; on the highest level graze cross-bred zebu cows who yield enough milk for the colony. It is self-sufficient too in poultry, eggs and meat; the patients get beef twice a week. In the well-equipped rehabilitation centre women are taught how to weave and crochet with their maimed hands, while men learn how to make shoes for maimed feet. In the hospital section we watched a weeping and homesick newcomer being comforted. Her face had been badly affected and one of the oldest nuns sat beside her on her bed, stroking her hair. In the out-patients department, catering for those well enough to live in their own huts, we watched dressings being changed and rejoiced when those with mere stumps left at the end of their arms unselfconsciously shook hands in accordance with Malagasy tradition. That, to me, was the greatest of the colony's many achievements.

Most cured patients are reluctant to leave and some become hysterical when told they must go home, despite the emphasis on self-help during their stay. One can understand why; the outside world offers nothing comparable to the emotional and material security provided by the nuns – with an extra saintly input from the aged priest.

That leper colony is a special place; one does not often encounter the combination that inspired the Garden of Eden legend – a fusion of natural beauty and human goodness. Back in the Landrover, I whispered to Rachel, 'If this is Christianity, I'll buy it!' But alas! it is only one aspect of Christianity. Another is the condemnation of birth-control by Christian leaders who should be exerting all their moral authority to help save the human race from the consequences of its own fecundity.

We stopped at the entrance to the Mandena Forest Station, where Mario wanted to show us the Malagasy pitcher-plant. But the Station was closed. This small corner of Madagascar has a wondrous number of 'exclusives'. The triangular palm flourishes nearby, over an area of some ten square miles, and is found nowhere else on earth. The very first Michelin tyres were made from the *intasy* – one of the local *Euphorbiaceae* – but as it refused to be cultivated commercially interest switched to the Brazilian rubber tree. The 'leukemia periwinkle' also evolved as a rare weed on a mountain overlooking Fort-Dauphin. It was first sent abroad, to Paris, in 1655, and soon spread all round the world – becoming, in Alison Jolly's words, 'a miracle drug of folk medicines, prescribed by herbalists on every continent'. Since 1958 scientists have been using an extract from this 'rosy periwinkle' in attempts to cure childhood leukemia but at present it achieves only a two-year remission and its side-effects are the destruction of natural immunities, degeneration of the nervous system and – sometimes – baldness. Yet Dr Jolly points out that:

'The Madagascar rosy periwinkle is going strong. Medically it is used in moderation and in combination with other drugs as one of the major weapons in the modern armoury against cancer. Biologically, it lets us probe deeper and deeper into the structures of life. Chemically, new compounds are still being discovered, and the known compounds are so complex they defy artificial synthesis. As a chemical factory the weed is still ahead of the biochemists . . . After 300 years cultivation and twenty years intensive analysis, the rosy periwinkle remains partly an unknown. Six species of the same genus still grow only in Madagascar, each with its own secrets. Twenty years ago the curative powers of the rosy periwinkle were a superstition of local healers. Twenty years from now perhaps we shall trace discoveries as important as the rosy periwinkle's to one of those related "unknown" species. Saving the wild is saving what we do not yet understand: the working ecosystem.'

Mario and family insisted on our lunching with them in a small restaurant near the market-place: rice, excellent casseroled chicken, less excellent casseroled beef and a superb selection of fresh salads. But during the meal my appetite was taken away by an item of news casually mentioned – the possibility that the multinational company, US Steel, might soon show renewed interest in the extraction of titanium north of Fort-Dauphin. This element is found in the territory of the mouse-lemur, the smallest of all primates.

None of the Malagasy understood my distress – nor, indeed, did Mario. If US Steel brought dollars and jobs to Fort-Dauphin, and improved roads and communications, was not that the most important thing? Why fuss about a minute animal that no one ever saw, a creature not even useful – like its bigger cousins – as a tasty dish or a tourist attraction?

I said nothing: the argument is too complicated for such an occasion. And ecology is so new as a set of ideas that we are all easily confused, in our different ways, by its psychological spin-offs. Some people, myself included, are more *genuinely* upset by the extinction of a rare reptile, bird, mammal or plant than by news of a major earthquake in Turkey, or a famine in Ethiopia, or a cyclone in Bangladesh. The destruction of something irreplace-able, a product of Nature's genius working over millions upon millions of years, can arouse an angry, helpless grief far more intense than any emotion provoked by human tragedies in far-off places.

This is an uncomfortable fact to think about, let alone discuss. Yet it *is* a fact. And it needs scrutinising. And Madagascar, more than anywhere else I know, forces one to scrutinise it. What is this feeling? Is it sheer muddled sentimentality? Or is it linked to that First World callousness which allows us to support the nuclear arms race and the global arms trade with our taxes and votes while millions throughout the Third World needlessly suffer and die? I used to feel guilty about my own apparently disproportion-ate reaction to news of yet another ecological atrocity in Amazonia or New Guinea – or Madagascar. But for me Alison Jolly has sufficiently explained and justified that gut-reaction in the con-cluding words of her superb book:

'The conservation of nature is not simply the conservation of our past – that which we did not create. It is also the conservation of our future. It is the conservation of all the forms of life that have not yet evolved, and of the understanding that we have not yet achieved, which may one day become mankind's reality.'

9

Journal of Missing Pieces

Fort-Dauphin. Friday, 8 p.m.

We have found a bashie, of course by chance. This afternoon, miles from the market-place, I noticed a newly painted red and white minibus parked outside a row of shanty-shops. It somehow had the air of a vehicle gathering itself together for a long journey. The cab doors were open, one man lay asleep across the front seats and another lay under the chassis doing mechanical things. I tried to waken the sleeper but he was in an alcoholic stupor. I bent to make enquiries of the mechanic but he merely jerked his legs convulsively in reply. I consulted the watching shopkeepers, who thought it quite likely the bus might leave for Fianar within the next few days. If I returned at sunset, they said, tickets might be on sale. A locked hut, between two of the shops, was the ticket-office.

At 5.15 all four of us peered through the broken rear door and shuddered in unison. The interior looks a veritable torture-chamber; that new paint is deceptive. Some of the warped metal seats face each other, windows are broken, floor-boards missing. 'Think of the *dust*!' said Rachel. 'My buttocks!' said Jamie. 'But we've no choice,' said Adrian. 'Let's get our tickets,' said I. 'And book window-seats,' added Rachel. Departure time is alleged to be 3 a.m. tomorrow. The bent and palsied ticket-seller, father of the driver, thinks we may get to Fianar in two days – more or less . . .

Andalatanosy. Saturday, 6 p.m.

I'm against starting a journey in the small hours. Midnight is OK – you don't go to bed. Dawn is OK – a reasonable time to rise. But 2 or 3 a.m. is inhuman. As we walked to Minnie by the light of the waning moon I felt like a disinterred *razana*. And the others looked like three disinterred *razana*.

It was raining lightly when we got to the ticket-office. Several *lamba*-wrapped passengers were huddled under the tin eaves. Seeing three men asleep in Minnie, the boys wrenched open the door, further damaging its hinges, and ruthlessly roused them. The driver moved under the eaves and went to sleep again. (His name is Andafiavaratra: we call him Andy.) The mechanic/co-driver began to load luggage on the roof. (His name is Randriamaromanana: we call him Randy.) There was very little luggage; the Malagasy are people of few possessions. The third man remained asleep, tightly curled like a cat on the front passenger seat with his hands over his face.

Nothing happened for the next hour apart from a slow accumulation of passengers. We each secured a window-seat and settled down in Minnie.

At 4.15 we thought we were off; instead we toured Fort-Dauphin to pick up three sealed mail-sacks, all of which looked empty, from dwellings that seemed to have nothing to do with the Post Office. Then we returned to base to collect more passengers. When every seat was taken we really were off – at 5 a.m. Beside me sat an unwashed youngish grandma; her three-year-old grandson has a pathetically misshapen head and a bladder problem. Beyond her sat grandpa, who *sucks* snuff, having poured the powder into the space between lower teeth and lower lip.

At 5.20 we stopped because one of the four hens under Jamie's seat had escaped and was trying to fly through a broken window. By then we knew what a manic driver Andy is. In the dawn half-light we took the tricky Ranopiso col road much too fast in a deluge of blinding rain: and Minnie has no windscreen-wipers. I untensed only when we had crossed the watershed and were descending to the rainless lands.

Soon came the regimented dreariness of a sisal plantation, this one still owned by a Frenchman living in Fort-Dauphin who employs 3,000 workers. Breakfast (coffee and buns) happened in Amboasary on the Mandara river. The coffee-stall was cat-dominated; two were tail-less, whether by accident or design (as it were) I couldn't work out. The next twenty-one flat miles to Ambovombe were poorly farmed; maize, millet and sorgho are the meagre crops. A few distant wind-bowed trees proved the strength of the south-easterlies; a few zebu and mohair goats enjoyed dew-watered grass; only one hamlet was visible.

At Ambovombe we acquired three seatless comrades, a young man and his sisters. Their two turkey-hens were tethered to the luggage-rack; this left them free to move to the edge of the roof and deposit excretia on anyone rash enough to lean out to admire the view.

Beyond Ambovombe we were back in the Spiny South, on a track so deeply fissured that even Andy had to slow down, though not enough for my ribs. On such a surface Fotsy never took Merk above ten mph but Minnie averaged twenty mph to Antanimora. Even our map, so keen on upgrading three huts to a village, acknowledges that this forty-mile stretch is uninhabited. There are no hamlets, no tombs. Not a solitary spear glinted among the grey-green expanses of didierea, cacti, aloes and baobabs.

Antanimora must once have been a French administrative centre; it has colonial offices, a large school, balconied villas in decline and about 2,000 inhabitants. Those we saw were strikingly handsome though rather aloof. A wide selection of fly-ridden meats was on offer, set out on little tables under a big *kily* tree. Chunks of stewed kidney and grilled liver, rounds of fried steak, lengths of tripe, huge boiled bones with lots of marrow and little meat, and local versions of hamburgers and sausages. 'They all look like turds,' said Jamie, turning his back on the luncheon possibilities of Antanimora. Adrian – braver – ate rice and zebu-stew in a dark shack reeking of rancid fat. Rachel and I roved further afield on a hopeless bun-hunt. Why bake when you can fill up on first-class protein?

Over the next ten miles the bush thinned and low blue hills, quite close on both sides, broke the flatness. The track improved slightly and we zoomed along at about thirty mph. Then suddenly Minnie was swerving from verge to verge, apparently out of control. When she jolted to a stop in the middle of the track Andy and several male passengers began to argue excitedly while Randy scrambled out and dived under the chassis. He emerged five minutes later brandishing a length of Minnie's guts. The steering had gone – he would have to return to Fort-Dauphin for a spare 'piece'. We *vazaha* looked round in wild surmise. How did he propose covering those 120 miles? Since Ambovombe we had had the track to ourselves. No problem – a truck from Ihosy would appear because today is Saturday. But, persisted Jamie, how and when would Randy *get back* from Fort-Dauphin? Naturally nobody had thought that far ahead. Jamie I fear hasn't yet brought his sense of time into alignment with Madagascar.

The next town was said to be close (three miles) and I went on alone, glad of this chance to walk. The noon sun was not too hot, the light breeze felt almost cool. This is a strange, strange place: not only the vegetation but the stones, the soil, the harsh bright light. Flacourt mentioned, among the riches of Madagascar, jasper, agate, bloodstone, garnet, chalcedony, topaz, amethyst. Around here you feel you are in the midst of them all as the sun draws nameless transient colours – not really colours, but flashes and glitters and sparkles – from rock and sand and pebbles and flints.

I can't help selfishly rejoicing at being stranded here in an isolated Antandroy community, though I hid my delight while overtaking forlorn groups of fellow-passengers. For those without spare cash to buy food, this is a real calamity.

Andalatanosy isn't of course a town – there's no such thing within 150 miles, going north. It's a friendly small village of wooden shacks and mud huts lining the track for a quarter of a mile. As I arrived Minnie arrived too, with our luggage, having been driven very slowly by a subdued-looking Andy. Had the steering gone a few hundred yards further on we would have crashed into a gully by the verge. Soon the expected truck came from Ihosy, stopped for lunch and didn't leave until 2.45 p.m., taking both Andy and Randy. Who knows when we'll see them again?

We lunched quickly – rice and zebu-stew – in the only eating-house. Then Rachel and I hastened to the weekly cattle-market on a eucalyptus-bordered expanse of sloping wasteland – though 'wasteland' is a silly word to use when ninety-five per cent of the land for hundreds of miles around is barren. *Vazaha* visitors can't be too frequent but we at once felt welcome. The main business was already over; only a few score zebu and goats remained, and a few dozen people. Good-looking folk, lean and graceful, with quick smiles and strong faces. But reserved – their friendliness polite, not chummy, yet with a readiness (depending on the *vazaha*) to develop the relationship. When we drooled over a lordly white billy-goat, his wool destined for the Ampanihy rug-makers, a young man – bare to the waist, using his blanket as a skirt – tried to do a deal and we entered into pretend sign-language negotiations which greatly diverted both children and adults. Here shorts have not yet replaced loin-cloths, though during this 'cold' season most men also wear long woollen or cotton blankets. Some women were smoking cigarettes as they stood around waiting for their husbands to join them on the homeward trek. All over Madagascar women smoke in public.

The atmosphere was not entirely unfamiliar; Antandroy tribesmen and Irish farmers have something in common – a certain look in the eye – as they consider the buying or selling of a beast. Most of these zebu seem in poor condition and many are plagued by bots, which evidently doesn't bother their owners. Now of course they are at their worst, as Irish cattle used to be in February. But I'm told they are in any case much inferior to African zebu because of their diet: the fact that millions of them can survive hereabouts – in *any* condition – is astonishing. The calf mortality rate – mainly from worms and scour – is about fifty per cent, though Madagascar is free of foot-and-mouth, rinderpest, brucellosis, tuberculosis and most of the African tick-borne fevers.

The southern Malagasy tribes are not 'professional' cattle people like Africa's Fulani or Masai. Here the herds' religious and social significance is far more important than their economic value. Many herds are half-wild, not part of their owners' domestic routine. They must be guarded only against rustlers, since there have never been any four-footed predators in Madagascar to necessitate the building of defensive corrals. At this season thousands of zebu are taken far from home, to be within reach of some big river that does not dry up completely during winter. Yet these tribes are neither pastoralists nor nomads; their way of life, like their vegetation, is peculiar to Madagascar.

We spent the rest of the afternoon walking for miles to the east of the village. The stony redness is flecked with evergreen scrub, or clumps of wild sisal or *raketa*, or spreading plants, close to the ground, their large leaves doggedly green amidst sharp grey gravel. High white clouds stood still in a violently blue sky: over this red land it can look even bluer than at great altitudes. Figures occasionally appeared in the distance, following faint footpaths into the folds of low smooth hills.

Tombs are more numerous than dwellings but only a few are affluently white-washed – making them the most conspicuous features of this landscape – and none has the elaborate paintings we've seen elsewhere in the south. From a distance most look like Connemara fields, surrounded by low drystone walls. But each covers a bigger area than a Connemara field and the whole enclosure contains hundreds and hundreds of zebu horns, relics of gargantuan funeral feasts. There are too a few ancient, neglected tombs – perhaps belonging to a different tradition? – as big as a two-storeyed cottage, skilfully constructed of small boulders with an echo of Inca cut-stone. These are beginning to disintegrate under the assaults of tree-roots and could easily be mistaken for piles of rock; suddenly to recognise them as man-made is quite startling.

Fertility and circumcision stones are also numerous: vaguely phallic slabs of rough-hewn granite standing alone. Again, if one didn't know their significance they might seem just another of this region's natural curiosities. In this area mass-circumcisions take place every seven years, when all the boys between seven and fourteen are done together. Merina boys are done soon after their third birthday – usually in hospital, nowadays, if the family can afford it. This ceremony is a private affair, like baptism – but much more important, even among practising Christians, because an uncircumcised male cannot be buried in the family tomb.

We had our map with us: I wanted to prove a theory about French cartographers. And sure enough, the 'villages' of Bekapitsa and Ikoroma consist, respectively, of four and five minute mud huts. These low thatched ochre oblongs, squatting on the ochre earth, remain invisible until one is almost beside them. Maize cobs lie on roofs, poultry scratch, goats are tethered to tree-trunk roof supports. Outside Bekapitsa's biggest hut stands a tar barrel converted to a stove – the ultimate in sophisticated mod cons. This, we found, was the chief's hut. As we approached both 'villages' the few inhabitants scuttled indoors, but Bekapitsa's chief felt it his duty to investigate us – a splendid character in a loin-cloth, aged about fifty with a shaven head and the muscles of a weight-lifter. ('All that beef!' murmured Rachel.) As we called a greeting he shouted to his daughter to bring his blanket and draped it ceremoniously around his shoulders before advancing to shake hands. He evidently assumed us to be lost and laughed kindly – he had a marvellous twinkle in slanting eyes. (A lot of Polynesian blood there.) He beckoned us to follow him through a carefully planned *raketa* maze; the prickly pear has survived the beetle quite well in this area. Then he had to dismantle a formidable *raketa* barrier to allow us from his territory onto a wide path. We shook hands over the fearsome thorns and I valued, not for the first time, this revered Malagasy custom. When there are no words in common a handshake can be an important method of communication – something much more than a formality. Once out of sight of Bekapitsa we left the path again to wander over a few more miles of undulating aridity.

In this climate shelter and clothing are not problems. Nor is food, in zebuland, though a balanced diet may be. Always the problem is water – but especially now, towards the end of the dry season. Twice we watched women filling buckets from depressions in the sand, patiently pressing their gourds to the dampness for long, long minutes – and chatting cheerfully while slowly the murky liquid oozed into the containers. The right to use a certain well – if well be the name for these reluctant puddles – is strictly confined to certain families. So the apparently haphazard scattering of villages we passed this afternoon is directly related to the availability of wells. When drought comes – but that doesn't bear thinking of . . . I've read descriptions of such paths as we walked on today littered with the desiccated corpses of those who had been trying to get to the nearest big town, where water flows. Yet these puddles prove the existence of ample water deep down, accessible to modern technology though not to the gourds of the Mahafaly and the Antandroy.

No wonder these people are what we condescendingly call 'feckless'. They cannot, by planning, safeguard their own or their children's futures. Everything depends on the weather. No amount of prudent forethought ensures survival when no rain falls. So they might as well enjoy the present – which they do, with zest.

Although this is not true desert, it has much the same effect on the Man/Nature relationship – here based not on co-operation but on conflict. There is little cultivation: just the occasional small patch of puny maize and millet. Only special people could thrive in this environment: brave, spirited, patient people. Yet one doesn't think of the Antandroy as *impoverished*. It seems the wrong word for the local condition. Being permanently threatened by drought is not at all the same thing as being poor; it is more like leading a dangerous life, as soldiers do in wartime. 'Poverty' refers to physical and emotional weakness, found in communities deprived not only of material essentials but of hope and self-respect, of any just share in what others around them have and they would like to have. But these Antandroy – with only their zebu, a mud shack, a woollen *lamba* – these are a people with enough. Poverty extinguishes a fire that should burn within man; you can see its darkness in the eyes of the urban poor. But a challenging environment such as this keeps the fire burning bright. They are proud, the Antandroy; and dignified, assured – free spirits. If it rains they know they can be happy. If there is drought, they know they must accept extreme hardship, and perhaps death. Yet survivors are never without hope for next year.

The series of major famines and droughts that began in 1931, after the beetles' destruction of the *raketa*, established a tradition of Antandroy migration to other areas of Madagascar where there is – or was – a demand for extra labour on sugar, coffee and sisal plantations, or logging concessions. Their physical strength and stamina was appreciated and they proved more reliable workers than might have been expected; always they wanted to save money to buy more zebu when they returned home. Not many settled for life in another region.

Back on a wide path, we overtook a laughing group dressed in bright new garments. (If a garment is clean hereabouts, it has to be new.) They were an elegant lot: two young men and two young women all wearing gay sarongs and blouses and wide-brimmed straw hats. A boy of about Rachel's age was bare-headed and wore his pink, white and gold blanket like an Ethiopian *shamma*, revealing strong slender legs. His handsome features were a good advertisement for the Bantu/Polynesian mix and he carried an extraordinary stringed instrument – a wooden box four feet long, two feet wide and one foot deep, its strings arranged in a series of ten 'M' shapes on either side. After much hand-shaking and many expressions of good-will and welcome (these we do understand by now, having heard them so often), we all walked on together – until joined by an *ombiasa*, apparently going to the same cere-mony. (Probably a wedding.) He suddenly appeared out of a *raketa* thicket, a grotesque figure with a bearded face under an enormous wig or headpiece of black goats' hair and laden with necklaces of charms. He too shook hands, but unenthusiastically; his presence seemed to cause the temperature to drop several degrees. We said goodbye then to the elegant ones and hurried on, passing a larger group – also dressed up – sitting by the side of the path drinking hooch and obviously waiting for our group.

Andalatanosy has a *hotely*: our eating-house. Behind the 'res-taurant' a row of mud cells, each with two pallets, faces a line of eucalyptus and a distant earth-closet hut – which, according to the fastidious Jamie, isn't half distant enough. (I have to admit I only got as far as the door, then retreated behind a tree instead.)

The boys have one room, other affluent passengers fill the rest – sleeping, it seems, three to a bed. The less affluent are sleeping in Minnie and Rachel and I have been given someone's bed in the *hotely*-owner's residence. It is in one corner of the living-room, which also acts as an extension of the restaurant, and a cotton sheet has been hung from the ceiling to give it a third wall. This is being written by the light of a smoking oil-lamp as I sit on the edge of the straw mattress feeling exhausted – but sleep is impossible with so many noises off. (Not so, happily, for Rachel: she sank into a coma of fatigue at 7.) Our long walk did no rib-damage but my left hand is now in rather an alarming and very puzzling state: swollen, extremely painful, yet the cut *looks* clean and seems to be closing up rapidly. Rachel has been scratching a lot this past half-hour – bedbugs?

Andalatanosy. Sunday, 1 p.m.

Yes, our first Malagasy bedbugs, looking (and feeling) the same as any others. Also lots of hen-fleas. But even without parasites it would not have been possible to sleep until after midnight. Relays of people were being fed; members of a very extended family, plus friends. The *hotely*-owner is Merina, like many of southern Madagascar's small business people, and his wife is a Betsileo. There was much laughter – incessant clattering of plates – loud chomping as people got through their hunks of zebu – some amiable drunkenness as the evening wore on. All the time I was within an inch of sleep but never allowed to get there. By 11 an odd frantic desperation was welling up inside me; sleep-deprivation is after all one of the most effective methods of mental torture. Then I noticed that things were sidling out of my pillow, which was stuffed with the dry flower heads of the mattress mint. I can't imagine what they were – mites of some sort – but they had an instinctive urge to lodge in my ears. However, this involuntary eavesdropping on Malagasy life was fascinating. The prevailing courtesy proved that the 'graciousness' I have so often remarked on has nothing to do with 'party manners' in honour of the *vazaha*; it's how the Malagasy are. Also, their language is soothingly musical to listen to, despite its ugly appearance in Roman script, and those family voices were full of affection. The frequent laughter was so infectious that often I found myself smiling – though what between bedbugs, fleas, mites, exhaustion and a wildly throbbing hand my personal situation wasn't all that funny.

Nine of us slept in that small room, which needed an open door by 5.45 a.m. when Father began to rouse his grown-up son and two adolescent daughters, the chef and waitresses. They weren't easily roused but Father worked on them persistently though gently. And he made sympathetic encouraging noises when at last they staggered off, shaking themselves and scratching, towards the kitchen shed at the back.

At 6.15 we (also scratching) set off to explore the area west of the 'road', beyond an abrupt 1500-foot ridge some five miles long. A cloudy sky then: perfect walking weather. This ridge is covered with round red boulders and bizarre vegetation – bushes, cacti, small twisted trees – none of which we've seen elsewhere. A narrow path took us over a low col onto a wide flat plain carpeted with glittering little stones. Here there was a wondrously tranquil, *hidden* feeling. Turning south, we walked parallel to the ridge, passing several tombs. Zebu grazed in the distance on nothing that was visible while egrets de-botted them; one boy-herd stood on a high rock, studying us from afar, leaning on his spear; a giant buzzard perched on a massive boulder poised on a solitary round hill. High on the side of the ridge, other flat boulders were surmounted by inexplicable constructions of stone – possibly more old tombs? But more likely altars; cocks and goats are still regularly sacrificed around here, as indeed they are in Imerina. Towards the end of the ridge, near three huts, we crossed tiny paddy-fields by a tree-shaded water-course: dry now, but it must fill up in summer. From another grass-thatched hut – isolated, *raketa*-hedged – came music and singing at 8 a.m. Not the end of an all-night party, just a family of five enjoying themselves. As we stood listening to a soft, plaintive solo, one daughter noticed us – a lovely girl, apparently pure Merina. Her father was the soloist, playing the *valiha*, another of Madagascar's many stringed instruments. This one is a five-foot length of bamboo, with fifteen wire strings stretched between two metal bands. Everyone came out to shake hands before we went on our way.

The cloud had become thin silvery layers, with growing patches of blue. We returned by a different route, meeting three zebu-carts slowly crossing the gravelly plain. As we approached, three little boys shrieked with terror, jumped to the ground and fled – leaving their zebu to continue alone and unperturbed towards (we supposed) the village of Ambatamainty.

On the outskirts of Andalatanosy we crossed a dried-up river bed where a mother and her two small daughters were filling buckets from another 'well', this one a pool some six inches deep so their task was comparatively easy. But the water looked feculent beyond belief – really it was thin mud. One hopes the sediment is allowed to settle before use, since this is our *hotely*'s well. Watching the little girls dipping their gourds I thought how miraculous, to them, would seem the taps we so casually turn on twenty times a day. We say 'flowing like water' to convey an extravagant or careless use of something. It's a phrase I dislike. Anyone who has ever suffered – even once, even a long time ago – from real tongue-swelling thirst can never again take water for granted.

Back at base we found Jamie looking like an ancient Greek. After a night of shivering misery he had just bought a pallium-like blanket. (But striped brown, white and blue, which I don't think pallia were.) A handsome lad, even at the worst of times, he now cuts a positively dashing figure.

It was 10.30 but nobody had news of Andy and Randy. Hymn-singing floated faintly from a few transistor radios up and down the street. There are two mini-churches here but no clergymen anywhere around. Lay readers take services occasionally but were not in action today.

The turkey-hens' male escort was squatting on Minnie's roof trying to coax his feathered friends to eat boiled rice. He looked several degrees more anguished each time they turned up their beaks at it. 'Would you blame them?' said Jamie – a bit of a gourmet, on whom the strain of the Malagasy diet is beginning to tell. Most of our fellow passengers were sitting in the sun holding animated converse. Adrian has decided that Madagascar's roads are what they are because the Malagasy *enjoy* this sort of thing – as do I. Who would ever have thought motor-journeys could be such fun?

I bought another bottle of stiffener for the upper lip – if possible more gruesome than the Tsihombe distillation – because the swelling had spread from my hand to my wrist and was bewilderingly painful. The boys then insisted on my stuping the cut to avoid general septicaemia. Having seen the source of our water, it seemed essential that it should be *boiled* for this purpose – not merely heated. Jamie accompanied me to the kitchen (a dark filthy shed) and emphasised '*boiled*' in French – not that anyone there spoke any, but we felt we'd done the responsible thing. We watched a wood-fire being lit in a tar-barrel and about a litre of brownish-green water being poured into a dirty coffee saucepan. Jamie longed to demand a clean saucepan but I restrained him; that would be an unreasonable request. A daughter then began last night's wash-up in a small basin of what looked like thick vegetable soup. Jamie broke into a cold sweat and went out for air. When Adrian arrived to give moral support he peered into two giant iron cauldrons, half full of cooked rice and zebu-stew – ready to be re-heated at lunch-time. Lunch-time has now passed; even Adrian didn't have any.

Fifteen minutes stuping helped but I'm more and more baffled; the cut itself looks perfectly clean and healthy. I hope it stays that way, after immersion in Andalatanosy's water.

At noon someone saw dust rising in the distance, away to the south. We gathered in the middle of the street and watched. It was another minibus, much more battered-looking than Minnie – but on this scene looks don't count. Randy leaped out, waving The Piece. Andy followed, shakily. He is an elderly man, with close-cropped grey hair, very small and slight and black-skinned and visibly ravaged by years of hooch. (I feel ravaged enough after only ten days of it.) He wears faded, ragged, filthy jeans and a torn blue *lamba* and his eyes have no whites – permanently bloodshot. As he stumbled onto the road he looked like a caricature of someone with a hangover. At once he disappeared behind the shack where I bought my bottle and we haven't seen him since. I hope Randy drives this afternoon. He has now been under Minnie for almost two hours; it seems the 'piece' isn't *quite* right . . . The other vehicle is very decently waiting for us.

As I was writing the above, sitting in the sun near Minnie, a deputation of under-tens crowded around to beg for another eye-rolling display – one of my few party tricks, and really only suited to company such as the present. In the middle of my performance a young man of about twenty came to sit beside me; I have adult spectators, too, though they pretend to be less interested. He's been around since we arrived, often staring at me intently; obviously dim-witted, but genial. Now I discovered his worry: he'd been told I was a woman but couldn't believe it. He spoke a few words of French, one of which was *lait*. Tapping my bosom, he enquired, 'Lait?' 'Oui! Oui!' I assured him, 'but a long time ago.' Unfortunately the top pockets of my bush-shirt are full of passports, note-books, maps, sun-glasses and other solid objects which strengthened his suspicion that I was lying, that no *lait*-producing facility lay within. He shook his head and repeated, 'L'homme!', at the same time unbuttoning my shirt. There was nothing at all offensive about this action; he was merely conducting a scientific investigation while incidentally causing paroxysms of hilarity among the population, young and old. But as he discovered '*Une femme!*' poor Rachel could take no more and fled the scene. Fourteen is a sensitive age in those areas. I, being at the other end of the spectrum, could afford to remain unmoved. At fifty-one it is quite safe to let puzzled young tribesmen peer down one's shirt-front; they are unlikely to be inflamed by what they see.

Now things are happening – Minnie's engine has growled – Andy has emerged – looks like we're off!

Isoanala. Monday, 4.15 a.m.

The events of the past thirteen hours have diminished my enthusiasm for Malagasy motor journeys.

We set off just before 3 p.m., the other minibus leading. Incredibly, Andy was driving – which put Randy in an understandably bad temper. Yet it took us three hours to cover the thirty-four miles to Beraketa; even Andy couldn't speed over such a surface. We stopped only once, for a few moments, near a minuscule settlement. Two little girls were selling revolting lumps of bone, fat and gristle, dripping grease from a steaming cauldron. (How did they know we were coming? By the distant dust?) These horrors were purchased with yelps of joy by most of our comrades who spent the next hour working on them, creating a remarkable concatenation of squelching, crunching, grinding, sucking and rending noises. My immediate neighbours were among the hardest workers.

This was the most truly desert-like stretch we've seen, a level stony plain for mile after flat mile with very little vegetation yet hundreds of grazing zebu. Rather dull yet reassuring in the circumstances; here it wouldn't matter if Minnie went wild again. Then dullness was banished as a saffron and scarlet sunset suddenly ignited over this immensity of blue-shadowed plain, its horizons seeming infinitely remote, as from a ship on the high seas. As the magical afterglow came – orange, brown, copper – lines of eucalyptus were silhouetted, marking Beraketa.

I know nothing about Beraketa, except that the name means 'Many Raquet Cactuses', raquet cactus being another name for the prickly pear. In total darkness we tripped several times over God-knows-what on our way to a dimly-lit eating-house. ('*This* is what happens when there's no moon!' said Rachel.) Unfortunately the eating-house was also a drinking-house and Andy and Randy settled down in opposite corners with a bottle each; they'd been bickering all afternoon. Already the air was very cold. We attempted congealed rice-mountains and tepid zebu-stew, then frantically went on a chocolate-hunt. The shop had a tame baby lemur on the counter and not much else. We left empty-handed and returned empty-bellied to Minnie.

Beyond Beraketa dense bush replaces bare desert and the terrain seems much more broken – as is the track. It's hard to write convincingly about Madagascar's Route Nationales. Minnie couldn't go above twelve mph between Andalatanosy and Beraketa, yet that stretch was like the M4 compared to what now confronted her. Since sunset Minnie II had been following us closely; her waiting at Andalatanosy was not altruistic. Only one of her headlights remained and that was askew, illuminating not the track but the weirdies in the bush on our left.

The quarrel between Andy and Randy had gone out of control; four times in an hour we stopped to change drivers. Now both were drunk, their behaviour at the wheel was equally manic and I was losing my nerve. (Something that happens to me much more quickly in a motor-vehicle than anywhere else.) Twice Minnie struck boulders – or something – that seemed to tear at her guts and certainly did my ribs no good. We wondered how many more such impacts the new steering 'piece' could survive. Twice we left the cratered track to force our way through heavily armed towering vegetation like savage giants determined to block our way. Here I longed for Fotsy with a deep and passionate longing; when we had to bush-bash he stayed in command as we weaved slowly through the opposing forces. Andy however favoured the direct approach and put Minnie to various obstacles as though she were competing for the Aga Khan Trophy. She reared and lurched as we bulldozed skyscraper termite-hills, and swayed and skidded as we pushed and scraped through thorns which made hideous noises (like forks on plates) along her sides. The turkeys' owners were in a frenzy; the young man shouted heartening remarks through a broken window and the two young women looked close to tears. Yet these detours were almost relaxing in contrast to our road-work; at least the bush to some extent reduced speed.

Back on the track, Randy insisted on taking over again. Then he
trod hard on the accelerator and I began to sweat with fear and
wish I'd sent Rachel off to Kerry for her summer holidays. When
Minnie struck an oblong boulder in the centre of the track we all
literally hit the roof: the top of my head is still swelling to prove it.
(I'd seen that boulder coming but Randy simply didn't notice it.)
Again we stopped – frightened angry mutterings among the
passengers – more incoherent arguing in the cab – somewhere
along the way we'd lost Minnie II.

Andy repossessed the wheel and we rattled perilously on, poor
Minnie now sounding as though she might at any moment finally
fall apart. Then again she was being noisily grabbed by dense
bush, but only on one side – we hadn't turned off the track.
Quickly we swerved to the other side – and back again. This
however was not unusual enough to cause extra alarm; we just
held tight, exchanging strained smiles. Nobody realised that
Minnie was totally out of control until the grinding smash came.

Thus far we'd all been admirably restrained, our protests never
exceeding muted exclamations of terror or condemnation. But
now we'd had it. Everyone tumbled out, shouting and screaming
and abusing the drivers. We were badly shaken, in more senses
than one; that crescendo jolt had unmended my ribs. Torches
were produced and when we saw what had happened we were
even more shaken. Curiously, a sudden silence fell. Minnie's right
wheels were suspended in the air over a gully – the drop scarcely
nine feet, but onto sharp rocks. She was jammed on the concrete
parapet of a bridge – a typical French parapet, just high enough
for us to have sliced off the top six inches (as we saw later) by the
force of the impact.

The eruption of fury that followed our odd little silence quickly
became an argument about how best to rescue Minnie. The
Malagasy are not a contentious people, whatever the provocation.
And though famous for words rather than deeds they do appreciate that words don't lift buses off parapets.

Meanwhile I was standing by the bridge trembling with a
mixture of shock, rage and cold – the wind was icy. In my view the
time had come to abandon Minnie and either camp where we
stood or walk back to Beraketa; I fancied a starlight walk, to calm
my nerves. It seemed to me, and still does, utterly suicidal to try to
get to Fianar on a road like Route Nationale No. 13 in a vehicle
like Minnie with two dipsomaniac drivers. But the younger

generation thought I was just having middle-aged heebie-jeebies and spoke to me soothingly, which I found intensely irritating. You don't need to be an elderly neurotic to see this Minnie enterprise as plain crazy.

But every Malagasy situation is saved, sooner rather than later, by pure comedy. My rage evaporated when Minnie II emerged out of the night at walking speed, for the very good reason that instead of headlights she had two men with small torches walking half-backwards some fifteen paces ahead of her. 'Half-backwards' may seem not to make sense but it precisely describes their method of progress.

During Minnie's rescue we *vazaha* stood around shivering – all except Jamie, cosy in his new blanket. When he nobly offered to share its warmth with Rachel the women passengers deduced them to be a young married couple and we went along with this to avoid giving an impression of *vazaha* lewdness. Our warm clothing was with the turkeys, still *in situ* and looking quite composed by starlight. Perhaps they are much-travelled.

Within less than an hour Minnie had been half-lifted, half-towed to safety by the combined brute force of Minnie II and the male passengers from both buses, plus the brainpower of one passenger from Minnie II who directed operations. Much deference was shown to this gentleman, evidently a person of authority.

I was praying Minnie wouldn't start – indeed, to expect her to seemed wildly unreasonable. But she did, though now she can move only very, very slowly, all the time in low gear. Given the state of the track, this is a most fortunate disability. We left Minnie II behind, waiting for the rising of the moon. Andy and Randy, though sobered by the shock, were quarrelling more abusively than ever, blaming each other for the collision. But the duel about who should drive was over; Randy stayed behind the wheel. Twice Minnie stalled on long gradual slopes and everyone had to get out to push her to the top. On the second of these occasions, at 11 p.m., I rejoiced on Minnie II's behalf: the waning moon lay like a golden melon-section above a jumble of black hills on our right. Minnie took more than three hours to cover the twenty miles from the bridge to this town. I suppose it *is* a town; we arrived at 12.15 a.m. and haven't gone exploring. The sixty-four miles from Andalatanosy took nine and a half hours.

For four of our passengers Isoanala is home; beaming with relief they melted away into the shadows carrying suitcases on their heads. 'Lucky devils!' exclaimed Jamie. The rest of us were told this was to be a half-hour stop and we crowded into a dark, draughty eating-house. Isoanala occupies the highest point in southern Madagascar and during winter nights is piercingly cold. Most people ate rigid rice and cool zebu-stew by oil-wick light, sitting on wobbly benches at three trestle tables. Jamie, Rachel and I abstained. There was no coffee but, ominously, lots of hooch. Andy and Randy began to drink again. Both produced driving-licences, apparently relevant to their furious argument. Randy – a tallish young man, much lighter-skinned than Andy – became so enraged he seemed about to strike Andy, though the Malagasy are not prone to violence. He then went from table to table, seeking passenger witnesses to his innocence – begging us all to support his guilt-free claim. Why is he so steamed up about this when *Andy* drove us onto the bridge? Through the language barrier we can see only an outline of what's going on; the Andy–Randy conflict is obviously old, bitter and complex.

Rachel and I drifted back to Minnie and failed to get at our rucksacks. Adrian had got his down when the luggage was unroped for the departing passengers; I'm never very keen-witted at midnight and missed that chance. Others followed us out but nobody could open Minnie's jammed rear-door. We stood disconsolate, with chattering teeth, till Jamie arrived to tell us departure had been postponed to 4.30 – which no one believed. We reckoned 6.30 soonest. My relief was great. Apart from their latest drinking-bout, Andy and Randy needed *sleep*: a thought prompted solely by the instinct of self-preservation. I'm long past worrying about those two on humanitarian grounds.

Adrian disappeared with his flea-bag to sleep under the stars – the reward of forethought! I looked for Randy to unrope the luggage and found him and Andy in a lean-to shed, sitting around a charcoal-stove drinking from bottles. They were still arguing, each presenting his case to the ancient little *hotely*-owner, whose private quarters these are. He is a mildly disquieting character who never smiles, shuffles instead of walking and wears a mis-shapen Homburg as old as himself pulled far down over his eyes. Randy ignored my desperate pleas; he was in any case much too far gone to untie knots by moonlight. Back in the 'restaurant' Jamie had on his 'El Greco' expression, accentuated by a raised anorak hood looking like a monk's cowl. He drew his blanket tightly around him and laid his head on a table, having first half-heartedly cleared a space of spilled rice grains and chips of zebu bone. Just behind him two gargantuan cockroaches paced slowly up the mud wall, rhythmically waving their antennae. We didn't tell him; his cross was already heavy enough. But we ourselves sat on a bench well away from the walls. By then the women, children and older men had formed one huddled blanketed mass outside, on the bleak mud-floored verandah. The eight men who stayed here in the restaurant finished all the hooch in sight before settling to sleep.

One of the pair sitting opposite Rachel and me looked not only booze-befuddled but furrowed and haggard with worry. Twice he produced from under his blanket a packet of nine grimy envelopes addressed to various small towns en route, including those behind us. The letters were not stamped so he must be a self-employed courier. Apparently he'd just realised that in several cases he'd overshot the mark. Repeatedly he thumbed through the envelopes, mumbling the names and addresses to himself and lamenting his error. His guilt was rather touching and I feel they may yet be delivered.

By now all around us are asleep; three make eerie bundles on a table, looking under their brown blankets like corpses hastily covered after an accident. Two more are lumped together in the middle of the floor; they kick spasmodically – creepy-crawlies or hooch-nightmares? Rachel and I have just Scrabbled for two hours, our numb and purple fingers scarcely able to manage the letters. The unglazed shuttered window and rough-hewn door are ill-fitting and we sit between door and doorless kitchen entrance. The courier woke once and stared at our Scrabble-board with a kind of terror; perhaps he thought we were doing *vintana* calculations, *vazaha*-style. The man beside him cherishes a large spanner, a priceless object in modern Madagascar, which he keeps close to his heart under his blanket. But now and then as he shifts in his sleep it clatters to the earth floor and without quite waking he gropes for it under the table. This routine triggered off the giggles which repeatedly afflicted Rachel and me until at last she slept. Jamie, on being disturbed yet again, accused us – not unreasonably – of being like Fourth Formers at St Trinians.

Early on I requisitioned the three flickering oil-wick tins so the room beyond our pool of light is all restless shadows, recalling a shot from the Dracula vault scene in a silent movie. Over the years I've written my travel-diary in some odd circumstances, but none odder than these. As I wrote the last paragraph a figure appeared in the kitchen entrance – a youngish bony woman, naked as the hour she was born, with long tangled hair hanging about her shoulders and a questioning expression. She stood for a moment in the faint oil-wick glow, leaning forward, her hands clasped under her chin, viewing this scene of misery and squalor. Then she vanished. I'm wondering now if I really saw her, or if Travels With Minnie have completely unhinged me.

Betroka. Monday, 7.30 p.m.

Travels With Minnie got off to a slow start this morning – and continued slow. We covered forty-eight miles today.

At 5.30 I decided to rouse Andy and Randy and found the latter sharing a blanket with one of the women passengers. No scandal: she's his wife – poor girl! A superbly tinted dawn – pale green, primrose, pale pink – but *icy*. Finding Adrian under a *kily* in the middle of a vast square (Isoanala is mainly that square), I dutifully shook him, announcing our imminent departure. But he, doubtless remembering another episode under a *kily* in Ampanihy, very sensibly ignored me and burrowed deeper into his flea-bag.

I roamed in search of something that wasn't reheated rice and zebu-stew. The population was still abed, apart from six hens, one bitch being pursued by seven dogs, and two small boys on zebu-carts going to fill tar-barrels from the distant Isoanala river. Minnie II wasn't visible (I worried vaguely about her) but a large empty truck had been abandoned outside another *hotely*. Three of its tyres were flat. That *hotely* was run by a family of dwarves. This wasn't a hunger hallucination: the others saw them later. They were welcoming and kindly; mother, father and two adolescent children, none above three and a half feet in height. Their fried pastries were not made today or yesterday, but perhaps some time last week. I bought the entire stock (fifteen) and ate five standing on the edge of the town, looking south. The rising sun glowed pink-purple on fissured mountain ridges and I could see Route Nationale No. 13 looking like a perfect reproduction of a dried-up mountain torrent. The nearby clusters of two-storeyed red-mud houses were reed thatched, their shutters just opening. By then I'd rather lost my grip on the tribal situation but Isoanala is, I think, in or close to Bara territory.

Back at the shack, the turkeys' escort was trying to tempt them to breakfast. Adrian was packing his flea-bag. Jamie was pale and moving stiffly, like one with a neck-cramp. Our fellow-passengers were happily chewing old bones, chatting and laughing as though they'd spent the night in Claridges. Andy was sitting on the verandah looking perfectly sober but very diseased. Randy was missing. Still there was no coffee. When I offered Jamie a fried pastry he turned a shade paler, shook his head wordlessly and moved away. Then Randy and his wife appeared, arguing; he wanted to drive, she was insisting that Andy must. When I approached them I realised why. In lieu of coffee Randy had been at it again. The fumes were almost visible and his speech was slurred; it was 7.10 a.m. Wife appealed to Andy, who nodded morosely and got behind the wheel. As we all took our seats Randy rushed round the corner of the *hotely* to be sick. Then he stretched out on the ledge behind the seats in the cab and went to sleep. His wife sat beside Andy. Jamie – in a front passenger seat, inches from Randy's calloused feet – noted, 'He has great chasms in his soles with bits of wood sticking out of them.'

The next two and a half hours were spent trying to start Minnie. Isoanala is on a hill-top and the drill was to push her down the slope, hoping the engine would do whatever engines should do before she stopped. When it didn't, everyone – except Randy (being asleep) and me (being disabled) – had to push her backwards to the top of the hill to try again. Where she habitually stopped I sat beneath a magnificent unknown tree and admired the road. Suddenly Route Nationale No. 13 was a reformed character, a wide smooth red-earth highway. When/if Minnie started, I reckoned we'd have no more problems. But the likelihood of her starting seemed increasingly remote; the engine's occasional weak strangled noises sounded more like a death-rattle than anything else. Watching her being pushed backwards for the fifth time, I marvelled at our fellow-passengers' good-humour. For three nights and two days they had had little sleep or food; they had escaped injury or death by a parapet's breadth; they had often been required to contribute man-power (and now woman-power as well) to assist Minnie – in our effete society people win medals for enduring much less. Yet they remained cheerful and relaxed. Perhaps Adrian is right and they actually *enjoy* journeys like this – or do they not realise that journeys can in fact be quite different?

Across the road two tame ring-tail lemurs were playing in the garden of a new government building apparently never used. An elderly exhausted passenger opted out of the sixth uphill push and came to sit beside me. This building is unused, he explained, because all the allocated funding went into the construction, leaving nothing for staff wages. And at Isoanala the road improves abruptly because the road-maintenance fund ran out here. He looked anxiously at my left hand, which I had just unbandaged to see what was going wrong. Today it is not only grossly swollen but badly burned; great blisters have risen all around the thumb. My stuping, it seems, was too thorough. Yet the cut continues to heal cleanly while the pain grows all the time worse. Last night however I discovered something helpful. Often I write leaning my head on my left hand and this position – hand held up – to some extent reduces the pain. Meanwhile my ribs are in a far worse state, post-parapet, than after the original break.

When Minnie's engine roared – she was half-way down the slope – a wild cheer rang out and five minutes later we were on our way. Andy was no longer sober; his morale had needed boosting after each abortive push. But the nature of the terrain, and Minnie's inability to go above fifteen mph – even on this comparatively good road – meant that we were quite safe.

By now we have given several nicknames, fortunately unintelligible to their recipients. Opposite Jamie sit two obese teenage sisters – so tall they must be Bara – who titter and whisper and nudge non-stop. The fatter and more irritating was soon named Heffalump by Jamie. I named the other Aphrodite though Jamie says she has quite the opposite effect. Heffalump suffers from car-sickness, which in no way diminishes her appetite. At each *hotely* she fills up with rice and zebu-stew, to be disposed of in due course through the window while Jamie shields himself from the spume with a sheet of plastic borrowed from Adrian. (Adrian is a practical lad; he travels very light, yet can produce all sorts of helpful objects.) The natty supercilious young man who never leaves a mysteriously precious bottle out of his hands is known as Smarty-pants. Of all the passengers, only he has been consistently petulant about poor Minnie's little mishaps. The baby beside Rachel on its mother's knee is – prosaically – Green-hat. 'Damp-end' would have been more appropriate; it is afflicted by unnatural thirst, catered for from a barrel-sized Thermos of rice-water, and its kidneys are in perfect working order. The plump nine-year-old boy who sits directly in front of me eats pocketsful of

rotten dried fish the way other small boys eat toffees. We call him
Fishy Fartz. He has digestive problems. 'Wouldn't you', said
Rachel, when I complained of their effects, 'if you lived on
decayed sardines?' As Jamie observed, 'Other people's internal
organs become awfully important on a trip like this.' At Isoanala
two bulky sacks had been stuffed under his seat – most unfairly, as
he is by far the longest-legged passenger. These caused him acute
problems (by now his buttocks are vying with my left hand) and
he was soon reporting, 'I have my knee in Aphrodite's crotch, but
she doesn't seem to mind.'

We crossed many miles of flat red grassland, then many more
miles of stony, scrubby, broken country where gnarled trees
marked three river courses – all dry. There were no bridges and
Minnie stalled at each attempt to escape from the rough river-
beds. Everyone out, much pushing – off again. In the middle of a
parched uninhabited plain we stopped to release the turkeys and
their owners. The moment the birds touched solid ground they
began ravenously to eat the rice produced from one of the girl's
shoulder bags.

Minnie's fourth stall was in a deep dip in the track. This time no
amount of pushing, backwards or forwards, did any good. Randy,
refreshed by his slumbers, went under and diagnosed a need for
two new 'pieces'. So Minnie II, who had caught up with us during
the first stall, went ahead to summon aid from this small town of
Betroka.

For a couple of hours we all sat or lay around in that hot
shadeless hollow. Quite a few, not surprisingly, slept. Heffalump
and Aphrodite, still tittering and nudging, collected the pale gold
feathery tips of seven-foot reeds growing in a dense mass by the
track. We were now in slightly less barren country and a few
stands of cane and bedraggled banana plants also grew nearby.
When Smarty-pants helped himself to a stick of cane all who
noticed looked disapproving. Even as he picked the cane he kept
his bottle between his knees.

The relief vehicle, Minnie III, brought two spare pieces but
only on loan. Eventually we set off in convoy: passengers in
Minnie III, Andy, Randy and luggage in Minnie I – who, whether
because of her replacements or her light load, kept up with us as
we scorched along at *forty* mph! Our new driver wore a brightly
patterned frilly shirt and did not at first sight inspire confidence.
He was very young, very short, with long arms, virtually no

forehead, yellow skin and buck teeth. 'Peking Man!' muttered Adrian. He was certainly more Chinese than Malagasy. But he was sober. And Minnie III was sound of wind and limb. Nothing else mattered. He was also, we soon realised, an excellent driver. For some reason the tittering sisters found him irresistible; they moved their seats to get closer and serenaded him as we sped along. Other passengers leant out of the windows waving their clumps of feathery reeds and chanting triumphantly, like so many football fans returning from a victory. Only then did we realise how the tension had built up with Andy and Randy as a constant threat to our lives and general well-being. Even the laid-back Malagasy must have felt the strain more than they betrayed.

Near Betroka something has been done about reforestation, though much more is needed. We passed many eucalyptus plantations, not too severely 'raided', before coming to the edge of the high Isoanala plateau. Far below lay tin-roofed Betroka in a flat grey saucer-valley, semi-encircled by rough blue mountains. We expected only to pause here, for a late lunch. Instead, Peking Man instructed us to report to the bus-office at 7 a.m. tomorrow, when he will drive us to Fianar in a repaired (allegedly) Minnie I. Good news! Since rising in Fort-Dauphin at 2 a.m. on Saturday morning I've had almost no sleep and last night Rachel only dozed for an hour. In all her fourteen years I've never seen her look so exhausted. And poor Jamie looks little better.

This dismal town – population about 5,000 – is another French imposition with no soul of its own. Wide, dusty, too-hot streets of decrepit European buildings – mostly 1950s – are redeemed only by a row of handsome Merina-style mansions, their balconies, shutters and eaves intricately carved. In the enormous market many stalls are as poorly stocked as the local shops. Inexplicably, the *vazaha* are creating a sensation like nowhere else in Madagascar. Scores of excited youngsters and quite a few adults followed us all over the Zoma, shouting, laughing and occasionally jeering. Atmosphere not as friendly as usual in this Bara territory. Most people are conspicuously darker and taller than the average, yet if you saw them among a crowd of Africans you'd know they didn't belong.

Like the town, this hotel feels left over: a place that no longer has a purpose. But by the standards to which we have become accustomed it is rather superior. The owner's relatives seem to have settled permanently into most of the rooms, all leading off a long, high concrete verandah. The one vacant guest-room has a double-bed; another was moved in for Rachel and me. The concrete floor is disintegrating; Jamie says it reminds him of Route Nationale No. 13. At sunset we were startled when electricity came on. Twenty minutes later it went off and a smiling youth arrived with candles. The 'toilet equipments' are a tap in the compound from which sludge trickles and a rusty tin screen round a hole in the ground. As I write a gale-force wind is clattering non-stop at a loose sheet of iron directly overhead but this evening an earthquake couldn't rouse the younger generation. An ability to survive longer without sleep is one of the advantages of middle-age.

On arrival we enjoyed an astonishingly good three-course meal. In restaurant kitchens, if nowhere else, the French influence endures. The bar stocks Fianar rosé wine (only); after hooch it tastes like St Emilion and a half-litre gave me courage for this evening's ordeal.

My sticking-plaster rib-strapping had to come off. Ever since the bridge incident it had been making things far worse and I couldn't face another night of it. Rachel was deeply asleep when the boys went off to dine at 7.30 but I tried to waken her: I couldn't unstrap myself. What followed was rather uncanny, like watching someone sleep-walking. Although it was impossible to rouse her I got through to her unconscious. She stood up – her eyes half-open, but like a blind person's not seeing – and exactly followed my instructions. I put the end of the plaster in her hand and said, '*Pull – pull hard!*' She did so, and as she pulled I turned round and round and round, all the time repeating '*Pull hard!*' It was very, very sticky sticking-plaster and an amount of force had to be exerted. I expected Rachel to wake at any moment and wonder what was happening: but she never did. This was fortunate because she's a tenderhearted creature and a few inches of skin came off too, leaving long raw stripes. I never before understood how flaying worked: now I know. One doesn't bleed because it's just the top layer of skin which presumably soon heals. This must have been one of the more effective forms of mediaeval torture and being partially flayed seemed a fitting end to today's instalment of Travels With Minnie.

Antsirabe. Wednesday, 4 p.m.

Last night in Fianar I was too pain-exhausted to diary-write so this is a double entry. Incredibly, we covered the 500 miles from Betroka to here in twenty-seven hours.

We started at 8.15 a.m. yesterday morning, with Peking Man in sole control of a cured Minnie, and by 1 p.m. had joined Route Nationale No. 7 at Ihosy. Over that last seventy-five miles of Route Nationale No. 13 the surface was again atrocious and we saw not one other vehicle. From Betroka we were climbing back into the highlands through the unexpected Massif d'Antaivondro, a desolation of vast brown sweeps below gaunt grey rock summits. Unexpected because recalling the Highlands of Scotland – so close to the Spiny South!

Ihosy looked attractive: tall nineteenth-century brick houses with much fine wood-carving. But it is low-lying and too hot and anyway my various pains left me interested only in finding more hooch. Which I did (twenty-five pence for a litre) in one of the many stalls surrounding the sandy square of the bus station. I drank while the younger generation ate and was in no condition, for the next few hours, to observe topographical details. Luckily I came to at about 4, just north of Zazafotsy. Here Erosion experiments with curves and the track climbs between scores of half-comical, half-awesome peaks – gigantic bulges of rock parodying monstrous rugger balls, cauldrons, hats, cakes, or domes. On the red-gold grass carpet below these mountains lie what look like fallen summits – barn-sized boulders, silver-grey and time-smoothed. During the sunset conflagration this landscape became utterly unreal, a world flooded and throbbing with shifting lights and colours – amber and ochre, vermilion and russet, bronze and purple. 'It's psychedelic!' said Rachel. And it was.

In Ambalavao – in darkness – we paused briefly to deliver a thin sack of mail to the Post Office. The zebu tribes of the south bring their animals to this famous cattle-mart for sale to their main customers, Merina and Betsileo dealers.

Fianar's bus station was surprisingly lively at 8.40 p.m. and we heard rumours of a taxi-departure for Antsirabe at 4.30 a.m. 'Early to bed!' said Jamie. We all shared a room in a rambling wooden-chalet-type hotel, pleasing to the eye but not to the nose. 'It's not *just* the loos,' Adrian noted. 'This whole place is saturated in piss.' Jamie retired at once (more Mally-belly) but the rest of us banqueted in what is said to be Madagascar's best restaurant, the Chez Papillon. This was Adrian's extravagant idea, vigorously supported by Rachel, and I was too pain-racked to fight for frugality. The manager hesitated to admit us: when we saw ourselves in a mirror we realised why. I think it was Rachel's piteously pleading expression – like a famished spaniel puppy – that caused him to change his mind.

Jamie had insisted on setting his Hi-Tek alarm for 3 a.m. – a minority decision. But events at the bus station proved him right. We were just in time to book the last four seats in a ten-seater Peugeot taxi (£20 each) which departed at 5.15 and arrived here in Antsirabe six and a half hours later – a journey I prefer to forget. But our friends' welcome made this arrival in Antsirabe feel like a home-coming.

My hand/wrist is now so painful that my ribs can't compete. Possibly it was sprained badly during one of the Merk mêlées? Anything could have happened in that truck while we were all climbing over each other; there were so many hurtful incidents one didn't pay any attention to exactly which bit of one's anatomy was being damaged by whom. In our guest-hut I unbandaged and gave serious thought to what Rachel, with deplorable facetiousness, called 'the matter *not* in hand'. The burn blisters have burst – so that side-issue, though still sore, may be disregarded. The cut had closed completely and showed no sign of 'matter in hand', yet the swelling was far worse. Studying it, Rachel repented of her frivolity and said, 'You *must* go to a doctor!' So I did, with a Malagasy interpreter and private misgivings. Why should one expect Malagasy hospitals to be any more efficient than Madagascar's other post-colonial institutions? But at least I might be able to get hold of some pain-killer less deleterious than hooch.

The doctor sat white-coated behind a fine wide desk – a self-important young man, slim and trim and dictatorial. My interpreter pointed out that the cut had healed well and never been infected, that the burns were to be regarded as an irrelevant ancillary misfortune, but that the pain was severe, persistent and might have been caused by a sprain. The doctor examined the cut, felt my wrist, nodded knowingly and wrote out a prescription for antibiotics. He then summoned a nurse, gave her instructions and despatched me to have the wound 'dressed'.

My interpreter was not allowed into the small cramped untidy treatment-room where another nurse was sitting cross-legged on a stool eating a sticky bun. The waste bins were over-flowing and a Geiger-counter for calculating bacteria would have gone off the scale. After a moment's consultation the bun-eater wiped her hands down the sides of her uniform, picked a sharp instrument out of a bowl of cold water and before I had registered her purpose was *reopening* the closed wound. I began to protest – then gave up. Fatalism took over; it is one of my strongest characteristics. The bun-eater was very gentle and, surgically speaking, skilful; the pain she caused was nothing to what I'm now used to. She made soothing noises as she worked away, while her colleague stood by me patting my shoulder. Then the bun-eater stood back and surveyed her achievement, looking puzzled. I gazed gloomily at that bone which I hadn't expected ever to see again. There was of course no trace of pus or any foreign matter. The bun-eater shook her head, laughed, dabbed some purple lotion on the new wound and rebandaged it. I thanked her, went to the office to pay the bill, refused to use the prescription for antibiotics and tried unsuccessfully to buy pain-killers – the supply had run out five months ago.

Back in our room I lay down, with my left hand *up* on the bed-head, and gave my ribs a chance to begin their remending before we take the train to Tana tomorrow morning. I'm sorry if this sounds racist, but in Tana I'm looking for a *French* doctor. Madagascar may have no man-eating beasts or poisonous snakes, but judging by results it's the most dangerous country I've ever travelled in.

Tana. Thursday, 9.30 p.m.

By this morning the swelling had spread to my elbow and Rachel had to do all our packing before Zanoa put us on the 1 p.m. train, laden with another of her *haute cuisine* picnics. Malagasy rail transport (what there is of it) is cheaper than road transport – only £2 each for our second-class tickets. And the train, though full, was not overcrowded with adults. There were however a prodigious number of small children and uncooped poultry; whenever possible, the travelling Malagasy seem to like their poultry to feel free. Rachel found the journey tedious, after the stimulating unpredictability of Merk and Minnie. I think she is missing the boys, with whom we had a farewell dinner last evening in a Vietnamese restaurant. We hope to see them again in England; they were the best sort of travelling companions.

We arrived at sunset and went straight to the bar of a big hotel near the railway station, most suitably named – given my condition – the Terminus Hotel. There Tana's *vazaha* residents tend to gather and my medical luck changed abruptly when a French resident entered our lives – one of those fairy-tale people who enjoy helping total strangers whom they may never see again. In response to my enquiry about European doctors our saviour downed his Antsirabe orange, fetched his car and within ten minutes was escorting me into a consulting room near the Lido Hotel.

I never discovered this physician's name though I would like to engrave it in gold somewhere. He merely glanced at my afflicted limb before reaching back to a shelf and handing me twelve capsules imported from France. 'Three a day,' he said. 'You'll feel much better by tomorrow morning. But no more illegal spirits. You're lucky you only have gout. You've been to the South?' I nodded, speechless. 'Then you've been drinking the sap of the *Cycas thouarsii* – the Malagasy call it "the Man-eating Tree". For years it's been killing Frenchmen – Europeans seem to have no resistance to it. Gout is the best thing it does to you. No, thank you, I don't require a fee from a foolish Irishwoman.'

10

Prostration on the Pirate Coast

We spent two days in Tana, where my improbable disease went as quickly as it had come. I used to associate gout with the *ankles* of a degenerate great-grandfather; I didn't realise it could also afflict the *wrists* of the virtuous. Now I know better.

In the Immigration Department we effortlessly collected our visa extensions. Someone in Fort-Dauphin had efficiently despatched all that bumph by Air Mad and no one took it amiss (perhaps no one noticed) that for weeks we'd been illegal immigrants.

In the Aeroflot office we were informed that we could *not* travel home on the prearranged date because so many Malagasy students were returning to Moscow University on that same date. Perhaps the following week, said the tall unsmiling Russian – or the week after that . . . I detest pretending to be a VIP but on occasions there is no alternative. We didn't have enough money to spend an extra week or two in Madagascar, appealing though the idea was. I applied the 'famous travel writer' pressure (my toes curling in my boots with embarrassment) and the Russian withdrew to an inner office to consult a person or persons unknown. He soon returned, crossed two students off the passenger-list and confirmed our bookings. Rachel was ravaged by guilt. 'Poor students!' she said. 'We *are* mean!' But, as I pointed out, the students were being stranded *at home*. Being an Aeroflot passenger dries up one's milk of human kindness. It's the survival of the fittest – or the transport of the toughest.

In the railway station we booked seats as far as Perinet (about half-way to the coast) on the daily train that departs for Tamatave at dawn. The forest around Perinet is an indri lemur reserve. From Perinet we planned an eighty-mile trek on Route Nationale No. 2; this would take us to Brickaville, where English friends run a sugar plantation and we could rejoin the train for Tamatave. The Tana–Tamatave one-metre-gauge line would be no less famous than the Darjeeling or Quito lines had not inaccessibility deprived it of that glory which is its due. In 1897 it was planned by a member of Galliéni's occupying forces, a commandant of engineers with a bold imagination. Like East Africa's railways, it was built by immigrant labourers, many of whom afterwards joined Madagascar's colonies of Indian and Chinese traders and shopkeepers. The line was completed in 1913. It climbs from sea-level to 4,225 feet in sixty miles and the difficulties of laying it on very steep gradients, through dense rain-forest, were compounded by the activities of *fahavalo* – bands of guerrillas who in this area continued for years to oppose the French conquest. Many of the station buildings look like small forts, which once they were. During the 1947 Uprising the line was repeatedly cut by latter-day *fahavalo*, who thus effectively isolated the capital from the coast.

In 1912 the Tana–Antsirabe line was built, as a link in a Tamatave–Tana–Fianar–Manakara system. But the work interrupted by the First World War was never resumed and Madagascar was left with two unconnected rail systems. To ensure that the Tamatave–Tana line would pay for itself, the French deliberately limited motor-traffic by neglecting the maintenance of Route Nationale No. 2 – a major mistake, say some experts. This policy greatly increased the cost of imported goods in the Highlands and made the industrial development of that region even more impractical.

Our carriage was packed, though not overcrowded. A pensive-looking Merina gentleman, aged perhaps forty, sat opposite me. He spoke accurate but rusty English and his choice of seat/was not, I suspected, mere chance. In Tamatave, where he was working as an engineer, opportunities to practise English must be few.

Mr Ralambondrainy was unusually confiding, for a Malagasy; he dreaded going back to work because his Betsimisaraka staff resent a Merina being boss of their department. This, we later discovered, is a not uncommon problem in Tamatave, Madagascar's nearest equivalent to an industrial city. It is an awkward fact of Malagasy life that the Merina and Betsileo are far more skilled, as engineers, technicians and mechanics, than any other tribe. Attempts to ignore this fact, by 'discriminating positively', usually have disastrous economic consequences. Most inter-tribal friction, according to our new friend, is found at the managerial level. When there is no competition for 'top jobs', Merina families settled in other tribal territories almost always live happily with their neighbours.

We recounted the Aeroflot incident, which prompted a vehement condemnation of the government for so foolishly allowing hundreds of young Malagasy to be exposed to Soviet indoctrination. 'The families of these students hate them going to Moscow,' said Mr Ralambondrainy. 'But free higher education in Europe is very tempting for poor people who can't send children to France. Parents feel they shouldn't block this advancement. Then they are disappointed when young people come home with degrees that Malagasy employers don't trust. Our employers always prefer a French training. By now they have learned how poor the Soviet training is – though maybe this is partly because Moscow University gets the less bright students. Not many Merina go there!'

Mr Ralambondrainy hinted that although the government is now genuinely struggling to be non-aligned it is finding it hard to escape from the Soviet sphere of influence. 'We are lucky that now Russia doesn't have enough money to bribe us. Madagascar has got so run-down I don't see how we can improve things without some help from outside. When a country is falling apart it isn't easy to stay non-aligned. But we are lucky in our President. He is one of the few leaders acceptable to all our peoples, which is his greatest strength. He comes from Tamatave but he went to Tana when he was twelve – to a Roman Catholic school. He is brilliant. He can hold his own with anybody and we are proud of him. But perhaps he has too many ideals that can't become realities overnight. We have tried to change things too quickly. Decentralisation is a good idea, but when it means giving power to villagers with no training it has bad effects. This is why corruption has become so bad throughout the lower levels of the administration. These people abuse power. Yet it is not fair to blame them: too much was expected of them too soon. A government minister detected in corruption would lose his job at once under President Ratsiraka. But the President can't control and supervise what goes on in every little town.'

Route Nationale No. 2 and the railway are never far apart. Usually the 'road' is visible, sometimes only yards away, sometimes miles – rambling down another heavily forested mountainside, or crossing a deep distant cultivated valley. Even I – no great connoisseur of engineering works – was awestruck by the things this railway does. For sheer dizzying melodrama it comes a close second, in my experience, to the Guayaquil–Quito line. And then there is the sudden joy of encountering what feels like a new world, as the *Hauts Plateaux* are abruptly left behind. Travel within Madagascar has the flavour of changing countries within a continent; the contrast between the flat arid Spiny South and the lush precipitous east coast is at least as great as any within Europe.

In 1977 – Mr Ralambondrainy told us – the Chinese launched in Madagascar one of their apparently altruistic 'Aid to the Undeveloped' projects. (He saw it as part of a global anti-Soviet campaign.) The object of their attention is Route Nationale No. 2, which they are rebuilding in style from coast to capital. This project is being 'played down', officially; our friend had been unable to find out the estimated cost, or how many Chinese were working on it. (He advised us to take no photographs, during our trek, in areas where construction teams were active.) The Chinese keep very much to themselves and, in their six years on the job – which may well take another six (or twelve) years – they have made no efforts to indoctrinate the local populations, ideologically. But they do try to inculcate the Chinese work-ethic as they train their Malagasy teams in the skills of road-maintenance as well as construction. They seem to believe that the reincarnated Route Nationale No. 2 can survive their departure. And of course, as we say in Ireland, there's no harm in hoping.

As we approached Perinet, Mr Ralambondrainy drily pointed out that during all the decades when road-transport was cheaper than rail, there was no Tana–Tamatave motor-transport to speak of; but now, when costs are reversed, there will be (at least for a time) an excellent road service. 'And if the people can't afford petrol to use it, then there will be no taxes to mend it – and soon it will be gone and the poor Chinese will be sad!'

At Perinet the up-train and down-train meet every day for lunch; it would be unfortunate if they met anywhere else. This single line system means that a delay to either train affects both. But delays are not extreme: rarely more than an hour or so. And meanwhile there is much, though not varied, eating to be done in shack *hotelys* clustered below forested slopes festooned in orchids. If you do not want a sit-down meal, rows of small tables offer strange buns, and even stranger bits of grilled or stewed innards – pigs', we surmised, since this is not zebu country. And if you are rich you can lunch in the colonial spendour of the Railway Hotel's restaurant.

This three-storeyed brick edifice, with a steeply pitched roof and exaggerated eaves, arose on the platform in 1938 and seems at first glance to be the station itself. In its youth it flourished; there were four passenger trains a day, Perinet was the base for a major French logging concession and also a regular stopping place for French troops, to-ing and fro-ing from coast to capital. Now the timber industry has dwindled – an ecological benefit but a social disaster – and few Malagasy passengers can afford Perinet's Ritz.

For the past ten years an enterprising but by now disheartened young Malagasy has been renting the hotel from the railway company. We admired Manjo, who has not allowed demoralisation to set in. None of our fellow-passengers ate in the high-ceilinged, wooden-pillared dining-room, but a dozen tables were laid – just in case – with spotless linen and sparkling glasses. At one end an attractively panelled bar stocked Antsirabe beer, at the other a baroque French wood-stove was kept burnished. (Perinet stands at almost 3,000 feet and often has winter night temperatures of 50°F.) Only the area's residual timber felling, and a local *vazaha*-run graphite mine – each industry employing about two hundred – keep the hotel going. Manjo blamed the savage exchange rate, more than any other single cause, for the fading of a tourist trade that was never brilliant. Happily Perinet still attracts an erratic trickle of scientists, many of whom spend weeks studying the endemic flora and fauna.

The senior waiter was a charming elderly Betsimisaraka, impeccably French-trained; his three junior colleagues, though equally charming, had a more individualistic approach to their tasks. One of these led us up a wide polished staircase, and down a long polished corridor to a small clean room with bathroom (of sorts) attached. Our large second-floor window overlooked many, many miles of forested hills, their nearby greenness shading away to distant blueness. Our door lock was broken, but locks are not important in Madagascar – except perhaps in Tana.

Unfortunately we did not have this room to ourselves. Beside the lavatory was a huge hole in the floor, part of the establishment's ingenious plumbing. And through this hole, each night, came a family of the noisiest and most brazen rats I have ever met. When I first heard them I switched on my torch (we had found batteries in Tana) and saw one eating our loaf of breakfast bread and two sitting on their hindlegs by my rucksack, pulling a bar of chocolate out of a side-pocket. When I shone the light on them and shouted threateningly they did not bolt, like properly brought up rats, but squeaked abusively at me and continued to pull. They were incorrigible; we had to learn to live with them. For hours they scampered and squealed and twittered, fascinated by the *vazaha* possessions even when no food was accessible. Yet in appearance, if not in character, they were ordinary brown rats who had obviously entered the country as illegal immigrants – *not* an endemic species.

The indri is Perinet's most celebrated 'endemic species'. This three-foot-tall, black and white, leaf-eating creature is the only tail-less lemur. Its rain-forest home, now shrinking rapidly, extends no farther north than the Bay of Antagonil and no farther south than the Masora river, probably because in this region alone is found some exotic essential plant. Like most lemurs, it soon dies in captivity. There are many Malagasy legends and superstitions about the indri – the *babakota*, the 'Man of the Forest', which possibly inspired the cynocephalus story told by Marco Polo, though he located this 'dog-headed man' in the Andaman Islands. (His geography, unless he had been to a place, was always a bit shaky: something we have in common.) I had hoped that by listening we might find the indri ourselves; their song can be heard over a two-mile radius. But we were warned that as they tend to sleep eighteen hours a day in winter we would be unlikely to find them without a guide; and so it proved.

One expects rain in rain-forests, or at least humidity and low grey skies. Yet it rained only at night during our Perinet interlude and the sun was just pleasantly hot as we scrambled up and down steep slopes covered in dense undergrowth, looking and listening for the indri. At this altitude the east coast forest is quite unlike the popular image of a rain-forest; and even lower down the escarpment, where it is much wetter and more humid, Malagasy rain-forest trees (ninety per cent of them endemic) never attain Amazonian stature. Around Perinet the majority are tall, gawky and pale-barked, like unhealthy adolescents. Rare they may be, but they cannot compete aesthetically with the truly superb trees of our own West Waterford woods. However, this forest makes up in interest what it may lack in beauty. Every turn of the path reveals some new oddity amidst the orchids, lianas, tree ferns, bamboos, palms and thorny thickets like barbed-wire entanglements.

On our second day we admitted defeat. By then we had several times heard the uncanny wailing of the indri but it was obvious we would never see them without guidance. We were on our way to the Bureau d'Eaux et Forêts – slithering down a precipitous path, having been more or less lost for hours – when we met two friendly, ragged, dark-skinned boys, aged seventeen and twelve. They seemed quite used to finding *vazaha* wandering through the forest yearning for lemurs. Yet they were at first endearingly suspicious; firmly, though very politely, they demanded to see our permits. Their protective attitude towards the indri appeared to be genuine: if not, they were excellent actors. Moreover, their offer to lead us to the indri had no hint of doing a deal, no suggestion of looking for our 'custom'. It recalled the helpfulness of the Ank-aratra Malagasy who had appointed themselves our guides be-cause the *razana* decreed one should help strangers. But of course they also enjoyed the excitement of tracking and the showing off of their skills – and of their close relationship with the indri, which was indeed remarkable.

'Tracking' is not really the *mot juste*; indri-finding requires patient study above all else and, once you know where and when to look, the groups living close to Perinet are easily enough seen. One has appointments with them, as it were, going to certain places at certain times. Our young friends instructed us not to talk and to move slowly and quietly. Then, on reaching particular trees, they made loud kissing noises and often the indri came to stare down at us with bright yellow eyes, apparently relishing our attention – alert, yet seeming aware that on these mountains of the Reserve they are at present safe. There are five in this family and we watched them eating, resting, grooming and jumping. They were much given to jumping *backwards*, great ten-yard leaps from tree to tree. But they cannot be described as hyper-active; when not asleep, most of their days are devoted to long munching sessions as they stuff themselves with leaves, picked deliberately – not just any old leaf, but the choicest within reach. Their hands and feet are enormous and their long muzzles give them a decidedly canine look. The general impression however is teddy-bearish, as they cling to slim tree-trunks, peering down – round, furry and cuddly.

During the indris' siesta hours we explored Perinet village: not a time-consuming activity. It is separated from the railway by a mini-ravine containing a narrow brown river spanned by three bridges; one was designed for motor-traffic but as it now is I'd prefer to cross it on foot. It leads past a large rusty-roofed church to a few muddy shack-lined lanes. Both shops were well stocked with manioc but not much else. Tattered banana plants sprouted all over the place and half a dozen paddy-fields occupied a mountain ledge. There is virtually no agriculture hereabouts for the sufficient reason that there is virtually no cultivatable land. Beyond the village we walked for miles over thinly forested slopes and saw one Malagasy blue cuckoo and two kingfishers by a stagnant pond. In denser forest we saw several minute sun-birds feeding from the foot-long bell-shaped cream-coloured flowers of a creeper. We also heard the Malagasy magpie robin – rarely seen because very shy – which has what must be one of the most melodious calls in the whole bird-world.

Returning from one forenoon indri appointment, we met four absurdly noisy French would-be indri-spotters – all Tana residents – whose third Perinet visit this was. They had not yet seen any indri which in view of their behaviour in the forest did not surprise us. Clearly they were Persons of Importance (possibly even VIPs), and an elegantly attired Merina guide, provided by the Bureau d'Eaux et Forêts, accompanied them. He was peeved to discover that we with our ragged friends had been doing so well.

We were extraordinarily lucky to have met those boys. There was a most pleasing closeness between them and the forest and the indri – and, eventually, ourselves. This set me quite a problem on the eve of our departure. To tip or not to tip? I abhor the intrusion of money into such friendships, yet this was a special case. If the indri are to survive, they must be seen by their human neighbours as a precious asset. Those boys needed no financial inducement to protect their beloved 'maqui'. But our tip would, we hoped, contribute to a general awareness throughout the area that 'there's money in tham thar *babakota*'.

Thirty per cent of all Malagasy live along the island's forested east coast, a territory twenty to sixty miles wide, divided into small sub-territories by unbridged rivers descending from the escarpment. The majority of these coastal people are Betsimisaraka, who came together and acquired their name only about two hundred and fifty years ago, long after Madagascar's other main tribes had established their identities. The east coast topography discouraged unity and for centuries each local ruler was independent, acknowledging no superior beyond his own boundaries. But Ratsimilaho changed all that and in so doing forged one of the most remarkable of Anglo-Malagasy links.

For some forty years, during the late seventeenth and early eighteenth centuries, scores of English pirates operated from Madagascar's east coast, making the Island of St Mary, near the Bay of Antongil, infamous as World Piracy Headquarters – nowhere in the Caribbean could compete. In *Madagascar Rediscovered*, Mervyn Brown describes the pirates' retirement years:

> 'Several dozen pirates lived as princelings or village chiefs in little communities along the north-east coast or some little distance in the interior, owing their position to their martial reputation and their ill-gotten wealth which often enabled them to marry the daughters of Malagasy chieftains . . . The favoured area for settlement was the stretch of coast from Tamatave to the Bay of Antongil. For the average pirate, starting life perhaps in a riverside slum on the Thames and having survived years of brutality and privation at sea, his 'retired' existence among the bamboos and the coconut palms, surrounded by his Malagasy family and ample supplies of meat, fish, exotic fruits and potent home-brewed alcohol, must have seemed closer to Paradise than he ever expected to see.'

These virile settlers procreated so assiduously that their descendants were regarded as a separate clan: Zana-Malata, children of the mulattos. Red or brown hair, and blue or grey eyes, are still common up and down that coast though the Zana-Malata have long since been absorbed by the Betsimisaraka.

In about 1712 Ratsimilaho, aged eighteen, emerged as leader of the Zana-Malata. He was reputed to be the son of an English pirate whose name – Tom – comes as a considerable relief to harassed writers on Madagascar. Tom married Rahena, daughter of the Chief of Fenerive, and Ratsimilaho was their son. Soon after he took over as leader of his own clan, Ratsimilaho received an urgent appeal from the Antavaratra, the people of the coast north of Tamatave (and so his neighbours), who were being intimidated by the Antatsimo, a clan from the Vatomandry region. The Zana-Malata and the Antavaratra together defeated the Antatsimo, more by cunning than force. Then the various small tribes of the northern coast united and elected Ratsimilaho as their king; whereupon he changed his name, as is the intolerably confusing Malagasy habit on achieving a throne, and became Ramaroma-nompo. After several more minor wars, and a few marriage alliances and treaties, Ramaromanompo was acknowledged as leader of a confederation of all the tribes occupying the coastal strip for four hundred miles north and south of Tamatave. He called this group the Betsimisaraka – 'the many inseparable' – and it has retained its distinct tribal identity, though its political unity did not long survive the death of the only Anglo-Malagasy king. Today the Betsimisaraka – a people of unmistakably Malayo-Polynesian ancestry, though darker-skinned than the Merina – form the second-largest tribe in Madagascar.

We left Perinet soon after dawn, while wispy clouds still mingled with the forested crests and the indri were singing. For miles we could hear their regular morning recital: short songs, long songs, sometimes only one or two notes. In the distance these calls – aural links with a time before Man existed – have a curiously disturbing beauty, but heard close to they resemble the high-pitched screams of a terrified child.

Rachel seemed subdued and admitted to a 'fluey' headache. I too was without the tiger in my tank, but for that I blamed the gout cure. To have relieved me so quickly it must have been a very strong drug and I am suspicious of, though *in extremis* deeply grateful for, modern medicines. Briefly I wondered if we should turn back and take the train, but Rachel said no – perhaps because she knew how much I had been looking forward to this mini-trek after so many days on wheels. I reasoned then that we did not really need tigers in our tanks for the eighty miles to Brickaville; Perinet is only thirty-three miles due inland, though 3,000 feet above sea-level.

Yet that day's eighteen miles were less downhill than we had expected. The muddy red track wound around, and occasionally up, a series of green mountains – some heavily forested, some covered in dense low scrub, all apparently uninhabited. But only apparently. Now and then a movement caught our eye – a glimpse of bright cotton – and we realised that quite a few invisible pathlets led steeply from the track to isolated huts standing on high stilts, embedded in the bush. These flimsy shelters, woven of bamboo and ravenala, are not made to last. This is 'slash-and-burn' territory, where after a few years each family moves on to fell more trees and weave a new home. Mountain rice, needing no irrigation, grows easily on this cleared and burned land, though the initial clearing is not easy for a solitary farmer with only his family to help. Soon such land must have rest: ideally, ten years rest, which now with the population growing so fast it rarely gets. And when tired land is planted the yield is poor. Less rice for more mouths . . . Beware, Madagascar!

At 3.15 we reached Beforona, the first village en route. All day we had seen only four vehicles (Landrovers or jeeps) struggling with a track so deep in mud that at times it was difficult even to walk on. In 1856 this same stretch prompted the Reverend Ellis to write: 'The road here was frightful: the soil stiff clay, with deep holes of mud and water. I could readily imagine why, in 1826, some of Captain Le Sage's men should have thrown themselves on the ground, declaring they would die rather than attempt to proceed further. It would require more than a lifetime to make even a passable road through this region.'

Beforona remains, as it was in 1856, 'a tolerably large village, situated in a swampy hollow, surrounded by woody hills'. But in Mr Ellis's day it was a regular staging-post between Tamatave and Tana, geared to looking after passing *vazaha* and their numerous porters and palanquin-bearers. Now *vazaha* travel by train and no one knew quite what to do with us. We had planned to walk on another few miles, having partaken of such refreshments as were available, and camp in a secluded spot. But as we drank weak coffee in a grotty *hotely* rain came with tropical violence. 'No camping in *that*!' said Rachel decisively, lest I might have forgotten our sodden night in the Ankaratra.

The *hotely* was constructed of bamboo stakes and ravenala fronds. Its walls were decorated with heavy spider-webs, two feet in diameter, suspended between three 1981 calendars and several faded advertisement pages from French and English glossy magazines. The giggling and tongue-tied young woman who served us had rotten teeth – unusual in rural Madagascar – but our large following of excited children seemed healthy enough. At intervals passers-by peered in at us, then hastily moved away through the rain, looking uneasy. It was time to produce Samuel's letter.

The spacious tin-roofed office of the People's Executive Committee had an unglazed window and a broken concrete floor. ('Why', asked Rachel, 'does Malagasy concrete always disintegrate?' A rhetorical question; she does not expect her mother to explain such phenomena.) The 'President' – neatly dressed, barefooted, unsmiling – sat typing at a rickety table in the centre of the room. (Was it just coincidence that he was much the fairest man present?) Behind him stood an immense rusty filing cabinet. On benches around the wall sat eight men, ragged and dark-skinned and looking oddly on the defensive. The atmosphere seemed strained, and I felt had been so before our arrival. Nobody greeted us or even looked directly at us. The President took Samuel's letter from me without raising his eyes and spent ten minutes reading it. Then, still without addressing us, he sent a youth to fetch Razafimahatratra – the village schoolmaster and, astonishingly, a fluent English speaker.

With Raza (as I shall take the liberty of calling him) we were back to Malagasy normal: smiles, handshakes, courteous greet-ings, warm welcomes. A tall young man from Moromanga, he wore smart clothes under a *lamba* but his feet looked as though they would hate shoes. The grinning scruffy youth who attended him carried both our rucksacks as we hurried through mud and rain, past a Post Office (pretty dormant for the now being) and a shack-like church, to another office. While Raza copied passport details into an exercise book the youth disappeared to organise our 'chamber'; some time later we saw four men carrying a double bed into a long timber building, like a warehouse, on the far side of the street. From two fly-blown electioneering posters President Ratsiraka gazed down on us and around the wall stood tall filing cabinets containing – Raza informed us – the identity cards of all the district's men, women and children. ('I thought people kept identity cards *on* them,' Rachel said afterwards. 'But we're in Madagascar,' I reminded her.)

That wooden building was a warehouse, some hundred and fifty feet long, standing above the mud on piles and once used for the pre-export storage of bananas and coffee. Ours was the middle one of three 'chambers' –fifty feet by twenty, with a high sagging ceiling of frayed sacking which billowed in the draught from three large windows. Remembering the *hotely*'s cobwebs, I trembled to think what might fall upon us. This room was empty but for our double-bed in one corner – as things turned out, the wrong corner. Soon however a group of breathless small boys appeared, bearing a table and chair; Raza had taken note of my profession. The door did not shut, never mind lock, but unlike our Merina friends these villagers had no security phobia.

We went shopping, leaving the children who were swarming all over the room in charge of our possessions. In Beforona's only visible store the Chinaman behind the counter was bent and stiff and wore a pigtail. He stocked dried beans, musty biscuits and a few bottles of that horrendous *limonady* which is our unhappiest memory of Ranohira.

At sunset Raza brought two candles and a box of matches and we talked about education and taxes. Our friend at the Railway Hotel had been fretting about his four small children, the older two already at primary school in Perinet – a waste of time, he said. Raza agreed that rural schooling is bad and rapidly getting worse; his ninety-three pupils were sharing twenty-seven textbooks – and one teacher. Clearly he himself was an idealist who could have had a good job in Tana. He said, 'The French ran an educational system to suit the Merina: this nobody denies. Now everyone gets an equal chance but the resources are much less so standards have dropped. We have a whole population badly educated instead of a small group well educated. Except in the Mission Schools, education is free for all right through university – but what good is that when it becomes so bad? Maybe it is better if parents have to pay something? So many are so keen on education they would willingly pay for schooling to raise standards. Some think it was good to take the ten per cent poll tax off farmers in 1975 because it was a French system. But the result? The farmers don't have *more* money but they work *less* – and produce less food. That way everything runs downhill – now we import rice which we used to export. And the government has less money for schooling. Free education for all is also a European system, like taxes – we are making a mistake trying to pick and choose which bits of a system we keep – we can't only have the nice bits. We are damaged too by world changes in prices for our main exports – coffee, bananas, vanilla, cloves. But our *most* dangerous problem is the decline in French-speaking. This is a disaster for a modern state. Malagasy is not suitable for studying science and technology – you cannot translate textbooks. And it's not only science and technology: we have few abstract nouns in Malagasy – our intellectuals as well as our scientists need French. For ten years we've been taught the importance of Malagasy and this is right – we must be proud of it. Yet President Ratsiraka himself always speaks French in public. We cannot pretend Malagasy is an adequate language for modern living. But now exam papers in all subjects are set in both languages and students can choose which to use – so there is not enough incentive to learn French well.'

To cheer Raza up, I told him something of Ireland's 'two-language' problems. I also happened to mention that in London we could find no detailed map of this area, such as we had for southern Madagascar. As a result, the following letter was delivered an hour later.

INFORMATION

'Dear Friends,

This is the village of Beforona, which is situated in the National Road Number 2 that connects Tananarive with Tamatave. Moramanga is 56 kilometres from here and Brickaville, about 95 kilometres. These are the villages you will see if you go to Brickaville: Marozeno, 8KM – Ampasimbe, 20KM – Antogobato, 35KM – Antsapanana, 65KM. (It is the village where you can see the road to Vatomandry and Matamoro, that means to the south part of the East Coast.)

The road is bad from here to Ranomafana and very good from about Antsapanana until Brickaville. You cannot see taxi in all of this part of the road.

There are Hotels in all of these villages except in Marozeno. I tell you that you can see only breakfast or lunch or diner in Hotels. But if you want to sleep, you would show the letter you've showed us to the chefs of the villages, so that they can make you beds and chamber (room).

Finally, no doubt about security. You can travel all the road in foot if you want. Don't be afraid. Generally Malagasy people, chiefly these ones who live in country, are kind.

So I wish you good evening and good travel.

Please, ask if you want some help.

Yours sincerely, Razafimahatratra.'

For me, that letter somehow concentrated the essence of Malagasy hospitality. It more than made up for our unquiet night at Beforona.

In the next section of the warehouse, a large family lived in the corner beside ours and the partition was of hessian nailed to a criss-crossed wooden frame. Malagasy towns and villages after dark give the impression of a people who are all asleep by 7 p.m. But we have evidence, gleaned the hard way, that behind their tightly sealed shutters they enjoy long evenings of cooking, eating, gossiping, singing, laughing, gambling, drinking, teasing and playing stringed instruments. In Beforona all these activities continued until 11. And, soon after, some misfortunate elderly wretch, lying on the other side of the hessian two feet from my ear, developed a persistent hacking cough.

Our plank bed was thinly strewn with loose hay but eighteen-inch gaps between the planks made this a rather mobile mattress. (There were similar gaps between some of the floor-boards, which is why I remained on the bed; who knew what eight-legged endemic species might emerge at dead of night from beneath the boards?) During a coughing respite I slept briefly, then awoke to find my head firmly wedged between two planks where the hay had fallen through. And Rachel seemed to be tickling my torso – curious behaviour, but then we both tended to become rather juvenile on these distinctively Malagasy occasions. I giggled feebly, as one does with a wedged head, and asked her to help me unwedge. But she was still asleep; the tickling sensation was being caused by romping rats. They continued to romp all night, squeaking shrilly as they chased each other up and down the hessian wall and across the floor and bed. Playful creatures, Malagasy rats. As more and more hay fell through, Rachel too woke up. We rose before dawn and were leaving Beforona as a wave of orange-red light broke on the eastern horizon.

All day the sky remained clear and soon the sun was slightly too hot. After the night's rain the ankle-deep mud somehow contrived to be at once sticky and slippy. Not far below, on our left, a mountain torrent foamed between smooth giant boulders – often more a waterfall than a river, so steep was the slope. We crossed four roaring tributaries, on bridges in varying states of disrepair. We met nobody. This was an inviolate region; its gradients have successfully defied even the hungriest of the 'slash-and-burners'. All around us cliffs and slopes and river-banks and ravines displayed an overwhelming abundance of rain-forest exotica. Immense trees supported surreal creepers and sprouted ferns of the most wondrous variety and delicacy. Bananas grew wildly in every direction, as plentiful (but not as accessible) as blackberries in Ireland. Giant ferns sprawled across precipices – nothing was bare, no inch of space not overgrown. We counted four species of bamboo. The giant forty-foot stands had arm-thick bases; a slender-plumed bamboo looked like bouquets of feathers; a single-stemmed arching bamboo looked like magnified croquet hoops; a creeper bamboo reached from tree to tree to tree above the track. All was green – a thousand shades of green, it seemed – but for the pale glow of tree-orchids, like dim torches hanging in the shadows, and the long orange spikes of *Buddlea Madagascarensis*.

Then we rounded a mountain to be shocked by two colossal bright yellow Chinese excavators, each at least ten times the size of the huts they were rumbling past. This was the tiny village of Ampasimbe; despite the mud, we had covered twelve miles in four and a half hours.

In the *hotely* – a two-roomed hut on stilts – we ate tepid gluey rice and scraps of cold gristly chicken. The proprietor warned us to be careful where we walked; the bamboo-stake floor was collapsing under the bamboo matting. He had a wispy beard (unusual for a Malagasy) and fifteen children (not unusual for a Malagasy). The youngest, aged one, was on his knee, being fed rice-water off a spoon out of a dirt-encrusted mug. It looked improbably healthy and very happy. Under our table lurked a fat puppy, evidently already aware that guests found the local chickens largely disposable. On the far side of the churned-up track three young women sat outside their shack on matting, expertly delousing one another. The coffee matched the chicken. There was nothing else to drink in Ampasimbe.

Beyond this 'main street' – the farthest point of the Chinese advance – we were watching a road being born. Several detours were necessary as the giant machines ruthlessly remoulded Madagascar to their will. We passed a Chinese camp, bigger than most Malagasy villages and sealed off from the natives by (suitably) a twelve-foot bamboo fence. The high traditional ceremonial entrance, square and gaily painted and hung with coloured lanterns, looked pleasingly pre-Mao. But when we greeted Chinese workers, or waved to them in their high cabs, they repeatedly snubbed us.

At Ampasimbe the landscape broadens out, though remaining very broken, and for several hellish miles we were on a half-made surface of loose sharp chips – much more trying than the mud – while on either side new raw red embankments reflected the fierce noon heat. Then, mercifully, Route Nationale No. 2 and the Chinese Highway diverged, where the former tackles a gradient that made no sense to the Chinese engineers. We rejoiced to be back on our muddy friend, in greener, cooler country, though here *savoka* has replaced the rain-forest on most slopes.

Savoka is what happens when the land must be allowed to go fallow after the rain-forest has been felled and the first rice crops grown. Given a chance, it regenerates into secondary forest, of which there was a great deal in this area. But after repeated burnings the completely impoverished soil is taken over by the traveller's tree, giant ferns, and thickets of low, heather-like scrub. Then it is doomed; it can never again be made cultivable.

To *vazaha* eyes, the Betsimisaraka version of 'agricultural land' seems no more than beat-up wilderness. Mighty hardwood trees lie where they were felled on the steep slopes. Mountain rice will grow anywhere, anyhow – given sunlight – and is sown around those tree-corpses too unwieldy to be coped with by one Betsimisaraka family possessing only basic implements.

Amidst the tangled *savoka* (beautiful in its way) grow twenty- to twenty-five-foot robusta coffee trees, looking like wild coffee – as well they might, for their owners give them no attention of any kind. Many are now more than forty years old and should be replaced. But why bother replacing a still-yielding tree? Young trees yield nothing for four or five years and few Malagasy look that far ahead. The local treatment of the coffee cherries also lowers profits. These are dried on a mat, then mortar-pounded to extract the beans; extraction with a huller, or by soaking the cherries in water, gives much higher-quality coffee.

Coffee was introduced to Madagascar from Réunion in the early nineteenth century and became commercially important in the 1930s. By 1939 Madagascar was the world's largest producer of robusta but production dropped disastrously during the chaos of the Second World War and the even greater chaos (for Madagascar) of the 1947 Uprising. The enormous east coast coffee plantations, then still being cultivated by forced labour, saw the worst of the 1947–48 violence and destruction. The national yield never fully recovered yet coffee remains the Betsimisarakas' most important cash-crop, each farmer owning a few trees. Some eighty-year-old trees are still fruitful, causing experts to suspect that the Betsimisarakas may after all be right; in the Malagasy environment perhaps forty years is not the limit of a coffee tree's useful life.

We rejoined the new road near a bridge in the making, a long high bridge ambitiously spanning a river gorge. From the mountain far above we noticed that the little blue-clad figures were moving much more briskly than the little brown-skinned figures. Even without their uniforms, one could easily have distinguished the Chinese from the Malagasy workers.

A sweaty, thirst-tormented climb took us over a pass – a wasteland of heath-*savoka* – from where the old road descended steeply to Antogobato. Near the village we again joined the new road, in the form of a brash utilitarian concrete bridge, just completed and looking painfully incongruous. It was 3.45 and we had covered twenty-two miles. We shed our rucksacks in Antogobato's only store – Chinese-owned, of course, and stocking Antsirabe beer. Clouds were building up; when we had quenched our thirst we would look for lodgings.

Rachel went to investigate the river's swimming possibilities (nil) while I sat outside the shop drinking fast and listening to the echoing boom of distant dynamite explosions as another hunk of Madagascar was 'developed'. Our last close-up view of Chinese road-building was in Gilgit, in December 1974, when the Karakoram Highway was being constructed. Only eight years later a friend of mine returned prematurely from the Western Himalayas. He could not complete his journey; he was too stricken by the multiple pernicious effects of that road on a region he had known and loved in its 'undeveloped' state.

In Antogobato I realised with a despairing kind of agony that yet again we had come on stage during a last act. The Tana–Tamatave track has become Route Nationale No. 2 since Sergeant Hastie from Co. Cork took Madagascar's first horses along it – and since the first LMS missionary (a sad pioneer, leaving his wife and baby buried near Tamatave) struggled towards the plateau – and since Mr Ellis in 1856 described villages and customs that today may be observed unchanged. But, being a Cinderella Route Nationale, it made little impact on the area's ecology. If however Madagascar ever develops industrially, and heavy truck traffic on the new Chinese Highway replaces the comparatively innocuous two trains a day, the impact will be incalculable. Air pollution, vibration, noise – their effects on such a unique region are not yet understood. 'Father, forgive us, for we know not what we do.' Yet there is still hope. As an island, Madagascar is far less vulnerable than the Western Himalayas. And given the ferocity with which the elements will repeatedly attack this Chinese road, it may never replace the railway. Its scarring bridges will survive, as many French bridges have done, but these are mere visual defacements. Nature, backed up by the Malagasy temperament, may succeed here in at least defending itself against modern technology, though it cannot prevent the ravages of the 'slash-and-burners'.

The store-keeper's wife was half-Chinese, half-Merina, petite and elegant; quite a startling sight hereabouts – as incongruous, in her way, as the bridge. She responded to Samuel's letter by inviting us to be her guests instead of directing us to the chief. Her elder son Joseph (aged seventeen, very tall, entirely Chinese-looking) then led us down a muddy laneway to the guest-annex, a one-roomed hut. On a little table in the centre of the floor lay two curled-up spider corpses the size of golf balls. I tried not to look at the walls while spreading our tent on the bed as a sealed sleeping bag. There were cobwebs like hammocks in the corners, and wide cracks between the planks through which any number of new recruits might enter during the night. 'You look quite pale,' said Rachel as we walked back to the store-cum-dwelling.

This was the only substantial building in Antogobato, a long two-storeyed wooden house with a pretty little front garden, symbolically overlooking the village's huddle of shacks from its commanding position near the bridge. Up and down the east coast, from Diego-Suarez to Fort-Dauphin, the Chinese dominate the local economy. Like Madagascar's Indian community, they have shown remarkable tenacity and adaptability in surviving the coming and going of a colonial power, the advent of Malagasy Independence and the evolution of Christian Marxism. They keep their heads down and get on with trading and money-lending, avoiding politics and obeying whatever set of laws happens to be in force. To them the Betsimisaraka bring all their coffee, bananas, lychees, cloves and whatever other cash-crops they may grow. (It would be more correct to say 'find growing'; apart from mountain rice for family consumption, crops tend just to happen in this prodigiously fertile region.) The Chinese buy everything, regardless of amount or quality, at prices fixed by themselves. Until the recent 'austerity' crisis, they also supplied simple consumer goods in their stores, and extra foodstuffs that would not otherwise be available in places like Antogobato. As money-lenders they provide both short- and medium-term credit and most peasants are permanently in their debt; when farmers deliver a coffee crop they are rarely in a position to look for cash.

But cash has never been important to them, so this is not perhaps as iniquitous a system as it sounds. It does however mean that by Malagasy standards the Chinese are very rich indeed, as was apparent the moment we entered the Chan-Dines' home.

Tamatave craftsmen had made the fine chests, cabinets and tables, using rain-forest hardwoods unknown outside Madagascar. The bottled-gas cooker, three-piece-suite, carpets, wineglasses and pure white poodle were French. The several transistor radios were German, the cameras Japanese. (But no films were obtainable, so next morning we left behind those of ours that fitted.) The food was Sino-French and that meal was one of the best we ate in Madagascar. There were two Betsimisaraka houseservants, who sat down to dinner with us: a pleasing touch.

Monsieur Chan-Dine was away in Tana on business. His great-grandfather, Madame Chan-Dine informed us, had settled in Tamatave; she made a point of stressing that he had not been 'imported labour' but was himself the son of a merchant. Her own Chinese grandfather had first settled in Tana, then moved to the coast. Aged forty-two, Madame Chan-Dine looked not much older than the eldest of her five children, a nineteen-year-old married to the son of a Chinese restaurant-owner in Tamatave and the doting mother of a four-month-old baby. Joseph and a thirteen-year-old daughter were at school in Tamatave; two other children were being educated in France. All the family were trilingual – Cantonese, Malagasy, French – though none could write Chinese.

This family clearly saw itself as having more in common with the French than with the Malagasy, despite Mamma being half-Merina. Before dinner the girls showed us a collection of French-language Peking-produced glossy magazines, depicting China's natural beauties, artistic treasures and recent industrial and scientific advances. They were understandably proud of their Chinese inheritance. Earlier, Rachel and I had been speculating about the relationship between the road-builders and the settled Chinese. During dinner I cautiously approached this subject, but my antennae told me it would not be tactful to proceed.

The Chan-Dines were a happy and loving family with a strong sense of hospitality; Joseph was ever on the alert to fill the goblet again. We had a choice of Fianar Rioja-like red wine and homemade white rice-wine. Having allowed both to gladden my heart to its core I felt quite nonchalant about spiders as we hastened to our guest-annex through torrential rain.

Beyond Antogobato we had the Day of the Ravenala, twenty-one miles dominated in memory – if not quite in fact – by the traveller's tree, Madagascar's most famous plant, now incorporated into the seal of the Malagasy Republic. *Ravenala madagascariensis* is such a familiar sight in ornamental and botanical gardens all over the world that many are unaware of its origin in the rain-forest of eastern Madagascar. A cousin of the banana, it has long since appropriated the deforested regions of this coast. It thrives where nothing else will, partly because its brilliant blue seeds are fire-resistant, partly because it apparently requires no nourishment from the soil.

We were now near sea-level and all day the heat was intense; for me this sufficiently explained our need to rest every few miles. We had left Antogobato at 7.15, after a scrumptious breakfast of packet toast, tinned butter and tinned marmalade, yet within an hour we were glad to stop where free bananas were available. In a 'lay-by' cleared of vegetation green hands were stacked by the ton, awaiting some Chinese truck, and dozens of ripe bananas lay discarded on the ground amidst hundreds of rotten fruit. Rachel sat in the shade of a red cliff sprouting miniature ferns while I scavenged – and tested a jack-fruit, which was unripe. As we ate, we wondered about the tall, leafless, blossom-laden trees that flamed nearby, soaring above the varied greens of coffee, bamboo, ravenala and banana. Was this the flame tree *Hildegardia erythrosiphon*, which flowers at the end of the dry season and is found only in Madagascar? I had understood it to be endemic to the west coast, but perhaps its appearance here is another symptom of the fast-changing ecology of the deforested east coast.

At 10 we stopped again, thirstily, at the long-drawn-out village of Ranomafana, surrounded by gentle *savoka*-green hills on which we saw our first clove-trees: tall, compact, cypress-shaped. Those were the property of individual farmers; the main plantations – many millions of trees – are on the coast north of Tamatave. Cloves were brought from South-East Asia in the 1820s and became the second most important Betsimisaraka tree crop. The Malagasy economy was badly damaged by the invention of synthetic substitutes in the 1940s; now the main demands are from India, for cooking, and from Indonesia, for mixing with cigarette tobacco.

Only one of Ranomafana's shops was open on this Sunday

morning and from a grumpy old Betsimisaraka we bought two large bottles of violently coloured ersatz fruit-juice; it had queasy-making and prolonged after-effects. Another enormous Chinese camp lay behind the main street and we passed several of the senior Chinese staff and their wives, out for a relaxing stroll in immaculate Sabbath boiler-suits, all carrying bouquets of the local flame-of-the-forest.

For miles the road switchbacked through low barren foothills, once covered in rain-forest of which the traveller's tree is the only survivor. Centuries ago these superb plants became the Triffids of the east coast, extending their power over hundreds of miles as all other trees vanished and playing an increasingly important part in the daily lives of the inhabitants. The ravenala's store of pure water is released by cutting deep into the thick base of the six- or eight-foot leaf-stalk some six inches above the junction with the trunk. (For this you need a spear, not a camp-knife.) Each stalk yields about two pints of the only *pure* water locally available. Apart from being a reservoir, the ravenala provides most of the building materials for east coast huts; leaves for roofs, stems for walls, bark for flooring.

Wherever we looked, between Ranomafana and Antsapanana, the ravenala's glossy bright green fans were standing erect, sometimes thirty feet tall, against the dark blue sky – on ridges of red clay, quartz rock or golden-brown heath. In many places it also grew level with the road, its giant leaves just perceptibly stirring and whispering in a small breeze from the coast. And occasionally it grew below the road, allowing us to look down on seed-pods each holding about thirty beans wrapped in a silky blue fibre. Travellers without ecological worries could walk through this region as Mr Ellis did, reflecting that 'the prevalence of this tree imparts a degree of almost inconceivable magnificence to the vegetation of the country.' But travellers aware of the causes of this prevalence cannot wholly enjoy the magnificence.

Antsapanana consists of little more than four Chinese *hotelys* yet being a road-junction it has an important air; an illegible much-collided-with sign-post points south to Vatomandry and there were two bashies and a truck parked in the 'main street'. It was long past lunch-time (3.15) and Rachel settled down to rice and very greasy stewed pork: singularly untempting fare, I reckoned, in the middle of that sweltering afternoon. I had three litres of beer, for which the young Chinese *hotely*-owner *under*-charged me because we are *vazaha*. From his powerful transistor radio on the bar-counter came a commentary in Malagasy on an African international championship soccer match but the locals seemed to have little interest in their country's fate. Only a few youths lounged on the verandah, or drifted in and out of the bar wanting to know the score. They bought no beer; it is too expensive for the villagers who in any case prefer rum – if they can afford it – or hooch. Hereabouts the latter is also made from cane and smells a great deal better than the gout-giving potions of the Spiny South.

Not far beyond Antsapanana the roads diverged for the last time. We turned onto the final stretch of Route Nationale No. 2 and were in the blessed shade of a remnant of rain-forest, pre-served by the intractability of the terrain. On either side of a long narrow ridge lay long narrow ravines, already shadow-filled and crowded with oil-palms, bananas, bamboos, cane, raffia-palms, ravenala and countless 'unknowns'. By 5.15 we had accepted the inevitability of sleeping *on* the track. Then suddenly the ridge widened, presenting us with a level grassy campsite, tree-encircled – a perfect farewell gift from the *razana*, to mark our last night's rest on the bosom of their Great Red Island.

This pocket of uninhabited land is in one of Madagascar's most heavily populated areas, yet after sunset nobody passed our site. Although we did not then know it, we were close to a seriously haunted village; the ghost – half horse, half woman – savagely mauls anyone foolish enough to wander around after dark. But throughout that night we were troubled only by heavy showers and at such a low altitude one can sleep quite well despite being sodden. The real inconvenience was felt next morning when our water-logged loads seemed double their normal weight.

Soon after sunrise we were on the move and within an hour had reached sea-level, where endless flat miles are given over to that cane-plantation whose manager we were on the way to visit. This was a built-up area; every ten or fifteen minutes we passed a hamlet of shaggy shacks and friendly people, some much taller than the Betsimisaraka. These, we later learned, were the descen-dants of the Mahafaly and Antandroy who fled north from the droughts and famines of the 1930s.

Here the humidity was beyond anything in my previous experi-ence, yet the locals imagined they were enduring a cool spell of mid-winter weather. At 7.40 we stopped in a hamlet almost big enough to be called a village and had a litre of beer each, as in

Tudor England, which made us feel happily depraved. (The only alternative was *limonady*.) *Vazaha* are no novelty hereabouts but our life-style seemed to puzzle the locals. The sort of *vazaha* who run plantations do not suddenly appear mud-covered out of the forest, carrying bulky loads, and sit around shamelessly swigging beer for breakfast.

With so many wage-earners in the population business was brisk for that little shop, though the amounts being purchased were minute: just enough for immediate use. Before the next meal the shoppers would be back; they have nowhere to store food safely, even if they were inclined to think ahead. Three men bought small bottles of rum and set off for work drinking on the wing. Not that we could afford to criticise as we went on our merry way, frequently saving each other from overbalancing; we weren't in fact drunk but the track had been churned to a quagmire by giant plantation tractors. In the fields on either side foremen holding long lists were shouting roll-calls and we were surprised by the numbers of women and children workers. Several brief heavy showers cooled us slightly and then a spectacular double-rainbow appeared ahead – the two arcs so broad, and their span so immense above the flatness, that the effect was quite flamboyant. Even the colours of the prism seem different in Madagascar.

For hours we plodded on muddily through the cane-fields. There was no shade along the track, though lush green groves surrounded each hamlet or village. We enjoyed two more beer-stops, the number restricted only by opportunity. At the second of these our host-to-be, Nick White, was well known to the young woman behind the counter. She called him 'Mr Wet'. As we neared Brickaville the villages became much larger and more substantial. By noon we were about two miles from the town – and then my left rucksack strap broke, ripping away from the canvas. When I swore at the shoddy quality of modern goods Rachel pointed out that 'rucksacks aren't *meant* to be mobile libraries!'

What would have been a disaster elsewhere seemed here a deliverance from heat-stroke; we now had an excuse to sit down and wait for motor-transport. All morning we had seen only tractors but within two minutes of our collapse a Peugeot van appeared – the timing was extraordinary – and we were rescued by Frank Wright, the Englishman in charge of the plantation machinery and a next-door-neighbour of Julie and Nick White.

He left us on their doorstep at 12.50 p.m. 'Just in time for lunch,' said Rachel crudely.

The Whites' kindness was not confined to three days of lavish house-hospitality. They also insisted on driving us to one of the east coast's few shark-free beaches at Mahambo, some thirty miles north of Tamatave. After a night at Le Recif, a Moro-Moro type hotel, we planned to continue up the coast by bus-truck to Foulpointe and Fenerive. We would see enough of Tamatave itself on the day before our departure for Tana, Moscow and London. We had learned that the bigger the Malagasy town (Tana excepted) the less time one wants to spend in it.

The main attraction around Mahambo is not the shark-free swimming, enjoyable though that is, but the vegetation. In the inland rain-forest ninety per cent of the species are endemic; along the coast – open to botanical influences washed up by the Indian Ocean – that figure is down to twenty per cent. Yet to our eyes everything growing along that shore-line looked gloriously outlandish; there are for instance about *forty* different species of narrow-fronded palms and pandanus. We also met the *Cycas thouarsii* of unhappy memory, which looks like a palm but is not. Alison Jolly has described it as 'one of the cycad group which links ferns to flowering plants, a kind of coelocanth of the vegetable kingdom'.

When the time came to sit by the roadside, awaiting onward transport to Foulpointe, neither of us, oddly, felt like leaving Le Recife. We are not natural beach-hogs and there was no snorkling, yet I only wanted to stroll through the endlessly fascinating shoreline forest, play Scrabble on the sand with my feet in the sea and swim four times a day. Rachel did not even want to swim – much. Normally she is a keen long-distance swimmer but here she stayed close to the shore like a nervy toddler. For some reason this goaded me to vicious irritability and I accused her of laziness. My temper seemed to be getting as short as my energy. Rachel retorted – 'I wish *you* wouldn't go out so far! How do the Whites *know* it's safe here? It's irrational,' she added morosely, 'to go pale about spiders and be so careless about sharks.' I realised then that filial devotion, rather than laziness, was part of her problem – and guilt made me even more irritable. Later I discovered that she had been reading too much Alison Jolly:

'There was a French lady who thought wading might be safe,

so she tucked up her skirts and stepped in, only to have a shark sever her foot at the ankle. Eleven species including the real maneater, the great white shark, patrol just offshore along Madagascar's east coast ... The beach shelves rapidly to deep, poorly inhabited waters. The sharks hang off the lagoon mouths, waiting for Malagasy endemic mullet, or perhaps an unguarded toddler, to stray out into the waves ...'

It says a lot for the strange beauty of the Mahambo region that we so enjoyed our three days there, despite unusual outbreaks of mother–daughter friction. We got to know the village quite well; a decrepit but friendly little place, pervaded by tropical take-it-easiness. Its inhabitants made the other Malagasy we had met seem positively dynamic. Mahambo is about two miles from the hotel, across weirdly vegetated dunes and through superb forest. Our frequent visits there were thirst-inspired. Le Recife hotel – not run (so's you'd notice) by anyone, and owned by an absentee *vazaha* named Frantz Cowar – charged *vazaha* double for Antsir-abe beer on the rare occasions when there was anybody around to serve the guests.

We left for Tamatave early one morning in an antique and unique minibus: unique because only half-full at Mahambo, though that happy situation soon changed. I remember little of our journey on 'the nylon route', so called because it is a normally maintained stretch of tarred road. An alarming lethargy was afflicting me; I could not keep awake. Rachel too was dopey, though less so; and she seemed to be developing Mally-belly.

We arrived at 9.30 a.m., which left us more than enough time to admire: 'the autonomous port of Tamatave which has just been enlarged. The wharfs have increased in number, some ware-houses have been blown down and replaced by more modern and functional ones, the protection dam has been extended, the plat-forms are well equipped and the hoisting engines numerous.'

First however we had to find a doss-house and buy train tickets for the next day. We consulted our Air Mad guidebook and ruled out the Hotel Neptune – '10 air-conditioned rooms with registered music, bath and WC. 10 new rooms expected soon. All the specialities of the French Midi region'. Then we decided to get our tickets first and on the way to the railway station chanced upon an Indian-owned doss-house where Rachel went to bed while I ticket-queued. Afterwards we both investigated Tamatave, though not in depth. The Malagasy suffer from a mass-illusion about this place; all over the island we had been told that whatever else we missed in Madagascar, we must not miss Tamatave. Yet even had we not been taking a jaundiced view of things we could have found little to admire in this decaying port, apart from a group of monumental banyan trees. And let us also mention – as our guidebook would say – that pervasive aroma of cloves which flavours the entire city and becomes quite dizzy-making as one passes certain 'functional warehouses'.

Rachel retired at sunset. I found a nearby bar-cum-brothel where I drank beer, which made me feel ill, while writing my diary. During the night Rachel vomited three times and my temperature soared. Yet I slept heavily, almost as though I were drugged, and had a series of vivid nightmares about *ombiasa* putting a spell on my publisher's office, which had moved from Picadilly to Fort-Dauphin, and bare-footed men with typewriters under their arms taking over my home in Ireland and telling me it was now a People's Executive Committee office. As we loaded up and set off for the railway station at 4 a.m. I had to face the fact that both Murphys were not merely off-colour but extremely ill – and getting iller by the minute.

This train was as overcrowded as Merk at his worst and none of the opaque windows would open. Acute nausea was one of our new symptoms and we realised that we could not possibly endure fourteen hours of what Jamie had so rudely described as 'ethnic pong'. We therefore sat on the floor at an open door between carriages, our legs dangling over the track. Twelve other seatless passengers, plus their luggage (much of it alive, as usual) were crammed into that tiny space. This meant that once we had taken up our positions – admittedly the most advantageous available – we could not move between Tamatave and Perinet, or between Perinet and Tana. It also meant that people tended to sit on us, not through any lack of consideration but because they had no alternative. In such situations everybody either has to sit on somebody or be sat upon. I was comparatively fortunate; the youth sitting half on my left shoulder and half on my rucksack cannot have weighed more than eight stone. The man sitting half on Rachel's shoulder and half on his wife's looked much heavier. He spoke enough English to remind us of our Southern friend, the Antandroy youth who unbuttoned my shirt. At intervals he tapped me on the head and when I looked around stared hard into my eyes and said, 'You man, yes? You engineering man?' My denials caused him to rock with laughter while Rachel and his wife winced. 'Yes, yes!' he insisted, 'I *know* you engineering man!' We decided that my bush-shirt, with its quasi-military look, must have created the engineering illusion. As the day wore on we both developed severe pains below our right ribs – and raging thirsts. Yet when I fetched two bottles of beer from the Railway Hotel at Perinet neither of us could drink it.

Between Perinet and Tana something went wrong with the engine and we stopped for over an hour on the side of a precipice. It was after 9 p.m. and Tana was abed when we walked very slowly up the long Avenue de i indépendance to the Hotel Lido.

Back in our now-familiar room, I decided the time had come to study urine-samples. Mine was the colour of Guinness, with a good head of green foam. Rachel's was the colour of Newcastle Brown Ale, with a less impressive head of yellow-green foam.

'Blackwater fever!' said Rachel.

'Probably not,' I judged. 'More likely hepatitis.'

And so it proved.

Next day – our last in Tana – Rachel stayed in bed while I toured the city saying good-bye to friends. I had to walk gingerly; the vibrations caused by each step seemed to send red-hot pokers through my liver.

Gervais from Antsirabe called to our room that evening with a farewell gift of a magnificent solitaire set – the board of some exotic wood, the pieces of polished variegated semi-precious stones. He could have chosen nothing more appropriate than those naturally beautiful products of his country.

Yet my most precious souvenir of Madagascar is a small packet of red earth such as the Malagasy take with them when they go abroad. They take it to ensure their eventual return to the Great Red Island. I took it for the same reason.

Bibliography

History of Madagascar, Rev. William Ellis, Fisher & Co., London, 1838

Three Visits to Madagascar, Rev. William Ellis, John Potter & Co., Philadelphia, 1859

Thirty Years in Madagascar, Rev. T.T. Matthews, Religious Tract Society, London, 1904

The Drama of Madagascar, Sonia F. Howe, Methuen, London, 1938

The Madagascar I Love, Arkady Fiedler, Orbis, London, 1946

Zoo Quest to Madagascar, David Attenborough, Lutterworth Press, 1959

The Great Red Island, Arthur Stratton, Macmillan, London, 1965

Taboo: A Study of Malagasy Customs and Beliefs, Jorgen Ruud, Oslo University Press, 1960

Madagascar, Nigel Heseltine, Pall Mall Press, London, 1971

Madagascar Rediscovered, Mervyn Brown, Damien Tunnacliffe, London, 1978

Madagascar Today, Sennan Andriamirado, Grijelmo, Spain, 1978

A World Like Our Own: Man and Nature in Madagascar, Alison Jolly, Yale University Press, 1980

Index

Century Travellers

☐	Wild Wales	George Burrow	£4.95
☐	Ride to Khiva	Fred Burnaby	£4.95
☐	Two Middle Aged Ladies in Andalusia	Penelope Chetwode	£3.95
☐	Equator	Thurston Clarke	£4.99
☐	Zanzibar to Timbuktu	Anthony Daniels	£3.95
☐	Thousand Miles Up The Nile	Amelia B. Edwards	£4.95
☐	Fragile Eden	Robin Hanbury-Tenison	£4.99
☐	A Ride Along The Great Wall	Robin Hanbury-Tenison	£4.99
☐	Sultan in Oman	Jan Morris	£4.99
☐	Cameroon With Egbert	Dervla Murphy	£4.99
☐	Muddling Through In Madagascar	Dervla Murphy	£4.99
☐	On A Shoestring To Coorg	Dervla Murphy	£4.99
☐	The Waiting Land	Dervla Murphy	£4.99

Prices and other details are liable to change

ARROW BOOKS, BOOKSERVICE BY POST, PO BOX 29, DOUGLAS, ISLE OF MAN, BRITISH ISLES

NAME..

ADDRESS...

....

....

Please enclose a cheque or postal order made out to Arrow Books Ltd. for the amount due and allow the following for postage and packing.

U.K. CUSTOMERS: Please allow 22p per book to a maximum of £3.00.

B.F.P.O. & EIRE: Please allow 22p per book to a maximum of £3.00.

OVERSEAS CUSTOMERS: Please allow 22p per book.

Whilst every effort is made to keep prices low it is sometimes necessary to increase cover prices at short notice. Arrow Books reserve the right to show new retail prices on covers which may differ from those previously advertised in the text or elsewhere.

Century Travellers

☐	Eight Feet in the Andes	Dervla Murphy	£3.95
☐	Full Tilt	Dervla Murphy	£3.95
☐	In Ethiopia On A Mule	Dervla Murphy	£3.95
☐	Where The Indus Was Young	Dervla Murphy	£3.95
☐	South	Sir Ernest Shakleton	£4.95
☐	Beyond Euphrates	Freya Stark	£4.95
☐	Lycian Shore	Freya Stark	£3.95
☐	Traveller's Prelude	Freya Stark	£4.95
☐	Jerusalem	Colin Thubron	£4.99
☐	Mirror To Damascus	Colin Thubron	£4.99
☐	Venturesome Voyages Of Captain Voss	J.C. Voss	£3.95
☐	Letters from India	Lady Wilson	£4.95

Prices and other details are liable to change
